The Soul of Russia

THE SOUL OF RUSSIA

I

THE

SOUL OF RUSSIA

BY

CHAS. T. BYFORD

London

THE KINGSGATE PRESS

4, SOUTHAMPTON ROW, W.C.

TO

K. M. B.

CONTENTS

AND dost not thou, Russia, drive away like a troika,
     not to be overtaken ?
The road smokes behind thee, the bridges creak,
Thou leavest all behind thee
The beholders, amazed, stop and say
     Was it a flash of lightning ?
     What means this blood-curdling course ?
     What is the secret power in these horses ?
     What kind of horses are you ?
     Have you whirlwinds in your withers ?
     Have you recognised tones from above ?
     Do you now force your iron limbs, without touching
        the earth with your hoofs, to fly hence through the
        air, as if inspired by a god ?
Russia, answer, whither art thou driving ?
     There comes no answer.
We can hear the little bells on the horses tinkling strangely,
There is a groaning in the air, increasing like a storm,
And the Russian land continues its wild flight,
And the other nations and kingdoms of the earth
Step timorously aside, without checking its career.
Russia, whither art thou driving ?

Dead Souls.—GOGOL.

PREFACE

MY aim in writing this book has been to
give to the English-speaking peoples a
concise view of the spiritual and religious forces at work in Russia to-day Like the
majority of travellers in the land of the great
"White Tsar," I have been interested by the
place that religion holds in the life of the people.
There are very few, even amongst the "intellectuals," who stand aloof from the corporate religious
life of the great Russian family.

This book is not written for the specialist
in comparative religion, or for the scholar well
advanced in the study of peculiar Russian sects,
but rather for those interested in the great and
terrific struggle, which has been in progress for
the last half century, for religious liberty and
political freedom in the Russian Empire.

I have purposely confined myself to the developments of religious life peculiar to the Russian
people themselves, and have thus omitted much
which might. have been written concerning the
Lutheran Church in the Baltic provinces and
amongst German and Lettish settlers in the large
cities and grain-growing belts, of the Roman

Catholics in Poland and Lithuania, of the Moham-
medans in the South-East and the Crimea, of the
Buriats and their "white horse" worship in
Southern Siberia, and of the semi-Christian, semi-
Mohammedan peoples of the Eastern frontier.
These all have their place in the religious life
of the Empire, but owing to the restrictive laws
against proselytising, they hardly affect the
Russian as such.

It has been my privilege to be the guest
of Lutheran pastors in the Eastern provinces and
the Crimea, and to study their work at first hand,
but as most of their services are conducted in
German or Lettish, they have but little influence, comparatively speaking, upon their Slav
neighbours.

In the chapters dealing with the Orthodox
Church I have not touched upon the great controversies which raged between East and West,
and the subsequent division of Christendom into
two great parties, for the simple reason that
Russia received a *ready-made* Church, and became the child of the Holy Eastern Communion.
Save in the Uniat controversy, the Orthodox
Church has had but little to do with the doctrinal
differences between Rome and Constantinople.

The limits of space have made it impossible for me to follow each of the various
sects in detail, in their rise and development,
but the bibliography at the head of each chapter

should be of service to any readers, if they desire to become more fully acquainted with the special phase of Russian religious life in which they are interested

As the book is written for the general reader, I have avoided footnotes, and have incorporated in the body of the work quotations from other authors, and wherever possible have acknowledged my indebtedness to them.

CHAS T. BYFORD.

FINCHLEY.
April, 1914.

THE SOUL OF RUSSIA

INTRODUCTION

"THE Russian nation," writes Dostoievski, " is a new and wonderful phenomenon in the history of mankind. The character of the people differs to such a degree from that of other Europeans that their neighbours find it impossible to diagnose them."

Great and far-reaching movements are taking place in Russia to-day, and the eyes of the Western world are looking anxiously towards her, wondering what will issue from the social, political, and economic changes which are hastening forward in that land.

Anatole France writes : "On the banks of the Neva, the Volga, and the Vistula the fate of new Europe and the future of humanity are being decided."

Pobiedonosteff, the late Procurator of the Holy Synod, gave expression to the ideals, hopes, aspirations, and feelings of the leaders of the greatest empire of modern times when, in a sentence, he declared, " Russia is no State; Russia is a world." In her steady advance, slowly, surely, and more or less silently, Russia is becoming the world-power.

Eastward and southward, ever in search of warm water and ice-free ports, Russia in the process is assimilating to herself, and absorbing into her national life, peoples of diverse races, languages, temperaments, and religions. Since the Crimean War she has absorbed whole nations, and the end is not yet.

Despite climatic severities, or perhaps by reason of them, recurring famines, internal disorders, political revolutions, chronic poverty among her peasantry, territorial expansion steadily proceeds, and with this external expansion and development, an addition to her population by natural causes, i.e by births over deaths, of about two millions every year.

Here and there, students of modern history and the movements of modern nations have discerned the facts; thus Dr. Sarolea, in his *Life of Tolstoi*, says: "The twentieth century will be the century of the Russian. Before it will have run its course, one fourth of the habitable earth, from the frontiers of Germany to the boundaries of China, from the ice-bound shores of the Arctic Sea to the sub-tropical ridges of the Himalayas, will be occupied by a homogeneous population of three hundred millions of people, the most formidable aggregate of civilised humanity known to history. No race has had a more tragic past, and no race seems destined to a more brilliant future. The slow, steady advance of Russia is one of the most impressive phenomena of history; and when the vision of mankind will be directed to the future, as to-day it is directed to the past, the schoolboy will one day be taught the epic of Russian expansion, as to-day he is taught the epic of Imperial Rome."

Her growing commerce and need for ice-free ports, her great industrial developments, her congested population in the old agricultural belts, her increasing contact with other nations, all make for this territorial expansion, but the most potent factor in this steady advance is without doubt the Holy Orthodox Church. Wherever the merchant, the trader, the prospector, the engineer, the soldier, the administrator goes, there also is to be found the priest. Manchuria, in the process of absorption, becomes a See of the Orthodox Church; Tcherkisses have in their midst the ornate outward evidences of the State religion, and even in Northern Persia, the "popes" are following in the footsteps of the army.

Finn and Tatar, Circassian and Chinaman, Pole and Lett, Kalmuck and Samoyede, Mongol and Yakut, are to be one, one in faith, one in submission with the Slav to the Holy Orthodox Church; bound together by invisible and almost unbreakable bonds, the bonds of a simple and common faith in the One God, the Father of mankind; One Lord, the Saviour of the World; One Church, unchanged and unchanging, the supreme

2

authority over life and conduct, worship and faith;
One Tsar, the vicegerent of God to the Russian
world.

"Everywhere from Kamchatchka to the Vistula," writes Von der Brüggen, " Russian Churches
and priests are maintained, even in places where
no religious, but merely a political aim, prompts
the Synod to spread propaganda. The comparison
of the Russian village priest of Tambov, or
Saratov, with his brother in orders in Poland,
Lithuania, Esthonia, is often surprising. Comfortable, large dwelling-houses, often horses and
carriages, fields and meadows, gardens, handsome,
cheerful Churches. The pope lives comfortably
on one thousand to one thousand five hundred
roubles salary or profit on his glebe land; he has
his nice schoolroom, is not obliged to 'bend his
back,' nor to drink brandy, nor to suffer hunger."

Brotherhoods are being founded amongst the
Orthodox all over Russia, collections are being
made in the Churches to help Lithuanians, Letts,
Poles, and others to become "Orthodox" and to
be Russianised; money has been granted to found
a Manchurian Bishopric, to build a great Church
in Pekin, with which to impress the Chinese, to
establish an Orthodox Monastery in Manchuria, in
order effectually to further the Russian advance
there. The supreme function of the Church, presumably, is to lead the people to discern between
right and wrong, between good and evil, to make

and keep the people simple, obedient, and united.

Despite schisms, reactionary and radical, conservative and revolutionary, atheistic and evangelical, the leaders of the Orthodox Church and the Russian nation keep steadily on their way; nothing deflects them from their purpose; all demands for reform are sternly and even severely resisted.

All attempts to revise the Church's creed are anathema. The ideal is the inflexible solidarity of the Church establishment and her absolute identity with the State itself.

"Once an Orthodox Russian, always an Orthodox Russian." Hence persecutions and prisons, beatings and banishments, confiscation of goods and deprivation of civil rights, are the lot of all those who dare to leave her fold.

It is the claim of the Holy Orthodox Church that it is the oldest and purest Church in Christendom, the only institution which has never changed or changes.

Her "popes" boast that it is the only permanent unchangeable Church in Christendom to-day. The power of the Church amongst the peasantry is undeniable. The Russian child is born and bred in the midst of religious observances, elaborate ceremonies, and gross superstitions, and that fact has an effect on his disposition and character not easily overestimated. His docile patience when suffering from the "ills that flesh

L

is heir to"; his lethargy in the presence of the
great crises of life; his adherence to primitive
methods of agriculture; his innate distrust of all
that is new and strange, can all be traced to the
primal influence of the Church upon his character.

"God wills it," is his invariable answer when
loss, disease, and death come into his experience.
And God to him is frequently but a super-Tsar.

"The Russian temperament," says Sarolea, "is
more extreme and more impulsive than the Western
temperament. Religious ideals take a firmer hold
in Russia than in any other country. No one who
has closely observed the religious life of the
Russian peasantry, no one who has spent a few days
with Russian pilgrims at Kiev or Jerusalem, will
doubt that the Russian people are to-day the most
religious nation in the world. Their soul seems
to come nearer to the simple truth of the Gospel,
and it is more nearly attuned to the doctrine of
renunciation. The Russian people seem more disposed to make sacrifices for what they believe to
be the truth. In Russia the age of martyrs is not
closed. Every class, every age, each sex, has had
its sufferers for the ideal. In hundreds and thousands Russians have given up their lives in the
cause of Christianity."

No student of Russian affairs can neglect what
is without reasonable doubt the greatest factor in
the life of the people—Religion A man may know
all that there is to be known about the Russian

people, in their peasant communes, town industries, social relationships, political principles, and even revolutionary ideas, but he will fail to grasp the inner secret of the Slav race until he has made a close study of the religious life of the nation. How he works, how he lives, how he thinks, may be apparently an open book to the student of the Russian character, but he will know very little about the peasant, after all, until he knows the religious side of him; and the religious side of him is all sides.

"Faith is as necessary to the Russian peasant as food and air." Nothing written about Russia can give a full or in anywise adequate view of the people and their problems, domestic and racial, which leaves out of account the religious life of the people. Russia is a world where nothing about her people can be rightfully understood without some fairly comprehensive outline of the part which religion plays in the life of her inhabitants and in the affairs of her government; for in Russia the Church is, on the one hand, a definite part of the government itself; on the other hand, a chief factor in the life of the people; on the one side, a rigid State institution; on the other, the beloved of the peasantry. In this statement one does not refer to the credal or philosophic basis of the Church, but to those external rites and ceremonies, customs and observances which play such an important part in the life of the peasant.

Throughout that vast Empire there are manifold outward evidences of the part which religion, as such, plays in the life of the ordinary people—Churches innumerable, wayside shrines, holy Icons, ragged pilgrims, black clergy, and parish "popes."

The Icon is everywhere, in custom-houses and passport offices on the frontiers, railway stations and restaurants, government bureaux and post-offices, on the saloons of the great river steamers and in the posthouses on the great main roads, in shops and warehouses, factories and offices, peasant houses and palatial mansions, university class-rooms and village schools, in vodka shops, and even in the basest dens of vice and evil.

Always and everywhere, from the White Sea to the shores of the Caspian, from the Vistula to the Pacific, in crowded cities and in the villages of the vast and lonely steppes, wherever the Russian has made a home, founded a settlement, or pushed forward the railhead into new territories, there is to be found the Icon, the Holy picture. It is the constant companion of the Russian in poverty and plenty, in peace and war.

It is the outward and visible sign or manifestation of a profound racial religious instinct, or rather, religious emotion, rather than an intellectual grasp of an intelligent faith. The Icon is a talisman against danger when travelling, against disease at home, and is the inseparable companion of the wanderer.

l

Another outward sign of their religious emotion is the constant crossing of themselves when passing Icons and shrines, and one another when about to part for some time. At railway stations and even tramway halts, on steamer quays and posthouse doors, one will see friends crossing one another before starting upon a journey.

The *moujik* in the *droshky*, tearing through the streets at a terrific pace, as if life itself depended upon the speed of his horses, will, without perceptible slackening of rein, cross himself as he passes a shrine or Church; foot passengers will uncover, cross themselves, and murmur a prayer every few yards where Church and outdoor shrines are in abundance.

How symbolic is this crossing! The forehead is touched where rested the crown of thorns; the side is touched where entered the cruel spear; and the passing of the hand over the body reproduces the Saviour's crucifixion on Calvary. All is done quietly and yet comprehensively.

Or again, watch the devotions of the people in the Churches. We pass through a crowd of oftentimes loathsome beggars —"little brothers of Christ"—crowded about the doors and on the steps of the sacred edifice, and upon entering we notice the blaze of candles before the sacred Icons. Here an officer, with dangling and clanking sword by his side, places a lighted candle before the Icon, kisses the painted feet of the saint, and then kneels

l

for a few minutes in prayer. Close by, a woman, well dressed, and evidently well to do, is pas-sionately kissing a sacred picture. Near by, a peasant, or street vendor, is kneeling, swaying in prayer, whilst ever and anon his long hair sweeps the floor as he prostrates himself before the Icon. A' girl of the poorer classes moves along on her knees towards the picture of a saint, and then, rising, literally covers the picture with her kisses, crossing and recrossing herself in the fervour of her devotions, what time her lips move incessantly in prayer.

The same profound religious spirit enters into every department of life. Before the peasant will dig a well, the priest will bless the spot, and when water is reached, the "little father" is sent for again. The site for a new house must be signed with the cross, and during the building each im-portant operation must receive a blessing. The first log placed in position, the completion of the thatch, the hanging of the door, all must be signed with the mystic seal of the Cross.

The "pope," with his distinctive dress, can be heard softly yet expressively reciting the prayer, whilst with hand outstretched over the place where the corner-stone is to be placed, he continues:

"May neither wind, nor water, nor anything else, bring harm into it; may it be completed in the benevolence, and free all those who labour on this building from all kinds of calamity."

l

The peasant, from the cradle to the grave, in all the diversities of his life, looks to the priest. When the locusts wrought havoc in the Eastern Provinces in 1906, the peasants sent for the priests to perambulate the fields and by their prayers stay the plague.

That there is superstition in all this reverence is undoubtedly true, as we shall see later Not only are the obeisance, the murmured prayer, the sign of the Cross, outward manifestations of the inner religious life of the men and women who perform them, but they are also a kind of incan tation, a formula of words and actions directed against the evil eye and the unseen powers of darkness, which, to the average Russian, are in the air about us.

The normal peasant or artisan ascribes evil happenings and frustrated purposes to evil spirits who have been let loose upon him or his by reason of his failure to duly observe any or all of these religious observances.

Pobiedonosteff, in his *Reflections of a Russian Statesman*, reaches the very core of this seeming religiosity of the people when he writes:

"What a mystery is the religious life of a people such as ours, uncultivated and left to itself We ask, whence does it come? and strive to reach the source, and yet find nothing. Our clergy teach little and seldom; they celebrate the services in the churches and direct the administration of the

l

parishes. To the illiterate the Scriptures are unknown; there remain the Church service and a few
prayers, which, transmitted from parents to children, serve as the only link between the Church and
its flock. It is known that in some remote districts
the congregation understands nothing of the words
of the service, or even of the Lord's Prayer, which
is repeated often with omissions and additions
which deprive it of all meaning.

"Nevertheless, in all these untutored minds
has been raised, as in Athens—one knows not by
whom—an altar to the Unknown God; to all, the
intervention of Providence in human affairs is a
fact so indisputable, so firmly rooted in conscience,
that when death arrives, these men, to whom none
ever spoke of God, open their doors to Him as
a well-known and long-expected guest. Thus, in
the literal sense, they give their souls to God."

It is these intensely religious people, orthodox
and unorthodox, cultured and illiterate, wealthy
and burdened with poverty, unspeakably filthy
in their homes, but frequently pure in heart,
and · not the few thousand "intellectuals,"
steeped in German economics and French political
traditions, who reveal to the non-Russian the ".Soul
of Russia." It is they alone who possess the secret
of the destinies of the great Slav race. In the
great Russian Empire, as we shall see later, we
find more phases of religious life. than perhaps in
any other country in the world. A bewildering

L

variety of religions and sects are to be met with in close proximity to one another, and their places of worship often stand side by side in the same town or village, and as a general rule, without giving rise to religious disturbances. In his relations with Moslems, Buddhists, Fetiches, the Russian peasant looks rather to conduct than to creed, the latter being, in his view, simply a matter of nationality. Indeed, towards paganism, at least, he is perhaps even more than tolerant, preferring to keep on good terms with pagan divinities, and in difficult circumstances not failing to present to them his offering.

Any idea of proselytizing is quite foreign to the mind of the common peasant, and the outbursts of zeal occasionally manifested by the clergy are really due to the desire for Russification, and traceable to the influence of the higher clergy and the government. This accounts for the fact that all over the land are to be seen the Orthodox Churches, with their pear-shaped domes and spires; and where the frontiers of the Empire are being pushed farther Eastward and Southward, one has seen the travelling Church, used by the pioneers of the Russian advance.

The general distribution of religions is as follows:

White Russians ... Holy Orthodox, Raskolnik, and Sectarian.
Poles . ... Roman Catholic and Uniat.

Letts, Esthonians, and Courlanders	Lutheran.
Tatars and Bashkirs	Mohammedan.
Kirghizes ...	Mohammedan, with the retention of certain Shamanistic practices.
Voyiaks, Voguls, Tcheremisses, and Tcherkesses	Interesting modifications of Shamanism, under the influence of Christian and Moslem beliefs.
Kalmuks .. .	Buddhists.
Tcherkesses . ..	Zoroastrians, and as above.
Yakuts, Samoyedes, and Buriats ..	Practically Pagans, the latter observing the ancient White Horse worship and sacrifice.

Amongst the minor bodies scattered through the Empire we find Hussites on the banks of the Volga; Molokani in the provinces of the South; Doukhobors in the South and in the Caucasus; Raskolniks have their stronghold in and around Moscow; Mennonites in Samara and Astrakhan; whilst the Stundists and Baptists are to be found in and amongst them all.

In addition to the regular recognised bodies who have a measure of State recognition, there are many fanatical sects, which have sprung into being from time to time, and have by their very excesses brought down upon them the strong and repressive hand of the government.

Such are the Skoptsi, Hleests, Castrates,

Nazarenes, and certain sects of Jews and Mohammedans.

According to the census of 1897, the population of Russia was divided religiously in the
following proportions:

Holy Orthodox	...	96,000,000 or 62 per cent.
Raskolniks	. .	2,000,000
Roman Catholics	..	12,200,000
Lutherans		3,750,000
Jews	. .	4,050,000
Mohammedans	... ...	12,150,000
Shamanists .		1,000,000
Sectarians	. . .	1,200,000
Buddhists and smaller sects		1,500,000

These figures are exclusive of Finland, which is
wholly Protestant.

The Russians are peculiarly susceptible to an
extravagant mysticism, and recent history, as well
as the records of former days, supplies many
instances of great Russian religious reform movements which have gone down in an orgy of
fanaticism.

With the spread of education, more frequent
intercourse with Western nations, a wider dissemi-
nation of the Scriptures, and capable interpreters
thereof, Russia will ultimately find her "soul"
and produce a great and enduring faith which will
make for the real uplift of the people within her
borders, and have a widespread effect upon the
contiguous nations of Europe and Asia.

L

SUPERSTITION AND CREDULITY

BIBLIOGRAPHY.

KENNARD . . . *The Russian Peasant.*

BARING . . . . *The Russian People.*

GRAHAM. . . . *Changing Russia.*

CONSTANT . . . *Religion.*

ROMANOFF . . . *Rites and Customs of the Græco-Russian Church.*

L

l

SUPERSTITION AND CREDULITY

SUPERFICIALLY Russia is an intensely religious nation. Evidences of the extreme religiosity of the people are to be met with everywhere. Not only in the great centres of population, or the "holy" cities of Moscow and Kieff, are the gorgeous externals of religion to be found; every little village has its Church; the golden domes shine in the morning light, a landmark for the weary traveller over the apparently interminable steppes. Usually the most magnificent building in the country town or village is the Church, and when one sees the noble edifice towering above the squalid homes of the peasantry, comparisons crowd upon the mind. What is the Church here for? What part does it play in the life of the people? What influence does it exert for their uplift? What good eventuates from it for these wretched peasants, too often hungry and poverty stricken, ill-clad and ill-housed? What comfort does it bring to their restless souls? Of what benefit is it for these poor creatures, many of them sodden with the all-prevailing "vodka," to gaze upon the showy outside of the gorgeous Church, and to be told that it is the Church of

L

God, the home of the Saviour, whilst next door, in the presbytery, they may perchance see the "pope" as drunk as one of the lowest of his parishioners, and know that at times he indulges in peculations and shameful bargains which are the very negation of his high calling. Glorious as the outside of the building may be, the interior, regarded as a place of religion for the practice of meditation, or for the receiving of spiritual food, is even more of a delusion. All is garish and glittering; magic and mystery surround one; all is calculated, and purposely calculated, and has been purposely calculated for centuries past by the priestly caste, to breed in the mind of the peasant fear and superstition. The building, and not the Lord thereof, the priest, and not his Master, is held in awe and fear.

The interior of the Church appeals to the senses, the fragrant odours of the incense, the range of superb Icons, the altar behind the Royal Gates, all these fill the mind of the peasant with mystery, wonderment, and awe; but his soul is starved.

The Church, externally and internally, is an outward manifestation of the place and power of religion in the communal life, but the whole tendency of the system is to debase the peasant, to divorce him from spiritual religion and evangelical truth. There is show outside—show inside—nothing more.

l

No one intimately acquainted with the Russian peasantry can deny that they are intensely religious. They go regularly to the Church on Sundays and holy days, cross themselves repeatedly when they pass a Church, or shrine, or Icon. They partake of the Holy Communion at stated seasons, at least once a year; they avail themselves of the Confessional, scrupulously observe the fast-days of .Wednesday and Friday, and even the long period of Lent; they are punctilious in their obedience to the 'demands of the Church, and will go on long pilgrimages to holy places, famous monasteries, and even to Jerusalem itself; but too frequently here their religion ends.

. Generally speaking, the peasantry are ignorant of religious doctrines and dogmas, and know but little of Holy Writ Of the inner religious life of the soul they have practically no conception. Ceremony usually suffices, and a childlike confidence in the saving efficacy of the ritual is normal. A peasant was asked on one occasion if he could name the Three Persons of the Trinity, and, without a moment's hesitation, answered, "Every one knows that; of course, it is the Saviour; the Mother of God; and Saint Nicholas, the Miracle worker." The peasant's answer represents fairly enough the theological attainments of a numerous section of the illiterate peasantry.

"The Russians, and especially the peasants, perform their religious observances in the most

l

matter of fact way in the world. But this in no way signifies either hypocrisy or necessarily super-stition—although they are superstitious (and scep-tical) with regard to signs and omens. The peasants are as a whole an intensely religious people, but often the signs and observances of their religion, the frequency with which they cross themselves, the candles they burn, are not necessarily expressive of their religion. They look upon these as something which must be done properly—a part of the ordinary duty of man, like going to the bath on Saturdays, putting on their Sunday clothes on Sunday, feasting during the Carnival, and fasting during Lent.

"They pay honour to their Lares and Penates much in the same way as the Greeks and Romans must have done to their household gods, because it is the duty of the Russian citizen; so the Russian thinks that to cross himself at certain places, to fast certain days, to burn a candle as a thank-offering for a successful bargain, to uncover his head before the holy image, are the things which he knows every real Orthodox Russian does, and a man who does not do these things is simply something else. A man who does not keep Lent and Easter is, in the eyes of the Russian peasant, a Turk or a heathen.

"The religion of the peasant is the working hypothesis taught him by life, and by his obser-vances of it he follows what he conceives to be the dictates of common sense consecrated by immemorial custom " (Maurice Baring. *The Russian People*).

Pictures have played such an important part in the development of the religious ideas of the Russian peasantry that, as a result, they have a very material idea of what God is like. In many of the pictures God is represented as a very benevolent-looking Russian official of high rank, seated upon a throne, apparently suspended in the heavens, surrounded with Apostles and Saints, after the fashion of an old-time Tsar with his Boyars at Court. One very favourite picture, supposed to be a copy of the original one of " The Last Judgment," as shown to Vladimir by the Monk Constantine (which partly induced the former to embrace Christianity), shows God passing judgment upon the quick and the dead, those who have not embraced the true faith being sent to the left, whilst the righteous find a place on His right.

Benjamin Constant, in his work on " Religion," relates that " when a Russian general in full uniform rode into the country in a part of Siberia but little frequented, he was regarded by the people as God Himself, and that the memory of his appearance got such a firm hold among them that when, ten years later, a Russian colonel came to the same place, he was greeted as the Son of God."

Hardly a year passes but some monk or

l

religious fanatic declares himself to be the Messiah, and invariably he will obtain a great following of men and women who will be prepared to go to almost any lengths to show their faith in him. Last year a cultured Russian passed through a town in Little Russia inhabited by Cossacks. He was asked the question, "Will you be so good as to tell us if you have been in the other world?" He was offended, since he supposed that the inhabitants meant to indicate to him that they did not believe what he had said. But the fact was that one of the inhabitants of the town had returned from a pilgrimage, and had told them that he had come from the other world, and those recently deceased in the town had requested him to bring greetings to their relatives. He had gone away again, laden with rustic presents, to the departed relatives of the credulous Cossacks. Now they wanted to find out from the Russian gentleman whether these gifts had reached their proper destination. In March, 1913, there was an extraordinary outburst of religious mania amongst the peasantry of the Black Earth belt in the South. A monk named Innocentius had acquired a remarkable reputation as a miracle-worker. In that part of Russia it appears that lunacy is very frequent, owing, it is supposed, to the use of unripe maize instead of leavened bread. By the ignorant and superstitious peasants this madness is regarded as possession of the devil, and as Innocentius was credited with the power of casting out devils, thousands of pilgrims came to his monastery, bringing their mad relatives or friends.

The place became "an inferno of the mad." At last the government banished Innocentius to another monastery in the extreme north of Russia, on a river called the Onega. His adherents confounded this name of the river with the Omega of the Apocalypse, and believing Innocentius to be the Christ Himself, they set out on foot to follow him to his place of exile, more than a thousand miles away. It was the depth of a Russian winter, and the sufferings of the devotees were indescribable. They were stopped in their march and sent back by train, begrimed by dirt, and nearly all frostbitten. The women and children were in hysterics. Many squatted on the floor of the railway vans, praying with open Bibles in their hands. Such incidents could be multiplied manifold. Episodes such as these are not at all uncommon amongst the Russian peasantry. Religion and its mystic power is so engrained in them, more as a thing to be feared than venerated, that it needs but little of its gloss to polish the most unlikely tale with the glitter of undeniable truth.

"One day a man of dignified mien, with long brown beard, dressed as a priest, and armed with a long pilgrim's staff as if to denote that he had travelled far—a supposition which was fostered by

the fact that his boots were worn into holes and
that he limped painfully at each succeeding step
—arrived in a village in the province of Orel, and
with wild enthusiasm narrated how that he had
been sent forward by the Emperor to choose a
village which contained a Church.   They were
duly flattered by reason of the holy man choosing
their village out of all the villages of Russia
for the reception of the " Little Father," and more
so in that they were accounted to be such men
of genius.   Further, they felt no small pride that
the Tsar should really be about to honour their
village with his presence.   Some few had their
suspicions, which were deepened when the holy
man said that it would be necessary for all the
villagers to provide food and cattle of one sort
or another to be presented to the Emperor, and,
further, that at least one hundred roubles must be
collected to present to the Church, for the meeting
was not only to be presided over by the Emperor,
but was to be quite unique in the history of
Christendom; also, not only would the food and
cattle be restored twentyfold by the Emperor, but
the Church would repay ten roubles for every one
collected.

" This was a bait indeed ; but the suspicious
ones still doubted the words of the holy man,
and finally asked the priest whom the Emperor was
about to meet.   This was the question which the
man of God awaited.   Said he, tearing his hair in

L

apparently frenzied wrath: 'O ye miserable un-
believers, ye of little faith, may God pardon you
for your faithlessness in doubting me, His messenger. The Emperor meets here no other than
God Himself.' The effect was astounding. All
were electrified, and stood dumb with amazement,
and the suspicious ones disappeared into the background, and hung their heads, ashamed that they
had been impious enough to distrust the messenger
of God Himself, and that they had almost gone
the length of rejecting the proffered visit of the
Creator. Money was immediately subscribed, and
not one hundred roubles, but two hundred, for,
said the simple peasants, 'if God will return us ten-
fold the gifts we give, then let us give two hundred
roubles instead of one hundred, and in like manner
the village was cleared of its cattle, its horses, its
goods of every description, and for the same subtle
reason.

"Rejoicing was rife, and the man of God
looked on, an expression of holy enthusiasm per-
vading his features.

"The goods collected, he suggested that it
would be advisable to drive all the cattle to a
large shed five miles away, when preparations
would be made to present them to God and the
Emperor a week from that date. 'Meanwhile you
must spend your days in prayer and fasting, and
on the seventh march with reverence to the spot
agreed upon.'

"The peasants did exactly as they were told, and fasted religiously all the week, and prayed mightily that their gifts might be acceptable to the august personages concerned, and more mightily still that all would be returned to them with ten times the amount added.

"Six days elapsed, and on the seventh day, in long procession, the peasants marched to the shed. Wonderful! As they approached, nothing unusual could be seen. 'God is mysterious. He will be there awaiting us with multitudes of angels. He can do things we wot not of.'

"They reached the shed. They entered the large folding doors, and, to their blank amazement, horses, cattle, and goods had all vanished. The peasants could not believe their senses, and many prayed that God would show Himself to them, but God did not appear, neither did the Emperor, and neither did the holy man of God, His messenger, and further, to this day they have seen and heard nothing of their money, cattle, or goods" (H.P. Kennard. *The Russian Peasant*).

There are a variety of superstitious practices connected with every phase of the peasant's life from the cradle to the grave. Many of them are undoubtedly of Finnish, whilst some are of Tatar origin. As soon after birth as possible, a child is swaddled in red and black bands, with the idea that these will prevent the devil from getting into the infant.

.᠎ Immediately upon a death taking place in a house, a glass of water is placed in the window, that the spirit may wash itself in departing.

A dead body is carried out of the house feet foremost, so that it may not return. At the burial of a peasant, after the usual religious cere-monies have been completed, many quaint usages are observed at the grave-side. Parings of the deceased's nails are buried with him in order to assist him to clamber out of the grave up to heaven, sometimes a piece of ladder, or a miniature ladder, is buried with him in order to aid the ascent.

Money is sometimes thrown in at the last moment, the idea being that Saint Peter may be unwilling to unlock the gates of heaven without a persuader in the way of coin of the realm.

When Peter the Great insisted upon the shaven chin, many of the "Raskolniki" saved their beards to be buried with them, so that when they arrived at the entrance gates on high they might be recognised and admitted by the guardians thereof.

"The baby of one of the peasant women was seriously ill. He refused to eat, lay in his cradle uncomfortable and sore. The dark gleaner seemed to be waiting for him.

"On the festival of Our Lady of Kiev, a visitor arrived. 'Tush, tush,' said she, 'bathing, swathing, medicines—all that is nonsense. The illness has nothing to do with these things. Some one of dark complexion has looked upon him with the evil eye.'

"The visitor prepared an immense *booblik*. (The *booblik* is a ring-shaped roll, rather thicker than a finger, sweet and crusty, with sometimes caraway seeds sprinkled upon it before baking.) Whilst it was still dough, that is, before it was baked, the old woman passed the naked baby through it three times in the Name of the Father, the Son, and the Holy Ghost. That done, the *booblik* was put into the oven. The baby was then washed in a mixture of charcoal ash and holy water. When the *booblik* was baked it was given to a black dog to eat; *and the baby from that day began to improve*" (Graham).

To do away with the evil eye, in which the Russians are firm believers, the "wise woman" takes a vessel of tepid water, in which she puts a cinder or two and a pinch of salt. If the cinders hiss very much, it is a first sign that "the servant of God" is really bewitched. Having said a prayer, she crosses the water, and begins to whisper another, of immense length and extraordinary mystery and incomprehensibility of language, while holding the vessel level with her chin.

In a few minutes she begins to yawn to an alarming degree—the second sign of bewitchment. When the prayer is finished, she crosses the water again, and taking a sip of it in her mouth, squirts it through her lips into the face of the patient three times, makes him drink a little, and finally washes his head and face with the remainder.

Charms against ague are very popular amongst the peasantry. In most cases they are worn round the neck on the same silken cord that the cross is suspended by, sometimes in a small bag, or rolled in a piece of rag.

1. A live spider, confined in a thimble or a nutshell, and tied up with a rag.

2. Incense, or rather, cinders that have been in the censer during three liturgies for the repose of someone's soul.

3. A blessed Easter egg that has lain on the Icon shelf for *three* Easters.

4. The "Zarranski" herb, sometimes placed at the head of the bed, or beneath the pillow, or worn round the neck.

5. The word Abracadabra. It is written upon a slip of paper with one letter missing in each line.

ABRACADABRA
BRACADABRA
RACADABRA
ACADABRA

The patient cuts off a line every day, and burns it, murmuring prayers and crossing himself meanwhile.

6. A Passion Candle that has been used at either Matins on Palm Sunday, Vespers on Holy Thursday, Vespers on Good Friday, or midnight service on Easter-day.

The candle-end is worn round the neck or a portion is fastened on the cross which the patient wears.

7. Camphor which has been prayed over by a "wise woman."

8. Water fetched at break of day, taken from a river in the direction of its flow. Strict silence must be observed in going to and coming from the stream, and on reaching home the Lord's Prayer, the Creed, and the sixty-eighth Psalm must be said three times over the water.

9. A certain way is to make a rag doll, whisper a prayer over it, and throw it into a neighbour's yard. The patient will lose the ague; the one who picks up the doll will get it.

These are only a few out of many, and all have a religious significance.

There is no doubt that religion is one of the chief recreations of the peasant, and plays a very real and important part in his life. In many cases, however, their religion is allied to gross superstition. Whilst they keep on good terms with God by closely observing the ordinances and ceremonies of the Orthodox Church, they also protect themselves from the evil which can be wrought against them by lesser deities. The peasant has peopled the homes, farms, baths, fields, woods, rivers, and lakes with spirits, many of them of a malignant or merely mischievous character. I am greatly indebted to Howard P. Kennard for much of what follows upon the superstitions of the Russian peasantry.

"It is generally understood amongst the Russian peasantry that swarms' of spirits—good, bad, and indifferent—wander at will through the Universe, and nothing will shake from them this belief, which, again, is sedulously fostered in their all too credulous brain by the iniquitous representatives of the Church. Every spot on the world's surface harbours these spirits; not even the sanctity of the Orthodox Churches is respected. These immaterial beings are, as a rule, the personification of evil, and the bitter and unrelenting foes of mankind. They penetrate into private houses, into human bodies, into holy edifices; they swarm in river, lake, and pond. They wander at will through forest and valley and across the boundless plains, bringing misfortune, disease, and every conceivable form of temptation in their train. Their number is legion, and they are blessed by the peasantry with all kinds of names—Tchort, Diavol, and others, all of which can be translated by the one word ' devil.'

"However, in different provinces, according to supposed misdeeds of the evil one, the name undergoes a change, and so in this way each spirit has some thirty to forty different names. With regard to the special attributes of the spirits, the popular peasant imagination divides them into the following distinct groups, and it is indicative of the

state of mind and the bringing up of our unfortunate friend, and of the moral and intellectual
teaching bestowed on him by the Church, that
the only subject he knows about is the subject
of these devils. If he does not know any minor
detail regarding the life of these devils, the history
of some spirit, he says, 'I will ask the priest';
proving that the source of his instruction is the
Church.   The following is a list of the spirits
as known to the Russian peasant and the ecclesiastical world, with a slight sketch of the attributes
of each one of them:

Domovoi	Household demon.
Domovoi dvorov .	Farmyard demon.
Bannik	Bath demon.
Ovennik .	Barn demon.
Kikimona	Hole demon.
Leshi	Wood demon.
Polevoi	Field demon.
Vodiavoi .	Water demon.
·Roussilki	Water fairies
Obvrotni .	Incarnations

"The Domovoi or household demon is that
one most commonly to be heard discussed by the
peasants at work and at rest, at market and fête,
on festival days and the holidays in honour of
any official function. 'What will the Domovoi
do to-day?' is the peasants' first thought.   What
can he do?   Much.   He haunts dwellings and plays
disagreeable tricks on unsuspecting housewives and
their husbands; but he can also be domesticated

l

and made almost harmless. However, he is none
the less feared, and the peasantry often allude to
him as 'grandfather.' Peasants, as a rule, tell
me that the Domovoi cannot be seen, but those
who have been honoured by a private view are
looked upon with nothing short of veneration. By
these the Domovoi is stated to be in possession of
a rasping voice, and to be covered with soft hair,
like the down on a baby's skin, even to the palms
of his hands. His principal occupation is to hide
in stores, cupboards, boxes, and moan dismally,
occasionally asserting himself by sitting on men's
chests while they sleep.

"The Russian peasant, after a heavy carousal,
and a consequent invasion by the evil Domovoi,
prescribes another bottle of vodka for himself,
and gets drunk again.

"Before any extensive culinary operations the
Russian peasant woman invokes the aid of the
Domovoi, and I have frequently seen her endeavour to propitiate the spirit in favour of her
sinning husband, who is out late at night on a
drinking bout, by placing outside the door provisions, such as bread and a bottle of *kvass*, in
order that the Domovoi may eat and imbibe, and
guide her husband's footsteps safely home.

"In family events of any importance, such as
marriages, births, deaths, food is placed on the
threshold both inside and outside for the Domovoi's
consumption, with the words: 'There for thee,

4

grandfather Domovoi; may your deeds be well
for us, and mayst thou aid us with thy kind
assistance, that our actions may prosper, our
children grow up, and our hens and pigs multiply.'
In return for all this attention bestowed on the
Domovoi, he, when in a friendly disposition, is
said to warn his hosts about impending trouble.
In what manner he does this I have never succeeded in ascertaining; but it would seem that
it is done through the medium of dreams. Further,
the Domovoi gives the peasant advice by means
of the same medium, and, strange to say, the
dream often takes the form of advice to steal his
master's wood, potatoes, and what not. This he
religiously proceeds to do, feeling absolutely justi-
fied in the performance of the deed, for one must
know the Russian *moujik* if one wishes to be
acquainted with the type *par excellence* of that
human being who can convince himself that is
right which he in his inmost conscience knows is
wrong, but which he ardently wishes to believe is
right."

Tolstoi, in his parable, *Master and Man*, brings
out this trait. 'Vassili really had believed that he
was being good to Nikita, for he could speak so
persuasively and had always been so entirely supported in his decisions by his dependents, that
even he himself had come to feel comfortably
persuaded that he was not cheating them, but
actually benefitting them.'

l

"The Domovoi dvorov or farmyard spirit, is a malign person who delights in tormenting domestic animals. It is owing to his evil influence that cows get weak and thin, horses get mutilated, and their tails cut. His appearance is that of a man, but covered completely with hair.

"He exercises complete dominion over the farmyard, and when the good Russian housewife takes a goose or fowl from the farmyard stock, she often practises deception on the Domovoi dvorov by hanging up the head of the fowl or goose in the poultry shed, in order that the spirit, when he counts his protégées, may not discover that one has been removed.

"The Bannik or bath demon haunts bath-houses, which, in consequence, are not considered safe after midnight. He hides under the shelves round the bath-house, is a very malicious spirit, and capable of the most outrageous crimes against the person, so in consequence the peasantry do all in their power to flatter him. At the time when the peasants bathe, it is known that the Bannik takes his bath at the fourth turn. This turn he usurps for his own, and peasants always, therefore, avoid bathing after the third, fearing that hot bricks may fall on them, boiling water may be thrown at them, steam scald them; and the method therefore adopted is to leave the bath-room, in the event of the peasants bathing singly, after the third turn to the exclusive use of the Bannik, for a period varying from twenty minutes to half an hour, and then after that period to return.

"In the Russian villages no one bathes after seven, that is to say, in those districts where the belief in the Bannik prevails, for it is an unwritten law, handed down from father to child for generations, that after that hour the Bannik takes possession of the bath-house, and invites the devil with his friends to wash. So much is this believed in that in many villages I have seen grown men and women afraid to walk in the direction of the bath-house, and you might offer them gold to walk past the door, but they would not accept it.

"The Ovennik or barn spirit. Village barns are ill-built wood constructions, and owing to the peasants' carelessness are frequently burned down; but simple and natural reasons are not admitted for these catastrophes. All evils of this nature are placed to the credit of the barn spirit. This evil personage sits in the darkest corner of the barn, and can be seen only once a year, during Mass on Easter-day, when he can be recognised by all who are foolhardy enough to endeavour to catch a glimpse of him, as a large black cat.

"He is well disposed as a rule, and much may be done to pacify him. In the winter, rather than that he should set the barn alight in order to warm himself, I have known peasants in the

Central Provinces of Russia burn each night a
small quantity of wood and straw in the open outside the barn, in order that the Ovennik may, if
he pleases, come out and warm himself, this too
in villages where wood has been scarce and poverty
prevalent, showing once more the depths of folly
to which superstition will lead them.

.   " The Kikimona lives in holes, and plays
tricks, and frequently is associated with the en-
tangling of skeins, the mixing of threads, and
the spoiling of spinning.   But the main function
of the Kikimona is the causing of epidemics of
disease.   To-day, in Samara, where the famine is
raging, and typhus and scurvy with it, it is safe
to assume that in the eyes of the peasantry the evil
time has been organised by the Kikimona.   In the
year 1891, the year of the great famine, the
peasants of the Kharkoff Government met, and
solemnly forwarded a petition to the Tsar, through
the hand of the Governor, to the effect that,
'seeing that that child of the devil, the Kikimona,
was absolutely and solely to blame for the terrible
want of provisions, would His Majesty take the
necessary steps towards the extermination of that
spirit.'

" The Leshi or wood spirit lives in the woods,
preferring more especially old, moss-grown, venerable firs.   His appearance is that of an old man,

l

his eyes burning with an unsteady flame. He grows at will into a person of immense size, or vanishes into thin air.

"While walking in his realms, he is taller than the tallest elms, but on coming into the open he can and does hide himself under a leaf.

"He is the despotic monarch of the forest, makes people lose their way, frightens them to death, and is reputed in many districts to have a terribly sensual nature, and to seduce women and girls indiscriminately. To some people he is very friendly, and will frequently bring game almost within reach of the hunter's hand, and lead him straight to their haunts. The peasants often bribe him extensively by leaving a dead hare or rabbit in the wood for his consumption."

"The Polevoi or field spirit takes the form of a peasant man, dressed in white. His body is black, eyes of various colours, and instead of hair, his head is covered with green grass. He is well disposed, but teases unmercifully, and especially annoys drunkards, his favourite hours for mischief being mid-day—a peculiar acknowledgment on the part of the peasant of his condition at that hour.

"Sometimes the Polevoi gets dangerous, and strangles the peasants sleeping in the fields. If the agricultural tools will not work, or if some part of the mechanism breaks, or if the soil is too

L

hard to allow of sufficient working, all these difficulties are put down to the account of the evil
Polevoi. He is again bribed by the peasantry. I
have seen an intoxicated peasant, before lying
down to sleep in the field, place another vodka
bottle, full of the stuff, by his side, and with the
words, ' There, that's for you, Polevoi,' sink to
slumber.

"The Vodiavoi or water spirit haunts lakes
and dangerous marshes. He keeps a strict guard
on his dominions, and it bodes ill indeed for those
who defy his wrath. Sometimes the Vodiavoi
takes up his abode in rivers and streams, and
frequently sleeps the night under the wheels of
a water mill. He can be seen sometimes as an
ordinary man, but with very long fingers, and
nails on his hands more like paws than ordinary
hands. His head is covered with long hairs; he
has a very long tail, and eyes which burn like a
red hot coal. He never comes quite out of the
water, but shows himself at half length.
"He drowns imprudent people bathing or
sailing on his domains, and delights in killing
those who never wear their baptismal crosses, and
forget God. Bruises, marks, wounds on the body
of a drowned man, are invariably taken as proof
of the torments inflicted by the Vodiavoi. He is
most disagreeable to millers and fishermen, but
some of the latter come to an understanding with

him, and get proofs of his friendship. But throughout Russia the peasantry believe that he requires
human victims for his daily food, and nothing will
convince them to the contrary.

" The Roussilki or water fairies are represented
as beautiful women and girls, young angels, singing and dancing in the moonlight on lakes, pools,
and streams, trying to attract men, whom they
torment and drown.   The most fervent belief in
the existence of the Roussilki, and the most
poetical stories and songs regarding their deeds,
are to be found amongst the people of little Russia.
They are credited with tearing fishermen's nets,
and it is believed that girls who drown themselves
through love become Roussilki.

"The Oborotni are either men changed by
sorcerers into animals, trees, or stones, or evil
spirits taking any form necessary to acquire their
object.   The most common form is that of a she
wolf, which may transform itself into a dog, a
cat, a bust, a stone, or a tree, and then return to
the image of a man.

"Obinenki.   Yet other spirits are supposed
to be devil's children, which are substituted in
the place of human babies profiting by some im-
prudence or forgetfulness on the part of the

mother. This belief does sometimes very great harm to quite innocent beings.

"One instance must suffice.

"A girl at the age of nine developed a hoarse guttural cough and a peculiar, rather vacant, expression of countenance. At the same time it was noticed that whatever house she entered there was sure to be illness. A consultation of the elders of the village was held, and it was decided that this unfortunate girl was no human child, but the child of one of the numerous devils, which had been placed as a substitute in the cradle during the period of suckling. A wise woman was called in to give her opinion, and without any hesitation gave it on the side of the majority. The mother was informed of the terrible decision, and such is the faith of the peasant in devils, and all things appertaining to them, she acceded to their request, which was that the wretched girl, in order to stop her wandering in the village and doing harm, should be chained to the wall of the house.

"This was done, and after a while the child became mad, but was kept chained to the wall for thirteen years, when she died in 1906."

The superstition of the Russian peasant is not alone in the Domovoi, but reaches beyond to the ordinary incidents of everyday life. When starting out on a business journey, for a woman to cross the road (it is always a woman) in front of

L

one will mean a bad market, even if not worse trouble.   There are varying degrees of harm brought about by a hare, cat, or a dog crossing one's path.

To neglect to clean the Icon, to replenish the oil in the sacred lamp, to forget to cross one's self when rising in the morning, to lay aside for awhile the baptismal cross, any or all of these will bring ill-luck or disaster to one's self or to one's property.

The "wise woman" is a power in every village. Sometimes she will brew a concoction of herbs, more frequently use mercury, and in liberal doses, but her usual method is by way of charms and incantations and mysterious rites.

THE HOLY ORTHODOX CHURCH

BIBLIOGRAPHY.

MOURAVIEFF . *History of the Russian Church.*

STANLEY . . *The Eastern Church.*

BLACKMORE . *Doctrines of the Russian Church.*

PALMER. . . *Dissertations on the Orthodox Communion.*

PARES . . . *Russia and Reform.*

GRAHAM . . *Changing Russia.*

SOLOVYOV . . *Otcherki iz istorii russkoi Literaturi.*

WALLACE . . *Russia.*

L

It must be manifest to every open mind that we have here no decadent or emasculated spiritual institution. A religion which has vivified and resuscitated nations : which throbs in the heart of one of the mightiest and most rapidly advancing of modern empires ; which commands the spiritual allegiance and gains the impassioned loyalty of the manhood of the Russian Empire, as no other Church does in any other land, is surely entitled to careful study by all those who feel interested in the comparative theology of the age.

DURBAN. *The New Orthodoxy.*

THE HOLY ORTHODOX CHURCH

EVERY Church of Christendom, like every race of mankind, has its own special genius and its distinct character. The Gospel runs itself into all manner of moulds, and whilst the essentials of prayer, faith, hope, and love are one, the outward manifestations of the spirit are as varied as the differing characteristics of men and nations. There may be unity in the Spirit, with diversity in the modes of worship. Amongst all Christians there may be the progressive spirit, ever seeking to comprehend some of the many things of which the Master said "Ye cannot bear them now," and a conservative spirit, which is content with that which has been handed down from father to son through many generations, and which has become crystallised in tradition and custom.

The Holy Orthodox Church in Russia, like Russia among the nations, has been the most conservative, stationary, even to stagnation, almost, of all the Churches in Christendom. No innovation has been allowed to invade the Russian Church for centuries. "No development, either in doctrine or in discipline, has ever disturbed the venerable and vast calm of the Holy Orthodox

Church." She is the true home of use and wont, custom and tradition; she is the true harbour and house of refuge for all those who are determined neither to go forward nor to go backward, but always to stand still.

"The straws of custom," says Stanley, "show which way the spirit of an institution blows. The primitive posture of standing in prayer still retains its ground in the East; whilst in the West it is only preserved in the extreme Protestant communities by way of antagonism to Rome. Organs and all musical instruments are as odious to a Greek or a Russian Churchman as they are to an old-time Scottish Presbyterian. Even the schism that convulsed the Russian Church almost at the same time that Latin Christendom was rent by the German Reformation, was not a forward movement, a protest against abuses, but against innovations."

The Russian Church is The One, Apostolic, Holy, Orthodox, Catholic Church, and all outside of her communion and obedience are schismatics and heretics. Protestants in the West are more or less used to the lofty presumptions of Rome; but the East looks down on us all. We are all dissenters and schismatics to her. Rome and Geneva, Canterbury and Edinburgh, are all in the same condemnation.

Balsamon says; "We excommunicate the Pope for all his errors; and with him, all the West who

l

heretically adhere to him. All the West are to be treated simply as so many schismatics, and an anathema must be provided for their abjuration."

That anathema is provided and pronounced in every Russian Church on the first Sunday in Lent; and that Sunday is known as Orthodox Sunday. On that day some sixty anathemas are hurled against all heretics and schismatics, from Arius of Alexandria down to our own day; on the other hand, for all the Orthodox, "Everlasting Remembrance."

The deadness of the Russian Church is not alone the result of the stolidity of the Russian character. The causes are to be sought for in her system. She has never been a missionary Church. The cry of the heathen has been to her unheeded. There has never been in her history, at least for the last three hundred years, a spiritual impulse to carry the Gospel to the regions beyond; and any Church which neglects that call is doomed to stagnation. The Church of Russia stands all the day idle in the market-place, whilst her sisters, in many forms of faith and practice, have gone out to inherit the waste places of the earth. When at long last she is stirred by a true missionary impulse, and gives herself with all the abandon of the Russian nation to the evangelisation of the world, then, and not till then, will she awake from her long sleep, and take her

place with the Churches of the West in the development of her "soul."

That the old spirit of intolerance and obscura-
tion is not yet dead may be gathered from the
following manifesto issued in 1908 by the Metropolitan of S. Petersburg, Antonius:

"The Orthodox Church is a divine institution.

"We teach that salvation can only be obtained
while abiding in fellowship with the Church. By
fellowship, we understand general prayer, Church
charity, the Sacraments, all one's activity sanctioned by the Church, good works done in the
Name of Christ and the Church, and not in one's
own.

"We agree that it is possible, though abiding
outwardly in the Church, to be a weak member
of the Orthodox Church, but it is perfectly plain
that a man who separates himself from the Church
breaks his fellowship with her, ceases to be one
with her in spirit. Separating himself from the
Church, a man separates himself from Christ.

"Thus teacheth the Orthodox faith. Except
of the Church, the Grace of Christ does not exist.

"Therefore, when the Orthodox Church
speaks of enemies of the Church, her meaning is
plain. Enemies of the Orthodox Church are all
those who profess any other religion, who deny
that the Orthodox Church is the only true source
of the Grace of Christ.

"Enemies of the Orthodox Church are all

those belonging to any other denomination--Raskolniks, Sectarians, Masons, the Godless, and so on.

"To leave the Orthodox Church, and be in enmity with her, is the greatest sin; for which there is no justification. No sin or failure of the clergy can serve as an excuse for apostasy. These must be warned and fought against while still remaining in the Church. But if any, in fighting against the evils existing in the Church, reaches so far as to fall away from the Church himself, he only proves by this that he is far worse than those whom he has been trying to convict of sin "

Russia took her faith and theology, her practice and ceremonies, over from the early monks of the Eastern Church, and she has hardly changed one jot or tittle from that day to this.

Nestor, the Monk and Annalist of the Pechersky Monastery, at Kiev, in the year 1116 A.D. declares that the Russian Church owes its origin to the travels of St. Andrew the Apostle, who, on his way from Sinope to Rome, crossed the Russian steppes, and from the summit of a low hill first saw the heights upon which modern Kiev has been built.

Planting his cross in the ground, he exclaimed to his companions: "See you these hills? On these hills shall shine the light of Divine Grace There shall be here a great city, and God shall have in it many Churches to His Name."

Whilst this legend accounts for the intro-

l   5

duction of ˙Christianity into the South by way of
the river Dneiper, Macarius, in his *Travels*, tells
of a saint (either Nicolas or Anthony) who was
thrown into the River Tiber at Rome with a
millstone round his neck, and on or with this
millstone, journeyed along the shores of the
Mediterranean, rounded Gibraltar, crossed the Bay
of Biscay, reached the Baltic by way of the North
Sea, and entering the River Neva, made his way
to Lake Ladoga, swam to the broad waters of
the River Volkhoff, and reaching the shores of
Lake Ilmen, found himself by the walls of
Novgorod the Great, the dominant republic of
Ancient Russia, and there won the people to
Christianity.

Both these accounts may be dismissed as
legends or fables, but they indicate that Christianity found its way into Russia along the banks
of the mighty rivers, and from thence penetrated
through the forests to the nomadic tribes on the
boundless steppes.

Muravieff, in his *Origin of Christianity in
Russia*, says:

"As far as we know, it appears that Oskold
and Dir, two Princes of Kiev and companions of
Ruric, were the first of the Russians who embraced Christianity. In the year 866 A.D. they
made their appearance in armed vessels before
the walls of Constantinople, when the Emperor
was absent, and threw the Greek capital into no

little alarm and confusion. Tradition reports that the Patriarch Photius took the robe of the Virgin Mother and plunged it beneath the waves of the Strait, when the sea immediately boiled up from underneath and wrecked the vessels of the heathen.

"Stricken with awe, they believed in that God who had smitten them, and became the first-fruits of their people to the Lord The Hymn of Victory of the Greek Church, 'To the Protecting Conductress,' in honour of the Virgin, has remained a memorial of this triumph, and even now among ourselves concludes the office for the first hour in the daily Matins, for that was indeed the first hour of salvation to the land of Russia "

The Patriarch Photius, in a circular letter, says: "Not only have the Bulgarians come over to the Christian faith, but also the nation of the Russians, who, proud of their successes, lately even exalted themselves against the Greek Empire, are beginning to exchange the impurities of heathenism for the pure and Orthodox doctrines of Christianity."

There is every likelihood that when Oskold and Dir returned home to Kiev they carried with them the seeds of a new faith, for in the Russian Chronicles of eighty years later there is mention of a Church in Kiev, named after the Prophet Elias, whilst there are also records that the Emperor Basil of Macedonia sent Bishops to Russia, who were called "Photian" Bishops.

l

In a catalogue of Sees subject to the Patriarch of Constantinople, the Metropolical See of Russia appears as early as the year 891 A.D. It is not, however, until the closing years of the tenth century that we have authentic accounts of the introduction of Christianity into Russia.

The Bulgarians of the Danube, the Moravians, the Slavonic peoples of Illyria, had already been evangelised about the middle of the ninth century. Cyril and Methodius had translated into Slavonic the New Testament and the service books used in Divine worship, and, according to some historians, even the whole Bible.

This early translation of the Word of God was a most potent factor in the early introduction of Christianity, for the missionary monks were by it enabled to expound the Gospel to the Russ in their native dialect and thus obtain a readier access to them.

That these early monks carried the Gospel far and wide, and had a hearing for their message, may be gathered from the fact that the widowed Princess Olga, who was Regent during the minority of her son Sviatoslav, had evidently been brought into touch with Christian teaching, for in the year 965 A.D. she undertook a journey to Constantinople, to learn more of the Gospel and the true knowledge of God, and to receive baptism at the hands of the Patriarch.

Nestor, the Monk, draws a very vivid picture

l

of the baptism, and in reference to Olga (she received the name of Helena on her baptism) says:

"She was the forerunner of Christianity in Russia, as the morning star is the precursor of the sun, and the dawn the precursor of the day. As the moon shines at midnight, she shone in the midst of a pagan people. She was like a pearl amidst dirt, for the people were in the mire of their sins, and not yet purified by baptism. She purified herself in that holy bath. and removed the garb of sin of the old man Adam."

Her son still clung to his heathen deities, and refused to embrace the new faith, but affection for his mother led him to agree, not only not to persecute the Christians, but to allow them to make open profession of faith under the protection of the Princess. During his many and frequent absences from home, mainly on military expeditions, his son Vladimir was confided to Olga's care, who sought to instruct her grandson in the true faith. Her efforts were apparently fruitless, for Vladimir became a ferocious prince, as notorious for his savage crimes as for his idolatrous zeal. The only two Christian martyrs mentioned by Nestor in his chronicle were Theodore and John, who were put to death because one of them had refused, out of filial affection, to deliver his son to be sacrificed by Prince Vladimir upon the altar of the god "Peroun."

The military exploits of Vladimir, and the consequent extension of his authority and influence, naturally led the Princes of neighbouring States to seek an alliance with him. To this end they sent envoys, partly political and partly religious in their mission. In about the year 986 A.D. a company of Mussulman Bulgars came to Kiev from the region of the Volga; they invited Vladimir to accept their faith and to conclude an alliance with their Prince.

"In what does your religion consist?" asked Vladimir.

".We believe in God," they replied, "but we also believe in what the prophet teaches, do not eat pork, abstain from wine, and after death choose seventy beautiful women for our wives." Whilst inclined to accept their faith, perhaps for the latter reason, abstinence from pork and wine was too much for him. "Drinking is the great delight of Russians," said he; "we cannot live without it." They returned to the Volga, having failed in their mission.

Later, the Chazarian Jews came to him and boasted of their religion and the ancient glory of Jerusalem.

".Where is your country?" asked the Prince. "It is ruined by God's wrath upon us," answered the ambassadors. "What!" cried Vladimir; "you come to teach others, and you whom God has rejected and despised! Do you wish for us

to embrace your faith, and suffer the same punishment? Go home; I do not accept the religion of
a people whom God has abandoned."

From Western Christendom, according to
Karamsin, came envoys. (Muravieff says, " learned
doctors from Germany ") " We have come to
tell you that your country is like unto ours, but
not your religion. We worship God the Creator,
you worship gods made of wood, created."
" Return home," replied Vladimir; " our forbears
did not receive this religion from you."

A Greek embassy had the best success of
them all. Many factors had been at work making
their visit more likely to be received with favour.
There had been a constant interchange of visits
between Kiev and Constantinople; the seeds of
Christianity had been sown by Oskold, Dir, and
Olga; many of the people had already accepted
the new doctrines, and had forsaken the idol
Peroun; and an alliance with the powerful Greek
Empire was politically a desirable thing.

Evidently the Greek Patriarch had heard of
the other attempts to win over Vladimir from
idolatry to a more spiritual faith, for he sent
a monk named Constantine, who, after showing
at some length the insufficiency of the other com-
peting religions for Vladimir's acceptance, pressed
upon him those judgments of God which are in
all the world; the redemption of the human race
by the blood of Christ, and the retribution of the

life to come. Nestor represents Vladimir as speaking thus of the preaching of the Greek monk. "He recounted to us with much eloquence what had taken place from the beginning of the world It was wonderful to hear, and excited the admiration of all. They assured us that there is another world beyond this, and that if anyone by baptism makes a confession of that faith which they have embraced, and die in this faith, he shall rise again after death, and never die more throughout eternity; but that he . who will not believe shall in that world be burned with everlasting fire."

Vladimir was undoubtedly impressed, but he still hesitated, and after dismissing the embassy, remained undecided as to his own action in embracing the new faith. After meeting his Council he decided to send envoys to Constantinople, to make observations upon each religion and to recommend to the people which they should accept.

On arriving in Constantinople the Boyars were taken to the great Cathedral of St. Sophia. The magnificent proportions of the building, the sublimity and splendour of the service, filled them with awe and wonder. The smoke of incense curled towards the lofty dome; chants from boyish voices resounded throughout the spacious building; patriarch and priests moved to and fro in glittering and gorgeous vestments; deacons and sub-deacons, with lighted torches in their hands, moved in procession, singing their hymns of praise. Every-

thing possible was done to impress the visitors.
Well might they report to their Prince "When
we stood in the temple we did not know where
we were, for there is nothing else like it on earth,
there, in truth, God has His dwelling with men;
and we can never forget the beauty we saw there.
No one who has once tasted sweets will afterwards
take that which is bitter; nor can we now any
longer abide in heathenism. If the religion of the
Greeks had not been good, your grandmother
Olga, who was the wisest of women, would not have
embraced it."

Vladimir was not yet ready to yield to the
enthusiasm of his Boyars, but, like many of his
ancestors, he determined to win his religion with
his sword. In attacking the city of Kherson, he
vowed that if he should conquer, then he would
be baptised. After a long and protracted siege
the city fell into the hands of Vladimir. According
to some historians, this was accomplished through
the treachery of a priest who had heard of the
Prince's vow. Vladimir demanded the hand of
Anna, the sister of the Greek Emperor, in marriage
This was granted to him upon the condition that
he embraced Christianity. After the lapse of a
few weeks, Vladimir was baptised by the Bishop
of Kherson, at Kherson. Many of the Boyars
followed their Prince's example. The marriage
was celebrated in the Church of the Most Holy
Mother of God, and upon his return home with

his bride, his twelve sons were baptised, the huge wooden idol, "Peroun," was thrown into the river Dneiper, and orders were issued for a wholesale baptism of the inhabitants of Kiev.

"Whoever, on the morrow, refuses to repair to the river for baptism, whether rich or poor, will be held as an enemy of the Prince." Nestor, describing the scene, says: "Some stood in the waters up to their necks; others up to their breasts, holding their children in their arms; the priests read the prayers; and when the whole people were baptised they returned to their homes filled with joy."

Vladimir, with his usual energy, began to build Churches in all the towns and villages of his dominions, and sent priests and monks to instruct the people in the new faith. He established schools for the children of the Boyars, and missionary monks were sent to Rostov, Novgorod, and even beyond the river Volga, preaching, teaching, and baptising the people.

By the year 996 A.D. the Gospel had spread throughout all Russia, and the first five dioceses were established and bishops appointed.

Vladimir died in 1015 A.D., and shortly after his death he was "canonised" as the guardian saint of Russia, being known as Saint Basil, whilst his grandmother Olga received the same distinction as Saint Olga.

The Russian Church, like the Byzantine, was

thus from its earliest days connected in a most intimate manner with the life and will of the prince or ruler of the State, a condition which has continued until this present day.

"As in all Eastern nations," says Dean Stanley, "so in Russia, the national and the religious elements have been identified far more closely than in the West, and this identification has been continued in a more or less unbroken form." Its religious festivals are still national; its national festivals are still religious. The Church has become part of the warp and woof of the national life.

THE RISE OF MONASTICISM

YAROSLAV, " The Princely Lawgiver," successor to Vladimir, founded two monasteries in Kiev, one for men, by the name of " Saint George," his own patron angel, and the other for women, named after the angel of his consort, " Saint Irene."

The Metropolitan Michael founded the Vidoubetz or " Come out " monastery, whilst the Boyars were also instrumental in founding religious houses upon their estates, but the real commencement of the monastic life in Russia can be traced to a simple and pious hermit, who made his own retreat a nursery for the monastic life. " Many monasteries," says Nestor, "have been founded by princes and nobles, and by wealth, but they are not such as those which have been founded

l

by tears, and fasting, and prayer, and vigil:
Anthony had neither gold nor silver, but he pro-
cured all by prayer and fasting."

Anthony, a native of Lubetch, south of Kiev,
visited the famous monastery at Mount Athos, and
there conceived a desire to finish his days in
monastic seclusion, but the Hegumen who ton-
sured him counselled him to return to his own .
country. Anthony obeyed, and brought back with
him the blessing of the Monastery of the Holy
Mountain. He visited the religious houses in and
around Kiev, but could not find the soul satisfaction
for which he craved, until at last he came to
the deserted cave of Hilarion, one time priest of
the Church of the Apostles at Berestov.

Here Anthony established himself, disciples
came to him, and subsequently they built the
Church of the Assumption · on the spot, whilst
the founder went some little distance away, and
excavated for himself another cell, where he could
in retirement spend his days in prayer. Anthony
nominated Theodosius to be the superior of the
brethren, and to him belongs the distinction of
founding the great Pecherski Lavra or Monastery.

Theodosius wrote out for the brethren—more
than a hundred in number by this time—the Rule
of the Studium Monastery, the strictest in all
Constantinople, which a monk had brought with
him from that city. Nestor the Annalist was
an eye-witness of the life and conduct of

ι

Theodosius, for he entered upon his novitiate in his seventeenth year, what time Theodosius established the Lavra.

The Pecherski Monastery struck its roots deep into Russian soil, and its influence was early felt, not only in monastic seclusion, the founding of other religious houses, but in the halls of princes and on the thrones of the great prelates of the Church.

Monks went forth from the monastery, preaching the Gospel to savage and nomadic tribes, many of them laying down their lives for the faith whilst engaged in their missionary labours. The germ of the monastery in Russia has always been the hermitage. These great institutions were founded by men who became the disciples of ascetic hermits, who, in withdrawing from the world, lived in caves and huts, and spent their days in meditation and prayer. Anthony, Hilarion, and Theodosius were imitators of the early hermits in Egypt, who, by the way, had the same names, whilst we have records of imitators of Simeon Stylites and the pillar hermits.

Even to-day the influence of the hermit and pilgrim in Russia is greater than in any other part of Christendom. As the hermits played such an important part in the rise and development of monasticism, it is worth our while to turn aside for awhile to see them as they appeared to contemporary historians.

Fletcher, in the *Russian Commonwealth*,

L

published in 1588, and quoted by Dean Stanley,
writes: "There are certain eremites (hermits)
who used to go stark naked, save a clout about
their middle, with their hair hanging long and
wildly about their shoulders, and many of them
with an iron collar or chain about their necks
or middles even in the very extremity of winter.
These they take as prophets and men of great
holiness, giving them a liberty to speak what they
list without any controlment, though it be of
the very Highest Himself. So that if he reprove
any openly, in what sort soever, they answer
nothing, but that it is *po grecum* ('for their sins').
And if any of them take some piece of sale
ware from any man's shop as he passeth by, to
give where he list, he thinketh himself much
beloved of God, and much beholden to the holy
man for taking it in that sort. The people liketh
very well of them, because they are as pasquils
(pasquins) to note their great men's faults, that
no man else dare speak of. Yet it falleth out
sometimes that for this rude liberty which they
take upon them, after a counterfeit manner by
imitation of the prophets, they are made away in
secret; as was one or two of them in the late
Emperor's time for being over bold in speaking
against his government . . . of this kind there
are not many, because it is a very hard and
cold profession to go naked in Russia, especially
in winter.

" There is one at this time that walketh naked about the streets of Moscow, and inveigheth commonly against the State and Government, especially against the Goudonoffs" (the authors of the serfdom of the Russian peasantry). Horsey (*The Travels of Sir Jerome Horsey* 1591) describes another, named Nicolas of Pskoff or Plescov " I saw this impostor or magician, a foul creature; went naked both in winter and summer, he endured both extreme heat and frost; did many things through the magical illusions of the devil, much followed, praised, and renowned both by prince and people. He did much good when Ivan the Terrible came to massacre the whole town as he had done at Novgorod.

"With his accustomed rudeness he sent to Ivan a piece of raw flesh as a present during Lent, and when remonstrated with he exclaimed, 'Thinkest thou that it is unlawful to eat a piece of beast's flesh in Lent, and not unlawful to eat up so much man's flesh as thou hast already?' Ivan trembled and cowered before the hermit, changed his purpose, and the inhabitants of Plescov were saved from his fell design."

No prophet of old, no reformer of modern times, could have delivered a more striking testimony in behalf of the true moral character of Christianity than the wild hermit with his raw flesh in Lent.

From the followers of such men the monas-

L

teries were founded, and in course of time acquired their own peculiar mission in Russian ecclesiastical and civil history.

In the troublous times through which Russia was passing, many of the monasteries became half sanctuaries and half fortresses, they were at the same time refuges of national life and monuments of victories won on behalf of an oppressed people against Tatar and Mongol invaders, and on more than one occasion proved to be the rallying-place of defeated and dismayed armies, which, with fresh courage and renewed strength, led by warlike monks, have gone forth to do battle against their conquerors and have been victorious in the strife. The most notable instance of this spirit is to be found in the history of the Monastery of the Troitza (The Holy Trinity), about sixty miles from Moscow. Founded in 1338, and greatly enlarged in 1360, it combines within itself the monastery, university, palace, cathedral, churches, and with its high and strong walls, entrenched about with a deep moat, there is added to all, and in a marked degree, the elements of a military camp or fortress.

In the suburbs of Moscow are two monasteries which have played an important part in the history of Russia. One is the great fortress of the Donskoi Monastery, near to the Sparrow Hills, usually supposed to commemorate the victory of the Don; and the other is the Simonoff

L

Monastery, on the banks of the Moskva, founded by a nephew of the Great Sergius. It was from this monastery that the final blow was struck against the Khan of the Golden Horde, who was then Ruler of Russia. The battle had gone against Ivan III., and he was resigned to his fate, when the Prior Bassian, with the Metropolitan Gerontius, came· to the prince, exhorting him to rally his army against the invaders. Ivan III. hesitated, and the Prior exclaimed: "Dost thou dread death? Thou too must die as well as others; death is the lot of all—man, bird, beast alike; none can avoid it. Give these warriors into my hands, and old as I am, I will not spare myself, nor will ever turn my back. to the Tatars." Ivan returned to the camp; Achmet fled without a .blow being struck. Russia was at last free from the Tatar, and for ever.

The long struggle between the Tatar and the Russ for the supremacy over the Russian peoples, and the fact that the Tatars were "heathens" to the Russians, led to a consolidation of the forces of the Russian nation and gave to the Russian Church a full share in the development of the life of the nation.

"One result of the Tatar yoke was the strengthening of the Russian religion. Religion took the place of patriotism, or rather, patriotism took the shape of religion, and became inseparable from it. The peculiar quality which stamps

L   6

the religion of the Russian people to this day was the result of the Tatar yoke. To this day in Russia Orthodoxy is the hall-mark and indispensable adjunct of patriotism."

This view-point of the Russian peasant and government explains much of the bitter and severe persecution which has been meted out to Dissenters and Sectarians from the earliest times.

The rise of Monasticism, the quasi-military activities of the monks in repelling the Mongol invasions, the consolidation of the republics and separate kingdoms into a Tsardom, the spread of the Church to the Sclavonic tribes, and the submission of the princes and boyars to Christianity, all led to the strengthening and consolidation of the power and influence of the Church.

In the fratricidal wars of the twelfth century, when princes and boyars were contending for the mastery, the only thing which served as a pledge for the general unity was the confession of one and the same Orthodox faith throughout all the limits ·of the kingdom. The Bishops, as spiritual judges in their dioceses, and the priors of the religious houses, which were continually increasing in number, served as mediators and peacemakers between the contending parties, and in the quality of ambassadors, went backwards and forwards without danger between the hostile camps. But the disorders of civil society had their effect also upon the affairs of the Church. Hitherto the Metro-

L

politans of Kiev had been appointed by the Patriarch of Constantinople, but the growing national consciousness led Isyaslov to declare that the infant Russian Church would not have a Greek again for Metropolitan.

A Synod of Russian Bishops was convoked at Kiev, and the assembly agreed to take the election of a Metropolitan into their own hands, without the Patriarch's having any participation in the matter. Clement, a monk of Smolensk, was chosen, and subsequently ordained by the laying on his head of the hand of Saint Clement, Pope of Rome, whose relics had been brought from Kherson by Vladimr

Thus, as Professor Bernard Pares, in *Russia and Reform*, shows, "In the Church there was unity of authority before it existed in the State."

By the year 1328 the centre of gravity of the Russian nation and Church was shifted from Kiev, by way of Vladimir, to Moscow Gradually, with the building of Churches, the commencement of the world-renowned Kremlin, the multiplication of monasteries and religious houses, Moscow became the very personification of the ecclesiastical history of Russia. Even to-day one will hear the peasants in far-off provinces speak of "our Holy Mother Moscow." So great is the affection of the people towards her—and she is dear to the heart of every Russian—that they refer to the great highways as "Our dear Mother,

L

the great High Road from Riazan, or Koslov, to Moscow." She has no legends of Apostles connected with her history; no records of valiant missionaries as from the banks of the Bosphorous; nothing save her central position to commend her; yet she has become the third great religious centre of Christendom, only being surpassed by Jerusalem and Rome.

John, Prince of Moscow, persuaded the Metropolitan Peter to transfer his residence to Moscow, which from that time became the ecclesiastical capital of Russia. Peter foresaw the future of Moscow, and persuaded the prince to commence the building of the stone Cathedral of Assumption. " If thou wilt comfort my old age, if thou wilt build here a temple worthy of the Holy Mother of God, then shalt thou be more glorious than all the other princes, and thy posterity shall become great. My bones shall remain in this city, prelates shall rejoice to dwell in it, and the hands of its princes shall be upon the necks of our enemies."

In that same cathedral, where John himself was buried, and in whose walls are interred the remains of the Metropolitan, the successors of John have all been crowned, not only as " Prince of Moscow " but as " Tsar of all the Russias."

.   The rise of Moscow signified the gradual consolidation of the Russian Empire, the unity of the Russian peoples, and the strengthening of

L

the hold of the Church upon the life of the nation. Gradually the rulers became the ecclesiastical as well as the political heads of the Russian Empire. " He who blasphemes his Maker meets with forgiveness amongst men, but he who reviles the Emperor is sure to lose his head."

The Emperor is the " Keeper of the Keys," the " Body Servant of God "; he is the " Holy Tsar," the " *Zembla Bogh* " (God on Earth), the " Pope of the Orthodox," the " Adjuster of the Earth," the " Peace and Goodwill on Earth."

The Tsar is the first person in the Church, the Metropolitan of Russia is the seond, and the monastic orders the third. During this period of consolidation of State and Church, the Metropolitans of Russia never rose to any great height of political importance. They always proved themselves to be the supporters, and never the rivals, of the throne.

Two great crises in Russian history occurred during this second stage in the development of the Church State, the first, the breaking of the Tatar dominion, and the second, the final expulsion of the Poles. Dean Stanley says: " As the deliverance from the Spanish Armada to the Church and State of England, so was the deliverance from the Polish yoke to the Church and State of Russia."

In this terrific struggle it was the Church which saved the empire, and the monastery of

Sergius which saved them both Moscow is crowded with religious memorials of that great deliverance, the greatest of them all being the famous " Redeemer's Gate," the chief entrance to the Kremlin, through which no one, not even the Emperor himself, will presume to pass with covered head. Over the gateway is the famous sacred Icon, which was carried before the victorious army, and is held in reverence by all the Orthodox until this present day. •

Muravieff, in his *History of the Russian Church*, gives us a long list of Metropolitans of the Church during this period, but none of them were men of outstanding importance in the ecclesiastical history of the nation. The chief interest centres in the struggles with the Tatars and the Poles, the gradual growth in number and in influence of the monasteries, and the development of the Orthodox Church as a purely Russian or national one.

The rise of the Romanoffs to power in the State, and the election of Nicon to the Patriarchate of the Church, indirectly led to the greatest upheaval in the ecclesiastical history of the nation. Tsar and Patriarch alike were responsible for the " Great Schism." Owing to the continuous copying and recopying of the liturgical books, many inaccuracies crept into the text. So long as the books were in manuscript they could be revised and the scribe held to be responsible, but with

l

the introduction of printing the errors became stereotyped. The Patriarch, noticing the in-accuracies, decided upon a thorough revision. He sent to Greece and Constantinople for the original manuscripts from which the early Russian text had been translated, and set about a thorough revision with characteristic Russian energy.

Although the work was necessary, it came late in the day. The people were wedded to the version in their hands, and consequently a revolt set in. Although Nicon was ultimately deposed from his high office, a Council of the Church approved of the revised liturgical books, and they were ordered to be recognised as the official text of the Church. In addition to the revision of the text, Nicon also introduced reforms in the manner of making the sign of the cross, in the spelling of the name of Jesus, and of saying in the creed, " The Holy Ghost and Life Giver," instead of " True One and Life Giver."

The fall of Nicon directly led to the abolition of the Patriarchate.

Its abolition was the next step of importance in the development of the Russian Church.

THE MOST HOLY SYNOD

A TREMENDOUS advance in the internal administration of the Church was made when Peter the Great in 1721 suppressed the Patriarchate, and in its place instituted the Most Holy Synod,

L

which has been from that time the ruling authority of the Russian Church.

The Holy Synod, whose constitution has remained unchanged since its formation, consists of the Metropolitans of Kiev, Moscow, St. Petersburg, and the Exarch of Georgia. In addition to the foregoing the Tsar nominates six Bishops, his chaplain, the chief chaplain of the forces, and the Procurator.

The Synod is practically under the authority of the Procurator, who must always be a layman, and who acts as an intermediary between the Tsar and the Synod.

The Synod is not a Council of Deputies from various sections of the Church, but a permanent college or senate, the members of which are appointed and dismissed by the Tsar. It has no independent legislative authority, for its legislative projects do not become law till they have received Imperial sanction, and they are always published, not in the name of the Church, but in the name of the Supreme power. A Council constituted in this way cannot display much independence of thought or action. From the time of Peter, the character of all the more energetic sovereigns is reflected in the history of the ecclesiastical administration. The Procurator is the most important and influential member of the Synod. He has the control and direction of all Orthodox ecclesiastical institutes, religious seminaries, and schools. He has a seat both in the Ministerial Council and the Imperial Senate. In all matters directly or indirectly affecting the State Church his opinion must be consulted, and he stands in every respect on the same footing as the Ministers proper. Pobiedonostseff was the most famous of all the Procurators. In his *Reflections of a Russian Statesman* he states his belief that " Religion should be used as a weapon to combat intelligence." As a kind of political confessor, he was able to see that his programme was carried out. He established such a tyranny over the whole Church system as to make it one of the most powerful engines for the realisation of his central idea.

He succeeded in instilling into the heir to the Throne his own belief in the ability of the Orthodox teachings to direct the destiny of Russia along the only path which could save land and people.

He also inoculated his pupil with that intolerance and hate towards Dissenters and Sectarians which were so characteristic of the later years of Alexander's reign.

His earnestness, his zeal, his conviction that Russian Orthodoxy and Russian Autocracy were called upon to make, not only Russia, but also the rest of Europe, happy and contented, had a strong effect upon Alexander III.

At all meetings of the Holy Synod the members

present take an oath as follows: "I acknowledge him (the Tsar) to be the supreme Judge in this spiritual assembly."

From the formation of the Holy Synod until this present time the Russian Church has remained stationary in doctrine and practice. There has been neither development nor growth; her servies and teaching have become stereotyped.

"The Eastern Church in general, and the Russian Church in particular, have remained for centuries in a kind of intellectual torpor. Neither the Slavonic nor the Russian world will be re-suscitated so long as the Church remains in such lifelessness, which is not a matter of chance, but the legitimate fruit of some organic defect." —SOLOVYOV, *Otcherki iz istoru Russkoi Literaturi.*

Every attempt at reform in Church ceremony, doctrine, or practice has been stubbornly resisted by the Holy Synod and the Higher Clergy, with the inevitable result that thousands of "in-tellectuals" have left the Church, and are openly or secretly antagonistic to religion, whilst amongst the peasantry whole villages have become Sectarian.

"It has often been made matter of reproach to religion that the most zealous defenders are not always the best of men. Russia in particular affords matter in support of this particular sarcasm. It is there that the most illiterate, the most degenerate sect of Christianity still sub-

ι

stitutes dogmas in the place of morals; miracles instead of reason; the performance of ceremonies instead of the practice of virtue. The principal cause of the vices of the people is the immorality of their religion, and he who considers that in the Russo-Greek Church are neither sermons nor exhortations nor catechisms will be at once of my opinion."—*Secret Memoirs of the Court of Catherine II.*

The Russian of the peasant class, being of an intensely religious nature, is bound in the order of things to get his religion somehow. The majority of the people find satisfaction in the Church ritual and ceremony. They are simply Orthodox. They have not the slightest idea of the great fundamental doctrines of Man, God, Sin, Salvation. To them, to be Orthodox is to be baptised as an infant; to wear a cross round the neck, next to the body; to possess a Holy Icon; to pray to the Virgin and the Saints; to walk in religious processions; to go on pilgrimage to some holy shrine, famous monastery, sacred city, or, chiefest of all, to Jerusalem, not to work on Saints' Days; to fast on Wednesdays and Fridays and during Lent; to go to the bath on Saturdays; attend the sacraments; to stand in Church during the service; to respond to the claims of beggars (little brothers of Christ); and to venerate bishops and high ecclesiastical dignitaries.

This is Orthodoxy to the average villager, the

L

height and depth, the length and breadth, of the peasant's religion.

" In Russia the Church has for foundation the mystical need of man; and for superstructure the mystical history of mankind, mystically interpreted. Prince and peasant take their place with equal convenience there, for they are in the Church by virtue of their manhood rather than by virtue of rank. The pity is that the professors in the Church are often found to be devoid of the instinct for the safe foundation. A great number are always to be found taking their stand on the miraculous, and building the whole edifice of the Church on materially misunderstood natural facts, making the aristocracy in the Church into religious cranks and the peasantry into superstitious clods. Let it be granted that miracles are possible; but God is not vulgar. Many Russian abbots would make of Him a veritable showman. Hence the discredit which comes down upon the Church I think miracle-worship is brought about by a contempt for the peasantry and a terrible inability on the part of the priests to win God's personal favour. Obviously, when a priest has the Grace of God, he needs no miracles to show forth the Word."

THE SUGGESTED UNION BETWEEN THE ANGLICAN AND RUSSIAN CHURCHES

ALTHOUGH the negotiations had no effect upon

L

the doctrine, polity, or general attitude of the Orthodox Church, yet it is of interest to notice that in 1721 Bishop Thebais, visiting the United Kingdom in quest of alms, suggested to the Anglican Bishops the idea of union between the Established Church of England and the Œcumenical Church, and as a result of several conferences he was the bearer of a letter from England to the Eastern Church Patriarchs. The inquiries of the British Bishops respecting certain doctrines and practices were replied to by a Special Council sitting in Constantinople, in which they referred to the unalterable foundations of the faith of their ancestors, on which alone the Eastern Church could receive them into her bosom. In the meantime the Anglican Bishops, through James of Alexandria, entered into correspondence with the Holy Synod, and sent to it their answers to the statement of the Patriarchal Council, with a request that they should be forwarded to Constantinople.

The Holy Synod, however, detected glaring heresies in the British document, especially in reference to the " invocation of saints and the reverencing of Icons," and in forwarding the papers to the Council at Constantinople, requested that they would preserve inviolate the traditional doctrines and practices of Orthodoxy, maintaining that it was impossible either to add anything or to take away anything from them. The Rev. R. W. Blackmore, in his Notes, explanatory of

L

Mouravieff's History of the Russian Church, deals
at length with the discussions between the two
Churches. Apparently the British bishops rejected two traditional points of Eastern doctrine
—the invocation of saints and the outward
reverencing of Icons

On the first point, the Bishops argued that
the "*worshipping*" of angels or saints, according
to the sense and practice of the Eastern Church,
was a deification of creatures, and consequently
a plain heresy and apostasy from the true faith!

On the second, that if the *worshipping* of
the creatures themselves was unlawful, much more
the *worshipping* of their pictures or images must
be so; and besides that, it was a direct breach
of the Second Commandment.

Upon these grounds they desired to have a
formal permission from the Synod to reject their
doctrines and usages; and yet at the same time
they signified that the Eastern Church might
continue to *worship creatures,* and *teach idolatry*
as before, without in any way thereby disqualify-
ing herself for their communion.

The Patriarchs, however, insisted upon the
doctrine of venerating and invoking the saints as
being primitive and scriptural, and that to reject it was heresy, inconsistent with Catholic
religion.

On these two points, however, there was
certainly no difference in the attitude of the

L

two Churches which would hinder or need have prevented Union, for the British Bishops most fully admitted the doctrine of the Intercession of Saints, and already practised what the Russian Church demanded. See Cardwell's Conferences, p. 388, for the following prayer appointed by the Archbishop of Canterbury:

" We beseech Thee to give us all grace to remember and provide for our latter end, by a careful, studious imitation of this Thy blessed saint and martyr, and all other Thy saints and martyrs that have gone before us, that we may be made worthy to receive benefit by their prayers, which they in common with Thy Church Catholic offer up unto Thee for that part of it here militant, and yet in fight with, and in danger from the flesh." Prayer to be used in all Churches on the day of King Charles the Martyr.

On the second point of the Icons, nearly the same reflections hold good, for the English Bishops rejected the opinion of the Icono-clasts, and admitted the use of images and pictures in the Church, and by no means denied that they, like all other things connected with religion, ought to receive a *certain* respect and reverence.

The death of Peter the Great brought the negotiations to an end, and it is useless to con-jecture what would have been the final outcome

L

if the personal conference mooted by him had been held in Moscow.

Many efforts have been made by Anglicans for a union between the two Churches, but all the advances have come from the West. The Rev. W. Palmer believed that the two Churches were almost identical in doctrine, and sought admission into the Orthodox Church, but on being told that he would have to be baptised *by immersion* (the Orthodox Church holds that baptism by immersion is necessary, and doubts the validity of any other kind; see Fortescue's *Orthodox Eastern Church*) he considered that it would be sacrilege to be rebaptised, and at last entered the Roman Church and submitted to the authority of the Pope (see Palmer, *Dissertations*, pp. 199).

Professor Pares, in *Russia and Reform*, asserts that some priests of the Orthodox Church maintain that there is but little difference between the dogmas of the two Churches.

The differences are vital, especially in the matter of the Sacraments, and there is little common ground.

The one thing in which they are in entire agreement is that they are both State Churches, governed by a lay and political body, although the authority of the State over the Church is greater in Russia than in England.

THE HOLY ORTHODOX CHURCH

HER SACRAMENTS.

BIBLIOGRAPHY

ROMANOFF . . *Rites and Customs of the Græco-Russian Church.*

MICHAELOFFSKY *A Short Catechism of the Russian Church.*

.

L

7

L

THE HOLY ORTHODOX CHURCH

Her Sacraments.

THE Russian Church is a child of the Greek. As we have seen, her conversion was accomplished in the tenth century by missionaries from Constantinople, and since that time the Holy Orthodox Church has hardly changed the rites, ceremonies, and order of the Sacraments, which were first drawn up by Cyril and Methodius in the early ninth century for the use of newly-converted Bulgarians. They have been scrupulously adhered to by the authorities of the Church with most conservative tenacity.

The Russian Church considers that two of the Sacraments are divinely ordained and "generally necessary to salvation," whilst of the other five "ordinances," four they own as sacramental, though hesitating to class them with the two of universal application, while the last they claim has Scriptural authority which cannot be easily explained away.

Baptism has always held a foremost place in the ordinances of the Church, and is usually

(always save in exceptional circumstances) by
immersion.

BAPTISM.

THERE are four distinct ceremonies performed
at a baptismal service, although it appears to be
but one service. These are, first, the Renunciation,
and confession of faith; secondly, the actual
administration of Baptism; thirdly, Baptismal
unction; and fourthly, the washing, with the
cutting off of the hair.

The service opens by the priest, who is not
yet in full canonicals, but is merely wearing his
cope over his ordinary dress, approaching the
child, who is naked, and blowing in its face,
crossing it three times over its brow, lips, and
breast. He then lays his hand on its head,
and reads over it a prayer, followed by
the exorcism of the devil, in which the Evil One,
with all his angels and legions, is commanded
to depart from the child. Another prayer follows,
addressed to the God of Sabaoth to defend him
from all spiritual and bodily harm, and to grant
him the victory over all evil spirits.

The priest then blows on the child's brow,
lips, and breast, saying three times, "May every
evil and unclean spirit that has concealed itself and
taken up its abode in his heart depart from thence."

Questions as to the renunciation of the Devil
and all his works are then put to the sponsors,
and repeated three times. As the questions are

L

asked all present turn their backs towards the East, i.e. they look towards the West, where the sun sets and from whence no light proceeds, but on the contrary, darkness and shadows, symbols of the Prince of Darkness; and on the last answer being given by the sponsors, " I have renounced him," the priest says, " Then blow and spit on him," setting the example himself by blowing and then spitting at the unseen enemy in token of horror and hatred of him.

The party then turn toward the Icon, and the reader repeats the Nicene Creed three times on their behalf. Before each repetition of the Nicene Creed the sponsors are asked:

" Have you confessed Christ ? "

" I have confessed Him."

" And dost thou believe in Him? "

" I believe in Him as King and God."

The priest then says, " Fall down and worship Him," and the answer is given, " I worship the Father, the Son, and the Holy Ghost, the Trinity consubstantial and indivisible," prostrating themselves at the same time.

" Blessed be God who desireth the salvation of all men, and that all may come to the knowledge of His truth. Now, henceforth, and for ever, Amen."

The Sacrament of Baptism follows. The priest puts on his full canonicals, gaudy and sometimes costly; lighted candles are placed in the hands

L

of the sponsors; the three on the font or baptismal
pool are lighted; incense is waved about; the
deacon chants a litany; the priest whispers a
prayer for himself. Then follows the benediction
of the water, which is performed by the priest's
immersing his right hand in it crosswise three
times, blowing on it, murmuring prayers all the
time, and last of all by making the sign of the
cross on its surface with a little feather dipped
in holy oil. He and his assistants then sing
" Hallelujah ! "

All is symbolical, mystical, and mysterious. The
font is a symbol of Noah's ark; the olive branch
is typified by the olive oil on the water.

The child is then anointed, the olive oil used
being a type of the inner healing of the soul by
by baptism.

The priest anoints the child on the brow,
saying, " The servant of God, A, is anointed with
the oil of gladness. In the name of the Father,
and of the Son, and of the Holy Ghost, now,
henceforth, and for ever, Amen "; on the breast,
" for the healing of thy soul and body "; on the
ears, " for the hearing of the Word "; on the
hands, " Thy hands have made me and fashioned
me "; on the feet, " that his feet may walk in
the way of Thy Commandments."

The priest then rolls up his sleeves well above
the elbows, the assistant holding back the wide
sleeves of the chasuble, and taking the child,

he stops its ears with his thumb and little finger, its eyes with the fourth and first fingers of the right hand, and with the palm covers the mouth and nostrils; with his left hand he holds the body, and then rapidly plunges the child face downwards three times in the water. Meanwhile during each immersion the words are repeated, "The servant of God, A, is baptized in the name of the Father, Amen; and of the Son, Amen; and of the Holy Ghost, Amen"; the immersion taking place at the mention of the name.

The child is then handed to one of the sponsors, the priest cleanses his hands by having water poured over them, and whilst he is drying them upon the towel he chants the thirty-second Psalm, "Blessed is he whose sins are covered," etc.

The priest then hangs the cross about the child's neck, saying, "The servant of God, A, is arrayed in the garments of righteousness." The little one is then dressed in a white garment whilst the deacon chants "Grant me a white robe, and Thou who art clothed with light as with a garment, most merciful Christ, our God."

Immediately afterwards the Sacrament of Unction begins.

Q.—"In what does Unction consist?"

A.—"The baptized person is anointed with oil, with the mysterious words, 'The seal of the Gift of the Holy Ghost' (*Shorter Catechism*)."

l

The idea of Unction took its origin, presumably, from the appearance of the Holy Ghost in the form of a dove after the baptism of our Lord. ·"It is not sufficient," says Bishop Benjamin, in *Novoe Skrijal*, "for the new believer to be immersed in water; he must be baptized with the Spirit also." Unction is the outward and visible sign of the inward and spiritual grace conferred by the "laying on of hands."

The service begins with the prayer:

"Blessed art Thou, O Lord God Almighty, the Fountain of Goodness, the Sun of Righteousness, shining on such as are in darkness with the light of Salvation, by the coming of Thy only begotten Son our Lord; and granting to us Thy unworthy servants purification by holy water, and Divine sanctification by Unction; and who hast mercifully admitted this thy servant to regeneration by water and the Spirit, and granted him remission of his voluntary and involuntary sins; grant him, O Lord and merciful King, the seal of the gift of Thy all powerful and adorable Spirit—the communion of Christ's holy body and blood. Preserve him in Thy holiness, strengthen him in the faith of the Orthodox Church, deliver him from the Evil One and all his snares, and keep him by Thy saving fear in purity and righteousness of spirit, that by every deed and word he may be acceptable to Thee, and become Thy child and the heritor of Thy Kingdom. For Thou art our God, the God of mercy and salvation, and to Thee be glory, to the Father, and to the Son, and to the Holy Ghost, now, henceforth, and for ever. Amen."

The priest then makes the sign of the Cross with the feather, dipped in a tiny bottle of holy oil, on the brow, eyes, nostrils, ears, lips, breast, hands, and feet, each time with the words, " The Seal of the gift of the Holy Ghost."

The priest, followed by the sponsors and friends, then marches around the font, chanting with the deacons and reader, " As many of us as have been baptized with Christ have put on Christ. Hallelujah ! "

The Sacrament of Unction concludes with the Litany for the Tsar, the Imperial Family, the baptised, and the sponsors.

The shaving of the hair follows, the theory being that as the child has nothing of his own to give, the first " sacrifice " to God is made by the cutting of the hair. Two prayers are recited, after which the priest takes a small wet sponge, and wipes the anointed places, saying, " Thou art baptized, thou art sanctified, thou art anointed with oil, thou art purified, thou art washed, in the name of the Father, and of the Son, and of the Holy Ghost. Amen."

The hair is cut in four different places with a small pair of scissors, making the form of a cross, the priest saying, meanwhile, "The servant of God, A, is shorn in the name of the Father," etc.

The sponsors collect the hair, press it, with wax from a candle, into a pellet, and throw it into the water in which the child has been baptised. If the pellet sinks, it is an omen that the child will not live long. Water and pellet are then thrown into a place where no impurity can reach it and no foot tread upon it. The whole service concludes with the same Litany, chanted after the Sacrament of Unction, the child is handed over to the parents, the fee is paid, and all adjourn to drink the baby's health, priest included.

At times, especially market-days, the priest will have thirty or forty babies to baptise at one time, and not infrequently all the boys will be given one name, and all the girls treated alike, irrespective of the wishes of the parents. Where there are so many to deal with it saves time and confusion only to have one name to remember and deal with.

Baptism by the laity is permissible in cases where the child is not likely to live until the arrival of a priest or other qualified person.

CONFESSION AND COMMUNION

THE rite of Confirmation is not observed in the Holy Orthodox Church. There is no long period

l

of waiting years between Baptism and Communion. Each baptised child receives the Communion about twice a year, generally at Eastertide and on its saint's day, whilst amongst the peasantry, the little ones are taken to the Communion and partake of the bread and wine whenever they are ill. To the illiterate peasant there is something magical in the " elements."

Confession usually takes place on Fridays, after Vespers. The penitent goes behind a screen, placed for the time in a corner of the Church. The priest awaits them, and on a cushion lie the Gospels and the Cross. The priest then addresses the penitent:

" Behold, my child, Christ stands here invisibly to receive thy confession. Be not ashamed, nor afraid, and conceal nothing from me—but without hesitation tell me what thou hast done, and receive absolution from Jesus Christ. Behold His picture (Icon) before us! I am only a witness, and certify before Him all that thou tellest me; if therefore, thou concealest anything from me, thou wilt be doubly sinful. Mark well, therefore, that thou leave not this ghostly hospital without receiving the healing that thou requirest."

The priest then puts " leading" questions to the penitent, and answers are given to them—" I have sinned " or " I have not sinned." The priests vary in their questions according to their own temperament and judgment of what is sin.

l

Full confession having been made, the penitent prostrates himself or herself before the priest, who lays his hand on his head and pronounces the absolution.

"Our Lord Jesus Christ, by the grace and bounty of His love to all mankind, pardon thee, A, all thy sins, and I, unworthy priest that I am, by the power given to me, do forgive and absolve thee from all thy sins in the name of the Father, and of the Son, and of the Holy Ghost. Amen."

The penitent is then "signed" with the Cross, and on rising from his knees kisses the Cross. He leaves a candle and a fee for the grace received.

A list of crimes and misdemeanours, 115 in all, are published in the Ritual Service Book, with the nature and extent of penances attached to each.

It is usual after Confession to abstain from all food and drink until the time for Communion. The communicants assemble in the Church and repeat after the priest the Articles of Belief:

"I believe, Lord, and confess, that Thou indeed art Christ, the Son of the Living God, who camest into the world to save sinners, of whom I am chief. I also believe that this is indeed Thy most pure body, and this Thy holy blood. I therefore pray Thee to have mercy on me and to forgive me all my sins, voluntary and involuntary, by word, by deed, by knowledge or ignorance, and grant me worthily and blamelessly to partake of Thy most pure Sacrament, for the remission of sins and for life everlasting. Receive me this day, O Son of God, as a partaker of Thy Last Supper. For not as a secret enemy I approach, not with the kiss of Judas, but like the thief I confess Thee, 'Lord, remember me in Thy Kingdom.' And may the Communion of Thy Holy Sacrament be not to my judgment and condemnation, but to the healing of my soul and body. Amen."

The priest takes a portion of the bread, which is cut into small pieces and soaked with wine, in the spoon, with a little wine, and puts it into the mouth of the communicant, saying, " The servant of God, A, communicates in the name of the Father, and of the Son, and of the Holy Ghost. Amen." Meanwhile the choir continually, by many repetitions, chants : " Receive ye the Body of Christ ; taste ye the fount of everlasting life."

The deacon holds a silk handkerchief under the chin of the communicant to prevent the possibility of a drop falling to the ground, and wipes it with his lips afterwards.

The communicant kisses the edge of the cup, crosses himself, and moves to a little table, where he places his fee, and then, kneeling before an Icon, continues in private prayer until the service is over. Sometimes after the final Liturgy the priest presents the Cross to be kissed by the devout and faithful Orthodox.

Usually the peasants go to Confession and Communion once a year, during Lent, some go twice; whilst those in Government employ— soldiers, sailors, workmen, scholars, officials—are sent or brought to Communion once a year, unless a professed member of a "foreign" religion.

ORDINATION

PRIESTS of the Russian Church are usually re- cruited from the sons of priests, free education in the Bishop's seminaries for sons of priests being one of the chief factors governing the selection of a vocation for the lad. After finishing his course the youth is first ordained reader. As a reader he is not considered to be an ordained minister. He is blessed by the Bishop, has his hair cut, as in the ceremony described in connection with baptism, and is allowed to wear the first of the canonicals, an alb, denied to the uncon- secrated lay-reader.

The next step is that of sub-deacon, when the candidate dons the scarf over his reader's alb. The ceremony takes place in the Church, and as the extra canonical garment is donned the Bishop says in a loud voice, "He is worthy," and the cry is repeated by the assembled clergy and choir,

As a full deacon the candidate receives the cuffs and a priest the vestment and stole.

Usually a deacon is ordained after the Communion service, showing that he is not indispensable to the administration of the ordinance.

Before the end of the service the candidate is led to the altar by two sub-deacons, and he is handed over to the full deacon, who speaks to the people the word " permit," i e., he asks their consent to the ordination of the candidate. The question is then put to the clergy, asking their permission to his entering the holy office, and finally to the Bishop, thus asking for his blessing. The whole of the clergy then pass in procession three times around the altar, the candidate kissing the corners of the throne each time, saying · " O God of Holiness, God of Strength, God of Immortality, have mercy on us." He then kisses the Bishop's staff and hand, the choir meanwhile chanting a psalm. The candidate then kneels down upon the right knee only, places his hands, crossed, on the throne, with his forehead between them, and whilst in this position the Bishop lays his hand upon him, pronounces the blessing, and the choir sing the *Kyrie Eleison*, those on the right hand in Russian, those on the left in Greek.

After prayers, read by the Bishop, he hands to the newly-ordained one the canonicals, one by one, accompanying each with the word *Axios* (" He is worthy ").

L

The deacon then kisses all his brethren, and is kissed by them, and he immediately enters upon his new duties.

The ordination of a priest follows the same order, save that it takes place earlier in the service, and the candidate kneels upon both knees, and at the conclusion the Bishop hands to him a *missal*, giving directions for the performance of Mass, Matins, and Vespers.

The prayer to be read at the end of the Liturgy is always said by the new priest, and he prays for his flock over whom he is to have charge, seeking for blessings upon them in this world and the next.

The consecration of a Bishop, Abbot, or other Church dignitary follows the same order, and they are robed in their canonicals in the Church, as with their brethren in lesser office.

MARRIAGE

An Orthodox Russian cannot marry an unbaptised person. Marriages with foreigners or persons of other forms of Christian religion are lawful, but the unorthodox party must bind himself, or herself, in writing, not to make objections to the baptism of any of their children in the Holy Orthodox Church. With the increase of intercommunication with other countries, this rule has been considerably relaxed of recent years, especially in the large cities, where many foreigners reside,

Marriages cannot take place during the Fasts prescribed by the Church, nor on Tuesdays, Thursdays, and Saturdays. Banns are published by the priest for three Sundays or holidays before the actual wedding-day. The bride, bridegroom, and witnesses sign the book before the actual ceremony takes place.

On the arrival of the bridal party at the Church, the choir sing, the "Royal" gates are opened, the young couple prostrate themselves three times, the whole party cross themselves, and the priest, in full canonicals, makes the sign of the cross over their heads while they bow before him. Two wax candles, ornamented with flowers and ribbons, are then lighted by the priests and placed in their hands. The boys, or servers, sway the incense, and the service commences.

After the Litany and prayers, the priest goes to the altar, and brings two plain gold rings, previously handed to him, and, taking one in his right hand, makes the sign of the cross over the bridegroom's head with it, saying:

"The servant of God, A, betroths himself to the servant of God, B, in the name of the Father, and of the Son, and of the Holy Ghost. Amen."

The ring is then handed by the priest to the bridegroom. The same formula is used in connection with the bride, with the change of names only.

8

The rings are then exchanged three times, signifying that their future joys, cares, intentions, and actions should be mutual.

A prayer follows, seeking God's blessing, and the Litany for the Tsar and Royal family.

Then comes the Sacrament of Marriage, or, in the Russian, the " Crowning."

A silk handkerchief is spread before the reading-desk, and the betrothed step upon it, at the invitation of the priest.   There is a popular superstition that whichever steps first upon the handkerchief will be *head* of the house.

The priest chants the one hundred and twenty-eighth Psalm, whilst the choir between each verse sing, " Glory be to Thee, O God, Glory be to Thee."

An awkward question is then put to the betrothed by the priest: " Have you ever promised yourself to another? " but the answer is printed in the service-book: " I have not promised myself, honourable Father."

After prayers the reader appears with a salver, upon which are two gaudy crowns, usually of plated silver, ornamented with medallions of Christ, the Virgin, and favourite saints.

The priest takes one crown in his hands, makes the sign of the Cross, with the crown, over the head of the bridegroom, saying: " The servant of God, A, is crowned with the handmaid of God, B, in the name of the Father, and of the Son, and of the Holy Ghost. Amen." The medallion of our Lord is then kissed by the bridegroom and the crown is placed on his head.

The same ceremony is gone through for the bride, with the necessary change of names. The priest then repeats three times, " O Lord our God, crown them with glory and honour," each time signing the bride and bridegroom with the sign of the Cross.

Afterwards the fifth chapter of the Epistle to the Ephesians is read, special emphasis being placed upon the last verse, " Let the wife see that she reverence her husband." More prayers and litanies follow, and the betrothed sip three times from the Common Cup a mixture of wine and water, reminiscent of Cana of Galilee. The priest then joins their hands, and they walk around the reading-desk three times, while the choir, sings.

The ceremony can be lawfully interrupted at any stage of the proceedings until the procession takes place.

The following address is then read:

" Be thou exalted, O bridegroom, like unto Abraham, and blessed like unto Isaac, and multiplied like unto Jacob. Walk in peace, and do rightly according to the commandments of God."

The crowns are then removed, and turning to the bride the priest says, " And thou, O bride, be thou exalted like unto Sarah, and rejoice like

l

unto Rebecca, and multiply like unto Rachel. Rejoice with thy husband, and keep the ways of the Law, as is well pleasing to God."

A short prayer follows:

"O God, our God, who camest to Cana of Galilee and blessed the marriage there, bless these Thy servants who have now united themselves in holy matrimony according to Thine ordinance. Bless Thou their goings out and their comings in, prolong their days in goodness, record their union in Thy kingdom, that it may remain pure, undefiled, and unslandered for ever and ever. Amen."

The husband and wife are then requested to kiss each other three times, and the benediction concludes the Sacrament. The party, led by the newly-married ones, then kiss the Icons, and general congratulations from friends are the order of the day.

EXTREME UNCTION

THE Sacrament of Extreme Unction is administered to adults only, to the dangerously sick who are in full possession of their senses, who are admitted subsequently to Communion of the Sick and its indispensable preparation by Confession.

It ought to be performed by seven priests, but in many places, and by far the larger number in Russia, one priest can perform it. Persons in good health are not eligible for the Sacrament, even if about to be exposed to great danger. Persons of other religions may be anointed with Extreme Unction if baptised and previously anointed with " The Seal of the Holy Ghost," according to the Office of Conversion.

When Extreme Unction is decided on, notice is given to the priest or priests and to such of the relatives as are likely to come and join in the prayers of the family. Strangers will sometimes come in uninvited: they consider their presence as a Christian duty. Occasionally, in such cases as consumption, the Sacrament will be performed in the Church, with more elaborate ceremonies than is possible in a private house.

In the house, a table, covered with a clean white cloth, is placed in close proximity to the Icon; a few wheat and grains or a dish of flour is on the table; in the dish a small empty wineglass is placed. Round this are seven little pointed sticks, in honour of the seven gifts of the Holy Spirit; on the top of each a morsel of cotton-wool. The priest pours a little olive-oil, mixed with wine, in remembrance of the Good Samaritan, into the wine-glass, and lighted candles are handed to every person in the room, including the other priests, if any. The incense is then lighted and waved about and around the table and towards the people. With face towards the Icon, the priest commences the service.

L

There are long prayers, litanies, psalms, and afterwards the benediction of the oil. The prayer of benediction is as follows: "O Lord, who by Thy grace and bounty dost heal the infirmities of both our souls and bodies, sanctify this oil to the healing of him who is to be anointed therewith, to the laying low of all passions and impurities of the flesh and spirit, and of all other evil, that by him Thy most holy name may be glorified—the name of the Father, and the name of the Son, and the name of the Holy Ghost. Amen."

The deacon reads James v. 10-16, and the chief priest present reads Luke x. 25, the story of the Good Samaritan.

Several prayers and a litany follow. When the last prayer is read the priest takes one of the little sticks, and dipping the end, wound with cotton wool, in the oil, anoints the sick person with it, using the sign of the cross, on his forehead, nostrils, cheeks, lips, breast, and hands, while he reads a prayer for his recovery, the patient devoutly crossing himself.

"O Holy Father, the Physician of our souls and bodies, who sent Thine only-begotten Son our Lord Jesus Christ to heal our sicknesses, and to save us from death, heal also this Thy Servant, A, of all his spiritual and bodily infirmities."

This is done seven times, and each time a fresh stick is used, and if possible by a fresh priest, if there are seven present, and by turns if only two or three.

Then follows seven readings from the Gospels and epistles by separate priests or in turns, each reading a different prayer after each reading of the Gospel.

The Testament is then held open over the head of the sick person by each priest present, whilst the senior in age or place reads a prayer.

The service concludes by the patient asking for a blessing and the personal forgiveness of the priest, and then individually of all present.

Then follows the Communion Service, preceded by a commendatory prayer for a sick person at the point of departure, called, " A form of prayer to our Lord Jesus Christ and to the most pure Mother of our Lord, at the separation of the soul and body of every Orthodox believer."

When the end is nearing, an Icon is placed at the head of the bed, or on the bench in a peasant's house, and a lighted candle is placed before it.

EASTER IN RUSSIA

WHILST the Sacraments touch the Russian peasant at certain great moments in life, such as baptism, marriage, and death, there are many festivals connected with the Church which affect him in the ordinary round of the year. The greatest of these is, without doubt, the Easter service.

l

Orthodox Russia for weeks has been preparing for the great day. The whole country has been apparently fasting during the long weeks of Lent; the majority have been religiously denying themselves of meat, and the men have even gone so far as to abstain from their beloved vodka. Easter Eve arrives, and after midnight the faithful are to be released from their long penance, everybody in the village, save a few, young, sleepy children and the Sectarians at the other end of the village street, sits up quietly waiting whilst the 'pope' burns incense and chants prayers before the Icons and the altar. Just before midnight almost everybody, at least, those who have any pretensions to Orthodoxy, gather in the dimly-lighted Church whilst the priest drones on, "Lord have mercy, Lord have mercy."

Just on the stroke of midnight, the Church crowded with peasants of both sexes, the priest, in an ecstasy of emotion, cries with a loud voice, "Christ is risen, Christ is risen," and the whole company take up the refrain, "Christ is risen," men and women saluting one another with the holy kiss, repeating meanwhile, "Christ is risen."

Outside the Church, those who have failed to find room within take up the cry, and from lip to lip the glad message flies, "Christ is risen." Some of the more daring spirits, or perhaps the less religiously inclined, begin to beat all manner of iron kitchen utensils until the din is terrific.

L

Gradually the Orthodox scatter and wend their way home, there to break the long fast by consuming an extraordinary variety of viands in immoderate quantities. By sunrise there will be few sober men in the place, vodka will have claimed its victims, and the men will be found in varying degrees of intoxication. To celebrate the dawn of the great Christian festival and the close of the longest fast in the Church year by getting thoroughly drunk, is a peculiarly Slavonic ideal of happiness.

The following day, Easter festivities will begin in earnest. Youths and maidens, decked in their " best," will promenade the village street, and a man, frequently a time-expired soldier, will play an accordion, the favourite musical instrument, whilst several couples will stiffly and solemnly dance the simple village dances.

The interior of the houses are bright with an unwonted cleanliness; the walls have been whitewashed, and festooned with branches of fir-trees.

Easter cakes, baked specially for the occasion, are to be found in almost every house, for the entertainment of the visitor, chance or expected. A portion of the Easter cake is commonly sent to the village priest by way of an Easter offering.

During the day, companies of peasants will parade the streets, carrying Icons, chanting psalms, marching with uncovered heads. Church bells will be clanging all day. A service will be held in the Church and at the close all will sing the national hymn, "Long life to the Tsar"; the "pope" will bless the ewer of water and will sprinkle it over the people inside the Church, and if there should be a waiting crowd outside, and there usually is, he will go on to the steps of the building and spray some over the waiting throng.

All over Russia, wherever the "Great White Tsar" holds sway, the same service will be performed at the same hour, thus making for the religious unity of the many diverse nations in modern Russia.

ON BEING RECEIVED INTO THE HOLY ORTHODOX CHURCH FROM ANOTHER BODY

ADMISSION to the Holy Orthodox Church is only permitted to those who have previously received the Sacrament of Unction, the third part of the ceremony of Baptism. The form of the words used preparatory to the ceremony of Unction are as follows:

.Q—" Wilt thou renounce the errors of the —— Church and its falsities?"

A.—" I will."

The deacon then intones, " Let us pray to God," whilst the choir respond, " Lord, have mercy upon us."

Priest.—" For Thy name's sake, O Lord God

l

of Truth, and that of Thine only Son and the
Holy Spirit, look down on Thy servant, now
desirous of being worthy of reception into Thy
Holy Orthodox Church and of the shelter of her
wings. Deliver him from all his former errors,
and fill him with true faith, hope, and charity;
grant that he may walk in the way of Thy Holy
Commandments, and do that which shall please
Thee, which if a man does them, he shall live
by them. Write his name in Thy Book of Life;
unite him to the fold of Thy heritage, that in it
he may glorify Thy Holy Name, and that of Thy
Son, our Lord Jesus Christ, and of the Life-giving
Spirit. And may Thine eyes look graciously upon
him for ever, and be Thine ears open to his
prayers; make him to rejoice in the work of
his hands, and in the confession and praise of
Thy High and Holy Name, and that he may
glorify Thee all the days of his life."

The candidate is then ordered to turn to
the West and sincerely and whole-heartedly to
renounce all former errors of doctrine and to
confess the true Orthodox faith.

Q.—" Dost thou renounce all the errors of.
thy former faith? and dost thou reject all that
is contrary to God and to His truth, and that
is damnable to the soul?"

A.—".I renounce all my former errors, and
reject all that is contrary to God and His truth,
and that is damnable to the soul?"

ι

Q.—"Dost thou renounce all convocations, traditions, and statutes, and all (here name of Church) teachers and their teachings, which are contrary to the Holy Orthodox Church? and dost thou reject them?"

A.—"I renounce and reject them."

Q.—"Dost thou renounce all ancient and modern heresies and heretics, which are contrary to God? dost thou reject them and condemn them to anathema?"

A.—"All ancient and modern heresies," etc.

The candidate then turns to the East.

Q.—"Hast thou renounced all errors of (here name of Church)?"

A.—"I have renounced them."

.Q—"Dost thou desire to unite thyself to the Holy Orthodox Church?"

A.—"I desire it with my whole heart."

Q.—"Dost thou believe in one God, who is worshipped and glorified in the Holy Trinity, Father, Son, and Holy Ghost? and dost thou worship Him as thy God and King?"

A.—"I believe," etc.

Then, after prostration, the convert repeats the Nicene Creed.

Priest.—"Blessed be our God, who lighteth every man that cometh into the world Repeat to us the dogmas, traditions, and ordinances of the Orthodox Church, which thou holdest."

A.—"The Apostolic and ecclesiastical or-

dinances which were established at the Seven
Councils and the rest of the Russian traditions,
statutes, and rules, I accept and confess; also
the holy writings and the prayers that the Holy
Orthodox Church has acknowledged and acknow-
ledges, I accept and acknowledge

" I believe and confess that the seven Sacraments of the New Testament—to wit, Baptism,
Unction, Communion, Confession, Ordination,
Marriage, and Extreme Unction—were instituted
by Jesus Christ and His Church, as the means
of receiving the grace and influence that they
convey.

" I believe and confess, that in the Divine Mass
the true Body and Blood of our Lord Jesus Christ
is verily received in the form of Bread and Wine,
for the remission of sins, and for the obtaining
of eternal life.

" I believe and confess, according to the understanding of the Holy Orthodox Church, that the
Saints in Christ who reign in heaven are worthy
to be honoured and invoked, and that their
prayers and intercessions move the All-Merciful
God to the Salvation of our souls. Also, that
to venerate their incorruptible relics, as also the
previous virtues of their remains, is well pleasing
to God.

" I admit that the Icons of Christ our Saviour,
of the Holy Virgin, and of other Saints, are worthy
to have and to honour, not for the purpose of

ı

worship, but that by having them before our eyes we may be encouraged to devotion, and to the imitation of the deeds of the Righteous Ones represented by the Icons.

" I confess that the prayers of faith addressed to God are accepted favourably by the mercy of God.

" I believe and confess that power is given to the Church by Christ our Saviour, to bind and to loose; and that what is bound or loosed by that power on earth, shall be bound or loosed in heaven.

" I believe and confess that the Foundation, Head, and Supreme Pastor and Bishop of the Holy Orthodox Church is our Lord Jesus Christ; and that from Him all Bishops, Pastors, and teachers are ordained; and that the Ruler and Governor of the said Church is the Holy Ghost.

" That this Church is the Bride of Christ, I also confess; and that in her is true salvation to be found, and that no one can possibly be saved in any other except her, I believe.

" To the Holy Synod directing, as to the Pastors of the Russian Church, and to the Priests by them ordained, I promise to observe sincere obedience, even to the end of my days.

Priest.—" Enter thou into the Church, leaving all thy former errors far behind thee; examine thyself, that thou free thyself from the nets of death and eternal misery; reject from this time

all the errors and false teachings which thou heldest
hitherto; honour the Lord God our Father
Almighty, Jesus Christ His Son, and the Holy
Spirit, the one true and living God, in the Holy
Indivisible and Consubstantial Trinity"

The choir chants the sixty-seventh Psalm, and
the novice prostrates himself before the Gospels
whilst the priest reads a short litany, the choir
chanting, "Lord, have mercy on us" between
each sentence.

P.—"Send down Thy Holy Spirit, and the
face of the earth shall be renewed."

Choir.—"Lord have mercy on us."

P.—"Turn Thee, O Lord, and be gracious to
the words of Thy servant." "The crooked shall
be made straight, and the rough places plain."
"Lord, save Thy servant, who putteth his trust
in Thee." "Be Thou to him a strong tower from
the face of the enemy." "The enemy shall not
come nigh unto him, neither the son of perdition
harm him." "Lord, hear my prayer, and let
my crying come unto Thee."

The priest then says:

"Rise, and stand firm, stand in fear."

The novice rises and says:

"This true Orthodox Russian Faith, which
I now of my own free will confess and sincerely
hold, I will confess and hold, with the help of
God, whole and undefiled to my latest breath, and
will teach and inculcate the same as much as lies

in my power; all its rules I will strivingly and joyfully perform, and will endeavour to keep my heart in virtue and innocence; and in token of this, my true and sincere confession, I kiss the Word and the Cross of my Saviour." The Gospel and Cross are then kissed.

Then follows confession, the novice prostrated with forehead on ground

Priest.—" Bow thy knees before the Lord God whom thou hast confessed, and received absolution of thy sins."

then:

" Rise, and as a faithful servant of Jesus Christ, pray to Him with us, that thou mayest be worthy to receive, through the Unction of Holy Oil, the grace of the Holy Spirit."

The Sacrament of Unction, slightly altered from that used at the Baptism of an infant, then commences. The oil used is manufactured in Kiev and St. Petersburg alone, and is blessed by the Metropolitan. The service proceeds as in the case of a child, to its conclusion, certain words only being altered to suit the different circumstances of the candidate.

Communion follows the Unction, and the novice is a novice no longer, but a fully-qualified member of the Holy Orthodox Church.

I

THE HOLY ORTHODOX CHURCH

HER PRIESTHOOD.

BIBLIOGRAPHY

ROMANOFF . . *Rites and Customs of the Græco-Russian Church.*

MURAVIEFF . . *History of the Russian Church.*

WALLACE . . *Russia.*

BARING . . . *The Russian People.*

OETTINGEN . . *Memories of a Village Priest.*

LANIN . . . *Russian Characteristics.*

TIKHOMIROF . *Russia : Social and Political.*

LATIMER . . *Under Three Tsars.*

WALLING . . *Russia's Message.*

127

9

PRIESTS AND CLERGY

ON MAKING EVERY DAY SACRAMENTAL.

"On rising from your bed, say : In the Name of the Father, the Son, and the Holy Ghost, I begin this new day. When I awake I am still with Thee, and I shall be satisfied when I awake with Thy righteousness, and with Thy whole image. While washing, say : Purge me from the sins of the night, and I shall be clean. Wash Thou me, and I shall be whiter than snow When putting on your clean linen, say : Create in me a clean heart, O Lord, and clothe me with the fine linen, which is the righteousness of the saints. When you break your fast, think of the length of Christ's fast, and in His Name eat your morning meal with gladness of heart. Drinking water, or tea, or sweet mead, think of the true quenchings of the thirst of the heart. If you wish to walk or drive, or go in a boat somewhere, first pray to the Lord to keep this your going out and coming in. If you see and hear a storm, think of the sea of passions in your own and in other men's hearts. And every day, in every place, work at the new creation which you yourselves are. Working with all your might at your proper and peculiar calling—work out your own salvation in every part of every day."

FATHER JOHN OF CRONSTADT. *My Life in Christ.*

THE HOLY ORTHODOX CHURCH

HER PRIESTHOOD.

NO account of the place and power of the Holy Orthodox Church can possibly be complete without attention being directed to the priests and clergy. The Russian priests are divided into two classes, called the "Black" or regular clergy (monks) and the "White" or parish priests. The "Black" priests are recruited from amongst men who have heard a "call" to service, and from the "White" clergy, who, having been widowed, or whose wives having retired into a convent, have entered a monastery to finish their days. The Bishops are always selected from the "Black" clergy, or monks, who form a large and influential class. The monks who first settled in Russia were, like those who first visited North Western Europe, men of the earnest, ascetic, missionary type. Filled with zeal for the glory of God and the salvation of souls, they took little or no thought for the morrow, and devoutly believed that their heavenly Father would provide for their humble wants. These monks main-

L

tained a constant standard of effort, a tradition of
a better world worth trying for, a tradition which
has never been wholly or even generally lost.
The instinct of reverence for that real sanctity
which illumined their lives passed as a permanent
heritage into princes and people. Amongst the
people there are and always have been men and
women who, without seeking any kind of ordination and without ever thinking of separating themselves from the Orthodox Church, have set themselves to do some difficult exploit for their special
salvation. Such persons ordinarily court no special
attention. One may go barefooted and wear heavy
chains beneath his clothes. The Russian word
for such exploits may be translated "moving on-
wards." It is a gospel of effort. Many will walk
the whole length and breadth of Russia in their
attempt to earn salvation. The monks, poor, clad
ofttimes in rags, eating the most simple fare, and
ever ready to share what they had with any one
poorer than themselves, performed faithfully and
earnestly the work which their Master had given
them to do. But this ideal of monastic life soon
gave way in Russia, as in the West, to practices
less simple and austere. By the liberal donations
and bequests of the faithful, and the grants of
lands by princes and boyars, the monasteries became rich in gold, in silver, in precious stones,
and above all, in land and serfs. The Troitza
Lavra, for instance, possessed at one time more

than 120,000 serfs and a proportionate amount of land; at one period in the history of Russia more than a fourth part of the entire population had fallen under the jurisdiction of the monasteries.

During the eighteenth century, the Church lands were secularised, and the serfs of the Church became the serfs of the State. On the establishment of the Holy Synod, the management of the monastic property was taken away from the jurisdiction of the Monastery Court, and placed under the superintendence of the spiritual authorities A special department was formed, under the Synod, called the "Kammer-Kontora," composed exclusively of the laity, for the purpose of looking after the collection and proper expenditure of the revenues derived from the estates belonging to the monasteries, some part of which was used for the upkeep of the monasteries and the maintenance of the clergy, and the balance to support schools and hospitals.

Peter the Great entertained the idea of fusing the property of the monasteries with that of the State, and of setting aside a fixed sum for the clergy, but his death interfered with this design. However, under Catherine II., most of his ideas were adopted and fulfilled. This was a severe blow to the monasteries, but it did not prove fatal, as many predicted. At present there are about five hundred monastic establishments For

L

the full account of the steps taken for the secularis-
ing of the property of the monasteries the reader
is referred to Oustreloff's *History*, vol. iii.

As in Europe, so in Russia, the story of the
monasteries and monastic life falls into three
chapters or stages.

First.—Asceticism and missionary zeal and
enterprise.

Second.—Wealth, luxury, corruption, and the
loss of ideals.

Third.—Secularisation of property and consequent decline.

In Western Europe, time and again, some
earnest and zealous monk has arisen, who, by the
founding of new orders, has sought to revive
the primitive monastic spirit and to lead his followers to the simplicity of the early days. No
such movement, however, has ever taken place
in Russia in connection with the " Black " clergy.
They have never deviated from the rule of St.
Basil, which restricts the members to religious
ceremonies, prayer, and meditation. During the
closing years of the last century there have certainly been reforms, but they have all come from
the civil authorities, imposed from without, and
never from within the monasteries themselves.
The monks, in their dislike of change,
simply cling to the traditional spirit of the
Church to which they belong; anything in the
nature of religious revival is foreign to her

traditions and character, she prides herself upon being above terrestrial influences.

Our concern here, however, is mainly with the "White" clergy or parish priests, who, being in close touch with the peasantry, have far more influence than the "Black" upon the "Soul of Russia." "Like priest, like people."

The Russian "White" clergy have had a curious history. In earlier days they were drawn from all classes of the population and freely elected by the parishioners. When a man was elected by the popular vote, he was presented to the Bishop, and if he was found to be a fit and proper person for the office, he was at once ordained; but this custom has fallen into disuse.

The Bishops, finding that many of the candidates thus presented were illiterate peasants, gradually assumed the prerogative of appointing the priests, with or without the consent of the parishioners, and their choice generally fell upon the sons of priests as the ones best fitted to take sacred orders.

The subsequent creation of Bishops' schools, for the education of the sons of the clergy naturally led, in the course of time, to the total exclusion of all other classes from the priesthood; thus the "White" clergy became a distinct and separate class or caste, legally and actually incapable of mingling with the other classes of the population. The fact that the clergy became an exclusive caste, "a Levitical priesthood," had a prejudicial effect upon their character, their habits, their outlook upon life, and their ideals.

The tendency to become a priestly caste was greatly strengthened by the intermarriage of priests with priests' daughters, the living frequently passing from the father-in-law to the son-in-law. In many cases the paternal and maternal ancestry for many generations belonged to the priestly caste. Until very recent years a wife would be found for the priest by the Bishop of a diocese, always a priest's daughter, the condition attaching to the union being that the bridegroom should inherit the living; sometimes his thus marrying meant that for years he would have to support his mother-in-law (the widow of the previous holder of the benefice) and her daughters. Romanoff, in his *Rites and Customs of the Graeco-Russian Church*, draws a picture of the young graduate from the seminary going the round of a number of parishes with a view to his selecting a bride and securing a living. The "deacon" cannot be "priested" until he marries; in the event of his wife dying, he is forbidden to marry again ("the Bishop must be the husband of only one wife "), and he usually retires to a monastery and therefore becomes eligible for the higher ecclesiastical offices. As a married man and parish priest he cannot rise higher than the equivalent of a rural dean.

l

Added to the " caste " system, another cramping influence upon the priest is that at a very early age he is taken from home, removed from the general life of the village or town, educated in a special seminary for priests' sons, having for his companions boys from homes exactly similar to his own and reared in the same atmosphere, and, above all, the instruction is of a very limited character, the chief subject being the mastery of the old or sacred Slavonic books.

In our estimate of the Russian priesthood of the present day we must remember the severe school through which it has passed, and also consider the spirit which has been for centuries predominant in the Russian Church. I refer to the strong tendency both in clergy and laity to attribute an inordinate importance to the ceremonial element in religion. E. B. Lanin, in *Russian Characteristics*, touches upon the way in which the parish priest confirms the peasant in his gross superstition, for a consideration·

" Priests who persuade their congregations to pay for the celebration of a special Church service to induce the Almighty to dispense with eclipses, and who allow themselves for a moderate consideration to be dragged across a turnip field in order thereby to touch the Divine heart that He may deign to make the turnips big and round, can scarcely claim to be considered the highest type of spiritual advisers."

Primitive man everywhere and always is disposed to regard religion as simply a mass of mysterious rites, which have a secret magical power of averting evil in this world and securing eternal happiness in the next. To this general rule the Russian peasantry are no exception, and the Russian Church has not done all that it might have done to eradicate this conception, and to bring religion into closer association with ordinary morality. The priest is merely expected to conform to certain observances and to perform punctiliously the ordained rites and ceremonies prescribed by the Church. If he does this without practising extortion, his parishioners are quite satisfied. He rarely preaches, or exhorts, or expounds Scriptures, and consequently has but little moral influence over his flock.

That the priests sometimes feel their position keenly and resent the charge of extortion may be gathered from the following petition prepared by the Metropolitan of St. Petersburg in 1905.

It is a human document, throwing considerable light upon the present relations between the ordinary priest and his parishioners. For the whole petition the reader is referred to the *Contemporary Review* for May, 1905.

"Both the ecclesiastical and the secular press remark with equal emphasis upon the prevailing lukewarmness of the inner life of the Church; upon the alienation of the flock from its spiritual guides, the lack of pastoral activity on the part of the clergy, who in the majority of instances confine themselves to the conduct of Divine service and the fulfilment of ritual observances.

"All the religious duties of members of the Orthodox Church were strictly regulated by the Synod. It was laid down exactly how one should comport oneself in Church, what attitude one should take before the sacred pictures, how one should spend festival days, go to confession, and see that the members of the Orthodox Church remained loyal to their faith. These efforts to subject to police prescription the facts and phenomena of spiritual life undoubtedly brought into the ecclesiastical sphere the mortifying breath of dry bureaucratism.

"The chief aim of the ecclesiastical reforms of Peter the Great was to reduce the Church to the level of a mere government institution pursuing purely politial ends.

"And as a matter of fact the government of the Church (under the Holy Synod) speedily became one of the numerous wheels of the complicated government machine.

"Regarding the Church merely as a component part of the State mechanism, Peter decided to set its servants to perform purely civil duties; and to the great misfortune of the parish clergy, he imposed upon it police and detective work. The priest was obliged to see that the number of

L

persons subject to taxation was properly indicated,
and in addition, to report without delay all actions
revealed to him in confession that tended to the
injury of the State.   Thus transformed from a
spiritual guide into an agent of police supervision,
the pastor entirely lost the confidence of his flock
and all moral union with them.

"A monthly stipend of from fifteen to twenty
roubles is not sufficient for the maintenance of a
priest, even if he grows his own corn; and he is
accordingly compelled to levy upon the parish a
number of obligatory contributions in connection
with the celebration of certain ritual acts.   This
has a painful effect upon the mutual relations
between the pastor and his flock.   In the soul
of the priest, monetary calculations awaken at the
most   unsuitable   moment   a   consciousness   of
pastoral impotence; this compulsory trafficking in
holy things withdraws from him every support
needed for practical activity.   The parishioners,
who are by no means always capable of appre-
ciating the degree of material need in which their
pastor lives, find occasion in such extortions to
class the priest with extortioners and vampires.

"Thus the clergy find it difficult to rise above
the level of merely professional performance of
ritual acts, and to become the true pastors of
the people.   For the people, on the other hand,
it is difficult to rally round the priest.

"The first condition is to discover means to

L

absolve the priest from the necessity of trafficking
with his parishioners on the occasions of the cele-
brations of a sacrament."

Over the vast area of Russia proper the
position of the priest is a degrading one, and no
wonder, for he is little better than a salesman of
spiritual benefits; he has no fixed charges, but
makes the best bargain possible, and as he has
the monopoly of his parish, his bargains are sometimes hard driven.   When called upon to baptise
infants, to marry two young people, to bury the
dead, to repeat masses for the soul of some relative,
he will haggle for the price like a man in an open
market.   This system of bargaining effectually
destroys the spiritual influence of the priest, and
causes his parishioners to seethe with discontent
with him.   The remarkable thing is that, despite all
these   coarse   and   soul-destroying   methods   of
ministration, the people crowd the Churches, thus
clearly showing that they dissociate the priest from
his office.

Frequently one will hear a peasant say, after
bargaining with a priest to say a mass for a dead
relative, to baptise a little one, or perform some
other priestly function:

" Hard-hearted pope!   Have you no pity on
the poor peasant? "

The *Chronicles of Leskoff* pourtray the position
and influence of the Russian priesthood in connection with the peasantry.

l

"The position of the priests makes any religious or moral influence on his parish well nigh impossible. The purest character, the best intentions, are checked by a Church government which only recognises the traditional and prescribed outward forms of the ritual, and prohibits every independent feeling and interpretation of the Word of God. To hunt sectarians is fashionable, and the priest must endeavour to track them if he is to be thought efficient. The truth is that everywhere, even in the Church, one feels the finger of the government and of politics. Which saint has to be evoked, in this or that case, this every deacon knows pat off, but the preaching of the Gospel, the cure of souls, so essential for the peasant, and in particular for the Russian peasant, this path is strewn with thorns for the priest by the Church authorities. The natural consequence is that the attitude of the peasant towards the Church is, like his religious life, purely external, consisting in customs, formulæ, ceremonial sacrifices. And further, the consequence is that, as soon as he is touched by the Spirit of the Gospel, he turns away from the State Church and becomes a sectarian. Then the Church steps in. As soon as there is a chance of political propaganda there is money for the priest, for the missions, for the Churches, for the schools. For the sake of a policy the Russian willingly starves, even in the religious sense."

L

The village priest is usually contented with his lot. As a rule he lives in a house built for him by the peasants; he receives, even in the smaller villages, a salary equivalent to about forty pounds a year; he has his glebe, and besides this, he is continually receiving additions to his income through marriage, birth, and funeral fees, and on every religious holiday (and they are very numerous in Russia) contributions of food and money from the peasants. The village priest does next to nothing, and is perhaps the best paid man in the village.

Nor does he seem to enter much into the lives of the peasants or help them in illness or distress. The commercial element is strong in the religion of the commune. So long as the priest discharges his usual priestly functions, the people are satisfied, while as a rule the priest is not disposed to do more than the work for which he is paid. The essentially material way in which peasant and priest view each other's functions is very characteristic of Russian society. The priest, as a rule, clings rather tenaciously to the past, and keeps a firm grip upon the re-sources of the Church.

The secession of any of his parishioners to another religious body is a serious matter for him. A woman in a West Russian village, before her marriage, was received into the Roman Catholic Church, and she was compelled to pay to her

L

former village priest the capitalized sum of her annual value to him.

The Russian peasant needs emancipation from the economic, as well as from the spiritual, thraldom of the Russian Church.

Maurice Baring, in *The Russian People*, gives one or two illustrations showing how the priest, in the minds of the peasants, is divorced from his office.

"I heard some soldiers discussing religion with a monk, and they attacked him on this ground; they said, 'The Church says there is only one religion, but that is a lie, because we know there are a dozen other religions, and that the people who belong to them worship God, and are just as good as we are. Therefore, all priests are liars.' A soldier one day boasted of having dragged a priest, drunk, from his bed in order to say Mass. 'We said to him,' the soldier said, 'Say Mass, you beast'; and he said Mass."

On the other hand, it has been my good fortune to meet with priests of the Russian Church who have had a real desire for the spiritual welfare of their flock.

At the close of a service one evening in September 1910, an aged priest came to me, and after greeting me with a "holy" kiss, said, "I welcome you as a preacher of the good Gospel of Jesus Christ."

The following quotation from the Russian of

L

M. Oettingen, *Memories of a Village Priest*, will
reveal the relationship that exists between peasants
and priest from the priest's point of view:

" He arrives—no inn, no reception. Where
does the sexton live? They showed me a miserable hut. And the verger? They pointed to
an even more wretched hovel. Let us drive to
the sexton. We drive thither and perceive a
small crooked Church, built of stone, enclosed by
a rotten wooden paling, and a dilapidated half-
open hut. We enter; the floor is of mud; the
two windows, fifteen inches high, are dim, the
walls damp, the corners covered with mildew.
The unfortunate couple are located with a peasant,
who has two rooms, and crams his family into
one. Then begins the bargaining with the commune as to who is to supply a dwelling for the
priest. After many entreaties, much bowing, and
painful humiliation on the one side, wise in-
structions and haughty bearing on the other, I
am sent for at the expiration of a fortnight. I
am to attend a parish meeting and to ask for
a home. I have to discourse for a long time, yea,
almost to beg them individually to be good enough
to give me some separate room. At last they
make up their minds, and I receive orders to
move into a peasant's house. The room turned
out to be hardly better than the peasant's hut,
and in this dirty hole the clerical couple had to
live henceforth with the old peasants. At tea-

time the sexton appears, but drunk. The priest asks him why he is drunk. 'You, "little father," have not settled down here. When you have been here a little more than a year you will drink more than I.' And truly it would not be surprising, considering the life which the priest has to live. Of money he has hardly any; he has to earn his living by baptisms, funerals etc.; he has to drive into the smaller villages of the neighbourhoood in order to earn a farthing here, to obtain a fowl and a little flour there, and sometimes he spends an entire day driving about in order to return home with twopence. This is the rule and not the exception, and the cry is always, 'Drink.' The parish gives him the so-called home, but as a sort of house-warming he has to supply a pail of brandy and to drink with them on peril of forfeiting their liberality and their affection. 'You have to deal with us alone; you must show us respect; if so we will grant you everything and respect you in return. But if you do not desire this, you had better pack up at once and go. Do not spare your back; it will be to your advantage to bow down before the parish."

It ·is easy to understand why drunkenness amongst the lower class of priests is rife, and why, according to the chief director of the Holy Synod, in the service registers of the priests there must always be mentioned " to what extent the individual priest is accustomed to consume in·

L

toxicating liquor." A demand not made upon any other class of official servant!

That there is immorality amongst both "Black" and "White" clergy is abundantly testified to by many well acquainted with the Russian priests, although one must not lose sight of the fact that there are many "popes" who are really concerned for the moral, social, and spiritual welfare of their flock. The fact that the priesthood is an appanage of a Government department tells against them tremendously and tends to degrade them.

Melnikoff, in a report to the Grand Duke Constantine, quoted by Wallace (*Russia*):

"The people do not respect the clergy, but persecute them with derision and reproaches, and feel them to be a burden. In nearly all the popular stories the priest, his wife, or his labourer is held up to ridicule, and in all the proverbs and popular sayings where the clergy are mentioned, it is always with derision. The people shun the clergy, and have recourse to them, not from the inner impulse of conscience, but from necessity And why do the people not respect the clergy? Because it forms a class apart; because, having received a false kind of education, it does not introduce into the life of the people the teaching of the Spirit, but remains in the mere dead forms of outward ceremonial, at the same time despising these forms even to

blasphemy; because the clergy itself con-
,tinually presents examples of want of respect to
religion, and transforms the service of God into
profitable trade. Can the people respect the
clergy when they hear how one priest stole money
from below the pillow of a dying man the moment
of confession? how another was publicly dragged
out of a house of ill-fame? how a third christened
a 'dog? how a fourth, whilst officiating at the
Easter service, was dragged by the hair from the
altar by the deacon? Is it possible for the people
to respect priests who spend their time in the
gin-shops, write fraudulent petitions, fight with
the cross in their hands, and abuse each other in
bad language at the altar? One might fill several
pages with examples of this kind without over-
stepping the boundaries of the province of Nizhni
Novgorod. Is it possible for the people to respect the clergy when they see everywhere amongst
them simony, carelessness in performing the
religious rites, and disorder in administering the
sacraments? Is it possible for the people to
respect the clergy when they see that truth has
disappeared from it, and that the Consistories,
guided in their decisions, not by rules, but by
personal friendship and bribery, destroy in it the
last remains of truthfulness? If we add to all
this the false certificates which the clergy give to
those who do not wish to partake of the Eucharist,
the dues illegally extracted from the Old Ritualists,

l

the conversion of the altar into a source of revenue, the giving of Churches to priests' daughters as a dowry, and similar phenomena, the question as to whether the people can respect the clergy requires no answer."

These words were written by an Orthodox Russian, well acquainted with provincial life, to a member of the Imperial family.

All priests are not like this. Many are honest, respectable, God-fearing, well-intentioned, fulfil their duties, strive to procure a good education for their children, take part in social movements, and strive to lead those in their spiritual charge to higher and better things.

During the past few years, priests, as individuals, or as members of the "League of Workers for Church Reform," have been trying to change the status and relations of the priests to the people. They have discovered the weak spot in their calling, and have been distressed with the lifelessness of the Orthodox Church. Hitherto every attempt on their part to get the authorities to consider and reform the abuses of the system has met with failure; the reformers have been jailed, imprisoned in monasteries, and exiled to Siberia and the Caucasus. Dr. Dillon, in the *National Review*, tells of one such, and he is but a type of many.

Petrov, one of the most famous priests in Russia, the Editor of *God's Truth*, a paper eagerly

L

read by the Russian peasantry, has paid the penalty of his temerity by being driven from out of the Church. In a letter to the Metropolitan of St. Petersburg, he states his position as a priest of the Church:

" The thing which our Holy Synod passed for the Orthodox Church and the composition of the Synod itself, can these be considered as at all the true Church of Christ? . . . We have to-day, after nineteen centuries of preaching, individual Christians, separate persons, but no Christianity; there is no Christian legislation; our customs and morals are no longer Christian; there exists no Christian government." After referring to the massing of armed men and preparing them for war as the very negation of the Gospel, he continues: "Christian morality would have been limited and little developed if it had no other end but the life and conduct of private persons without throwing light on the organisations, the rulers, the life and conduct of societies and States. ' But that is politics ' says the clergy; ' our business is religion.'

" True politics is, in fact, the art of the better organisation of·life in society and the State; but is not the Evangel, with its doctrine of the Kingdom of God, the science of the better organisation of life, of society, and of the entire State? . . . Christianity has become the State religion before the ·State has ceased to be pagan. . . . Chris-

l

tianity itself is accused. Defects are sought for in the doctrine of Christ; this is wrong, for it is the fault, rather, of the higher clergy, which, in spite of the triumph of Christianity, has not been able to resist the seduction of power. It is not the clergy that has influenced the State, but on the contrary, it has borrowed from the State its external brilliance, its organisations, its means of action, its constraint, and its non-spiritual punishments.

"The ruling 'regular clergy,' with its cold, heartless, bony fingers, has stifled the Russian Church, killed its creative spirit, chained the Gospel itself, and sold the Church to the Government. There is no outrage, no crime, no perfidy of the State authorities which the monks who rule the Church would not cover with the mantle of the Church, would not bless, would not seal with their own hands. What power would the voice of the Church possess were it raised in genuine Christian words? Such words would become the voice of the Eternal Gospel truths addressed to the conscience of the country. They would strike every heart, they would penetrate into every corner, they would chime above the thunders of revolution, above the clamour of execution, like the voice of a Church bell through the howling of the tempest.

"In the Church the creative power of truth became withered, dried, and anæmic; separated

L

from life, the thought of the Church was condemned
to turn about in the world of abstract dogma and
theological discussions.   God was reasoned about
without being introduced into life itself.

" The majority of the lower clergy is ignorant,
poor, dulled;   nobody occupies himself with its
moral welfare.   It is crowded by the reigning
monks into a corner; it has its arms tied; it is
deprived of the liberty to think, to speak, and to
act.   They who are so near to the masses of the
people, to the centre of life;   they who see all
its misery, the deprivation of justice from which the
whole country suffers;   who hear the ceaseless
groans that rise from below; who are choked by
the tears of the people, blinded by the sight of
the   frightful   nightmare   created   all   over   the
country by the impious violence of the reigning
power;   they have not even the right to speak
of the sufferings of their flocks; not even the
chance to cry out to the violators, ' Halt ! '

"Indeed, according to the opinion of the
monks, who are at the same time the reigning
dignitaries of the Church, all that goes against the
State goes against the Church, against Christ, and
against God.   This is to reduce the great work
of salvation of humanity to the petty rôle of
bodyguard to the temporal autocratic organisa-
ton. . . . The Church is the universal union, the
organisation of all humanity, above nations and
States.   For to the Church none of the existing

l

organisations of the State are invariable, perfect, permanent, or infallible.

" Such an organisation is the work of the future, expressing one's self in the language of the evangel, it will be the future Kingdom of God. An organisation in which everything will be maintained, not by external violence, but by a common interior moral bond, in which there will be neither exploitation, nor arbitrary government, nor violence, nor master, nor workman; where all will support equally the burdens of life and all will profit equally from its good. This is the task of the Church, but the organisations which exist at present, whether they are autocratic or not, are worth nothing. Their only difference is in the degree of uselessness; one is more, another is less useless; yet our old, expiring organisation is the worst of all that exists in the Christian world."

We need only to add that during the past ten years hundreds of priests have left the Orthodox Church and have entered into secular callings, to show that a new spirit is abroad, and that thinking men, with the real passion for the welfare of their parishioners at heart, cribbed and confined by the ecclesiastical hierarchy, are finding their true sphere outside the fold of the Church and away from the dominant and arrogant spirit of the most Holy Synod.

All elements of the people recognise that something of the greatest import is going on in Russia's

religious thought. It is unnecessary to show how
general this recognition is, since the Government
itself, moved by the higher clergy, has proposed
extraordinary measures to put it to an end.

SEMINARIES

A CLERGY training school, or seminary, will not
admit pupils above the age of sixteen; some enter
at fourteen. The younger may finish at nineteen;
others stay till twenty-three. The more talented
will pass on to a religious academy for four years,
and can obtain the grade of student (a simple
certificate of residence and study), candidate, or
magistrant. The candidate who would become
a magistrant must send in a thesis, which will
be tested in a debate between him and his
examiners. Candidates for the priesthood sometimes serve an apprenticeship. A term of two
or three years may be served as a " psalm singer,"
or parish clerk, or as teacher in a parish school.
Vacant benefices are advertised. Any one who
has the degree of candidate may apply. The
parish is allowed to petition in favour of one who
has been a clerk or teacher in it. The deacon,
who may not celebrate the Eucharist, is adminis-
tratively under his priest, the priest under his
Bishop or Archbishop. " Archbishop " is a personal
title without reference to a local jurisdiction, so
that a Bishop may become an Archbishop without leaving his See. Bishops and Archbishops

L

are under their Metropolitan. All alike are subject to the Synod.

A boy or a man may attach himself to a monastery and become a "servant." At thirty, —not before—he will perhaps become a monk, either on the official list of the establishment, or as a supernumerary. He may also become a deacon, then a priest, and later an archpriest. Bishops, Archbishops, Metropolitans are all archpriests, and as such are equal; it is a kind of army rank, and has nothing to do with administration. Amongst the monks, the Archimandrite is also an archpriest; he wears a mitre, and can be selected as the head of one of the greater monasteries. The lesser monasteries are ruled by Hegumens or priors. The heads of the three historic *lavras* or greater monasteries are the three Metropolitans. These are the Cave Monastery at Kieff, the Trinity Monastery near Moscow, and that of St. Alexander Nevsky in St. Petersburg. Each Metropolitan has a lieutenant through whom he rules.

L

ι

THE HOLY ORTHODOX CHURCH

Icons or Holy Pictures.

BIBLIOGRAPHY.

WALLACE . . . *Russia.*

GRAHAM . . . *Changing Russia.*

VILLARI . . . *Russia under the Great Shadow.*

L

l

THE HOLY ORTHODOX CHURCH
Icons or Holy Pictures.

WE have already referred to the almost universal prevalence of the Icon in Russia, and undoubtedly the worship or adoration of the Icon has a greater influence upon the religious life of the nation than the priests, when considered apart from their special office.

Not only are the Icons to be found in the Churches, homes, business houses, and railway stations, but the peasantry carry them about with them. They are a kind of talisman against ill-luck and evil.

Whilst spending the summer of 1905 in the Crimea, I witnessed the return of a troopship with war-worn troops from the Far East. The majority of the men were severely wounded, and a pitiful procession passed from the quayside to the market-place, where they bivouacked for a few days.

No sooner were the men settled in their places than they began to bring small Icons from their blouses and trousers' pockets, and placing them upon the ground, returned thanks to the Madonna or their favourite saint for a favourable voyage and a safe return to Russian soil.

Even whilst bathing in the Black Sea and in

public *bania* (baths), I noticed that the men never removed from their necks the little medallion, sometimes suspended by a slender gold cord, but more often a piece of common thread. The Icon is a continual reminder to the Russian that his God is not locked up in a Church, but that He is with him everywhere, on the battlefield or out in the wide steppes, in the little home or in the cabin of the great steamer.

To the Russian, the Real Presence is in the home, as well as in the most stately cathedral or sacred monastery. In all finite and material things the Icon reminds the peasant of the infinite and spiritual.

Whatever may be the right view of the abstract question respecting sacred pictures or Icons, and the showing of outward respect towards them, even though the peasant's attitude of mind be that commonly classed as idolatry, the Russians cannot be reasonably blamed for reverencing a usage which they received together with Christianity itself, and the first introduction of which was made, in part, at least, the instrument of the conversion of their Prince Vladimir.

An Icon is a pictorial representation of the Saviour, of the Saviour in the arms of the Madonna, of the Madonna herself, of a particular saint, most frequently, Nicolas the miracle worker, the favourite saint of the bulk of the Russian peasantry. Many of them are executed in an

l

archaic Byzantine style, with a yellow or gold background, and they vary in size from a small medallion of about an inch square to several square feet. Very often the whole picture, with the exception of the face and hands of the figure, is covered with a metal plaque, of gold, or silver, or brass, embossed so as to represent the form of the figure and the folds of the drapery. Thousands of them are manufactured, to be sold to the peasants for a few copecks each, whilst others are of priceless value, the frames and filigree work being covered with diamonds, pearls, and precious stones.

Amongst the hundreds of Icons in the Kremlin at Moscow is one of the " Most Immaculate Mother of God," carved and overlaid with gold set with rubies, and a curtain of satin worked with pearls. Many of the Icons have solid gold frames; sometimes they have curtains; others are glazed; whilst some are in the form of a triptych, and have hinged doors.

In some districts of Northern Russia, where primeval paganism or fetishism has not yet died out, the Icons are sometimes hung with the images (very crude in workmanship) of cows, sheep, horses, or in the case of human beings being ill, of arms, eyes, ears, legs, etc., as a gentle reminder to God that the owner of the Icon needs His especial intervention on behalf of that particular piece of property or part of his anatomy.

11

ι

Icons are of two kinds—Simple and Miraculous (*tchudotvorny*). The former are manufactured in great quantities, literally by the thousand, and are to be found in every Orthodox home, from the Palace of the Tsar down to the vilest hovel of the poorest peasant.

The Icon is generally placed high up in the corner of a room, facing the door, and frequently a small oil lamp and sometimes a candle is kept burning before the one in the room most commonly used. I have even seen an eight-candle power incandescent electric lamp in full glow in broad daylight.

An Orthodox Christian, upon entering a room, will immediately remove his hat, bow in the direction of the Icon, and cross himself with the sign of the Cross.

Before and after meals, the same short ceremony is gone through by all the participants of the meal. On the eve of Saint's days a lamp will be kept burning before all the Icons in the house, if the householder be an enthusiastic and devout Orthodox believer.

The peasants will refer to the Icon as God, and firmly believe that all happenings in his life are related to his own personal treatment of the picture. If he has a stroke of luck, he ascribes it to the Holy Icon; if he is pursued by ill-fortune, then, of course, he has neglected to keep the lamp burning; maybe he has forgotten himself in

L

a bad temper, and has used vile language in the Presence; possibly he has omitted to keep the frame clean, or he has been imbibing too freely of "vodka" in the neighbourhood of his God.

In the Churches and shrines the favourite pictures of the saints are worshipped by thousands of people, and made the object of their veneration on all important occasions in their lives.

Standing one day in St. Isaac's Cathedral in St. Petersburg, I watched the almost ceaseless procession of the tourists of many nationalities who had come in to see its great gilded dome, its massive red granite pillars, the wondrous bronze doors, cast in bas-relief, the priceless relics over against every altar, the tomb of Christ, marvellously wrought; but stones, bronze and gold, colour and perfume were of little interest compared with the people coming and going, passing to and fro, some ardent worshippers, others careless and indifferent, some being piloted around by a "guide," primed with stories concerning the facts and legends of the sacred edifice and the holy pictures.

In one part of the huge cathedral Divine service was being performed by a priest, of whom it could be said "that Solomon in all his glory, was not arrayed as one of these." He had a musical voice, and rapidly intoned the gospel for the day, and the prayers. The "server," in ordinary civilian dress, stood by the side of the

L

altar, a group of people were close by, some very
poorly clad, some in mourning garments, whilst
here and there a *moujik* stood in humble attitude
by the side of an erect military officer or prosperous
merchant. Several women knelt upon the cold
stone floor. Many candles were burning upon
huge many-branched candelabra placed before the
sacred Icons. In less than ten minutes the whole
service was over, the priest withdrew, passing
out of sight through the " deacon's door," and the
servitor took up the collection, receiving the gifts
of the faithful upon a red baize-covered platter.

One woman held my attention. Dressed in
black, though not in mourning, evidently fairly
well-to-do, she knelt throughout the service.
Thrice she touched the marble floor with her forehead, she frequently crossed herself, *and was the
only one of the company which contributed to the
collection.* Immediately after the service she
entered the small chancel and visited the Icons
one by one! at each picture she raised herself
upon tip-toe, and impressed a long, passionate kiss
upon the feet of the saint; her adoration of the
saints being completed, she placed several candles
in the candelabra, and took her departure.

An officer in full dress, with sword rattling
upon the pavement, approached one of the pictures,
and I noticed that he not only took the precaution
to rub the glass with his handkerchief, but deli-
cately and lightly kissed the picture in the corner,

L

quite close to the frame. In a modern English Church he would probably be an advocate of "individual" communion cups upon hygienic grounds.

One thing in the cathedral puzzled me. Near to the entrance door an official was selling, amongst other things, wax candles of varying lengths and thicknesses.

These were purchased by the worshippers and, after being lighted, were inserted into the sockets of the candlesticks. After genuflecting before, and subsequently kissing, the Icon, the worshipper would pass to another sacred picture and burn another candle, or leave the building.

Every few minutes a liveried servant would emerge rapidly from one of the many doors, and quickly passing by the candelabra, would hastily remove a handful of candles, many of which had not been consumed more than half an inch, and quickly extinguishing them, retreat to his hiding-place, then, opening a huge chest, would unceremoniously thrust them in.

I saw one such chest, about three feet long, two feet deep, and two feet wide, almost entirely filled with candles, only about one-eighth part burned.

What is done with them?

To what subsequent use are they put?

The only solution which occurs to me is that they are returned to the candle factory to be

L

melted down and fashioned anew into candles. If so, the profits in the traffic must be enormous, for hundreds of candles were bought and lighted during my brief stay in the building.

Another scene comes before me as I write. A village church in far-off Samara. The little building is crowded with peasants in their sheepskins. Over and above the perfume of the incense is the all-pervading smell of the crowd. The priest, deacon, and server are conducting worship; the service comes to a close, and the men and women, following one another in rapid succession, move to the sacred picture and kiss the feet of the saint, meanwhile crossing themselves and murmuring, " God have mercy upon us." The Icon plays a most important part in the religious life of the Russian peasant. The influence of the picture is always with him.

The " Old Believers " have in their hidden sanctuaries in the forests and in their homes many ancient Icons and pictures—a perfect revelation of the mediæval spirit with which Russia was impregnated at the time of the Great Schism. Nothing made since that time has any value for them; they are wedded to the old. As works of art they are very crude, but the hold they have upon the Raskolniki is stronger than the more modern Icon upon the ordinary Orthodox, if that were possible.

The wonder-working or miraculous Icons are

L

comparatively few in number, and are always carefully preserved in a monastery or Church. The method of bringing them into existence is worth recording, if only to reveal the superstition frequently connected with the worship of the Icon. A monk, or priest, or even a layman will have a vision that in a certain spot there is hidden an Icon "not made with hands" Journeying to the spot indicated he will generally find the Icon buried beneath the mould, or possibly hanging upon a tree-branch. The sacred treasure is then carefully removed to a Church, and the news of the discovery spreads like wild-fire. The whole countryside seethes with excitement. Thousands of pilgrims flock to prostrate themselves before it. Innumerable candles are blessed and lighted before it. Some of the people are apparently healed of their diseases, and soon pilgrimages are organised for miles around.

The Holy Synod is then officially informed of the great discovery, details of its finding are reported, and recognition is sought for. If recognition be granted by the Holy Synod, the Icon is treated with the greatest reverence Thousands from all parts of Russia flock to it, weeping, wailing, and singing as they go, seeking healing for their bodily ills and peace to their souls from the newly-discovered miracle-worker.

Instances are on record of important or ancient Churches, desiring to augment their funds,

L

consulting the Synod beforehand as to whether, if an Icon be found, it would receive recognition!

Stephen Graham, in *Changing Russia*, says: "But the Church which is founded on the wonder-working Icon is a commercial Church; it knows that the greater the miracle, the more the money cast into the treasury. The wonder-working Icon or relic is well in its place; if the Icon and the relic have such powers, they have their special place and significance in the Church. The heavens did not open at Bethabara that the people might open their mouths, or it would go on opening there now when the pilgrims visit it to be baptised. But the singular event of the Gospel story has its definite place. It is an accompaniment of the life of Jesus; it is not that life itself."

The Russian Church cannot afford to take its stand on miracles. If ever there comes a revolution in the land, the Church will suffer immense tribulation through the imputation of superstition, idolatry, simony, and corruption. The good part of the Church will be overwhelmed with that which is diseased.

Some of the miraculous Icons have fête-days instituted in their honour, as, for instance, the Kazan Madonna. A few of them are connected with some great event in Russian history. The Vladimir Madonna is reputed to have once saved Moscow from the invading Tatars; the Smolensk Madonna accompanied the Russian Army in the great campaign against Napoleon in 1812; and when the French were at the gates of Moscow in that year the citizens pressed the Metropolitan to take the Iberian Madonna, which may still be seen at one of the gates of the Kremlin, and to lead them out, armed with axes and hatchets, against the enemy.

The Iberian Madonna is the most famous of all the Icons, and is kept in a small chapel in the Voskres Senskaya Ploshtchad, between the two arches of the gate leading to the Red Square.

"It is a copy, executed in 1648, of a much older Icon preserved in Mount Athos. No good Orthodox Christian ever passes it without doffing his hat and crossing himself many times, and every day large numbers of people enter the chapel to pray before the holy picture.

"Whenever the Tsar comes to Moscow, before entering the Kremlin, he visits this shrine and prays before it. One may see the most important people in the land doing homage here and kissing the Icon—generals in full uniform, councillors of State, nobles and noble women of the highest rank, rich merchants, not to mention crowds of humbler folk. Many miracles are attributed to the Iberian Madonna, among others, the conversion of an infidel, who, on scratching the picture, saw blood flow from the wound; the scratch is visible to this day, to bear witness to

L

the truth of the story. The Virgin is adorned with a crown of brilliants, and quantities of pearls and precious stones, including some of great size, and a network of pearls, and the robe is covered with the usual silver plaques. Every day the image is taken from the chapel, placed in a large closed coach, drawn by six black horses, four abreast and two in front, one of the latter ridden by a boy postillion. Inside, opposite the image, sit two priests in full vestments.

"Priest, driver, footmen, and postillion are always bareheaded whatever the weather. It is carried to the houses of people dangerously ill, provided that they can pay a fee of fifty to two hundred roubles (£5-£20), or to assist at family festivals, the inauguration of new buildings and shops, and other similar functions. In the case of a new building a temporary shrine is erected in the courtyard, before which the priests hold a service. During its absence from home the Icon is replaced by a copy, to which great virtues are also attributed. When the coach drives past, the people prostrate themselves before it, touching the ground with their foreheads in abject humility. One day, as the vehicle was rolling along, I saw one of the priests put his head out of the window and spit into the street. The action was characteristic, and the fact that it was not resented shows what a wide gap there is in the eyes of the Orthodox between the Church he venerates and

L

its ministers whom he despises. The Icon is a large source of income to the Church, not only from the fees which are paid when it is sent for, but also from the offerings which most of the worshippers leave when praying at the shrine itself.

"Icon worship has a firm hold upon the Russian peasantry. Every saint is supposed to cure a particular disease and to confer special benefits. Frequently in the Churches, the people, instead of listening to Divine Service, will wander about, preferring to worship their own particular and favourite Icon. To many they do not realize that God exists somewhere and beyond and independent of their picture.

"The worship starves the 'soul,' materialises the Deity, and divorces a living faith from the moral code."*

* Villari, *Russia under the Great Shadow.*

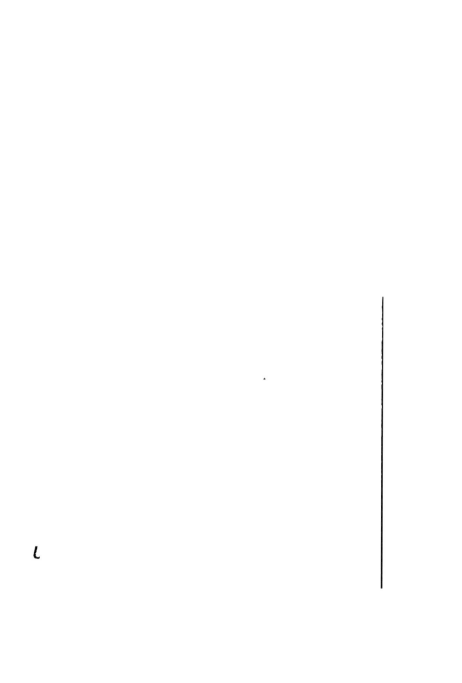

THE HOLY ORTHODOX CHURCH

Missionary Activity.

BIBLIOGRAPHY.

STANLEY . . . *Lectures on the Eastern Church.*

MOURAVIEFF . . *History of the Russian Church.*

STEAD . . . . *The M.P. for Russia.*
Petersburgskia Viedomosti, April,
1897.

ZILLIACUS . . . *Russian Revolution.*

GRAHAM . . . *Changing Russia.*

KROSSNOGEON . *The Constructive Quarterly, Dec.,*
1913.

L

THE EXILE'S SONG

MISERY.

Was it for this, God's light flattered me,
  An exile, spurned, sunken in deepest sorrow,
Only to know man's venomed calumny
  Will pierce my soul afresh on each fresh morrow?
Dark the horizon; sits forbidding gloom,
  A hopeless melancholy, on yon day dawning;
Fear grips my heart, the seal of coming doom
  Stamps on my soul the dread of to-morrow's morning.
Was it for this that God's light flattered me?
  Hot stream the tears across my careworn cheeks.
Shall youth's young dream of happiness quite shattered be?
  Oh God! 'tis false: a voice within me speaks,

JOY.

Speaks, and lo, the future is unfolded—
  Beckon me the woods to come and play,
Frolic in their depths in sweet oblivion,
  Scatter darkness with the light of day,
Wander in the wilds in the midst of roses,
  Listen to the whispering of the brooks,
Hear the nightingale at even warbling,
  Sleep 'midst the mossy-bedded nooks.
There, in solitude with nature,
  The caves my covering, the sun my heat,
Rags my clothing, bare shall be my feet.
  Hills, shedding tears of joy eternal,
Weep in never-ending stream,
  Lazily the rugged rocks o'erleaping,
Music to my life's long dream,
  There sweet repose will never leave me,
Far from wickedness and vice,
  Waiting till God's voice shall call me,
Home—to Peace and Paradise.

L

THE HOLY ORTHODOX CHURCH

MISSIONARY ACTIVITY

DEAN STANLEY, in his *Lectures on the Eastern Church*, writes, "The Russian Church is not a missionary Church, neither has it been a persecuting one."

In the sense of foreign missions, that is, missions beyond the frontiers of Russia or beyond the pale of Russian political influence, Stanley may be right, but the story of Russian territorial expansion is inextricably bound up with the missionary activities of the monks of the Orthodox Church. His reference to it not being a persecuting Church may have been true when he delivered his lectures in Oxford fifty years ago, but the attitude of the Church to other religious bodies has changed for the worse under the malign influence of Pobiedonosteff.

Some idea of the early missionary activities of the Church may be gathered from the *History* by Mouravieff and the MSS. of Baron Rosenkampf. The Monk Lazarus founded his monastery in the fourteenth century on the shores of Lake Onega for the conversion of the Lopars, and at the same

L

time the monks of Balaam proceeded to the Conversion of the Carelians.

Not only spiritual instruction, but even the occupation and colonization of the northern and eastern districts of Russia was forwarded by the multiplication of religious houses. Thus every monastery which extended the boundary became the nucleus of a new pale of settlements, and even a stronghold of defence.

Great Perm was added to Russia by a single monk, through the preaching of the name of Christ. St. Stephen, penetrated with an apostolic zeal, felt his heart pained at the gross heathenism of the inhabitants of Perm; he went alone to preach Christ in the deep and silent woods, and by faith overcame all the opposition of the heathen priests. He founded there his first Church, and from thence, little by little, the Gospel spread further eastwards. Thus, gradually, the monks pressed into Siberia, and paved the way for the growth of the Russian Empire. But we need not to go back to the fourteenth century. The same policy is in force to-day in Manchuria and Mongolia. Churches are being built, monasteries establaished, and bishoprics formed. At the centre of all this activity is the policy of "Russification." The vital connection between Church and State, and the policy of a Church State in Russia, has led the Church, through the Holy Synod, to establish missions amongst the non-

L

Russian subjects of the Tsar, and to severely persecute those who refuse to commune with her.

Madam Novikoff (O.K.), writing to the late W. T. Stead, declares that "Greek Orthodoxy is the soul of our Government, and the great link between the Government and the people. But devotion to our faith is immeasurably superior to any worldly consideration. Russia is more of a Church than a State, more of a religion than a nationality. We are first Holy Orthodox, and then Slavs, and then Russians."

Missionary enterprise is essentially Slavophilism. To make the Russian people one,—to bind together Slav and Finn, Pole and Lett, Tatar and Circassian, Armenian and Siberian, and in process of time, Chinaman and Persian too, by the invisible and unbreakable bonds of a simple and common faith,—the roots of which run back unbroken through the soil of centuries— this is the ambition of the Church Statesmen of Modern Russia.

Tsar Alexander III. was the most uncompromisingly zealous champion of the three Slavophile principles: Autocracy, Orthodoxy, Nationalism; one king, one religion, one law; and he was firmly determined to enforce these principles in their strongest and most unmistakable sense.

Running parallel with the missionary enterprise, if not actually fused with it, is the glorification and aggrandisement of the Russian Empire.

L   12

The Bishops of Rome early conceived the design of building up an Universal Christian State, theocratic in government, with the Pope as the Representative of Christ on earth, in which all the civil authorities should be subject to the subordinates of Christ's Vicar on earth. The Eastern Church followed a contrary policy; they remained true to their earliest traditions, and never dreamed of a world-wide Church State. From the time of Constantine she had been accustomed to lean upon, and to look to, the civil authorities for support; she had always beeen content to play a secondary part, and never resisted the tendency to form separate National Churches, with a large measure of freedom in the government of their own dioceses. From the beginnings of the fifteenth century, in Russia especially, the head of the State was also the ruler in ecclesiastical affairs.

.With the abolition of the Patriarchate under Peter the Great, and the formation of the Holy Synod, the Holy Synod became the highest ecclesiastical authority. Theoretically the Orthodox Church has no visible "Head" or "Pope." Christ is the Supreme Ruler. His mind is known through the Synod.

Those who are at all acquainted with the inner history of Russia are aware that there is practically no clear line of demarcation between that which is temporal and that which is spiritual, and that the civil authorities have no scruples in

l

using the religious organisation for purely political ends.

The inevitable result of this use of the Church has been that "missionary" activity is not the direct outcome of a passion for the religious welfare of the non-orthodox, so much as a policy to bring the non-Russian within the orbit of the ideal: one King, one religion, one law. This policy has also had an ill-effect upon the parish priests, for whilst they have lived upon a plane little higher than the peasants themselves, their "missionary" brethren have had houses and lands, money and power granted to them in abundance.

The contrast between the conditions of life of the priest in a village in Riazin or Tambov and in Lettonia or Courland is most marked

The occasional use of the ecclesiastical organisation for political purposes has now become the settled policy of the bureaucracy. The activities of the Church are mainly along the lines of Russification. One or two illustrations of this policy will suffice:

In 1887 a number of priests, well furnished with State funds, were sent to the Lettish and Esthonian peasants to conduct a campaign in these provinces. Their policy was not the conversion of individuals, but to obtain the consent of a majority in any given village to embrace the Orthodox faith, and then to declare the whole

L

village as Orthodox.   One of the priests, who had been able to secure a large number of "converts," was rewarded with a civil decoration—the only fitting recompense for such service.

Those of the "converts" who attempted to attend their own Lutheran or Baptist Churches found their way barred by the Russian law, which makes it a penal offence for any one to leave the Holy Orthodox confession.

Pastors who received their parishioners or Church members, or who consented to marry them according to the rites or customs of their Church, were sent to prison; one pastor, universally respected, died before the sentence could be carried out.

In 1904 similar tactics were inaugurated against the Lutherans and Baptists in Finland.

The *Petersburgskia Viedomosti* for 1897 relates that:

"In April last, in the villages of Semlianka and Antonofka, in the district of Bousoulok, five children, varying in age from two to eleven years, were taken away from their parents in virtue of Article 39 of the legal code. The Baptist Sectarians petitioned that the children should be restored to them. At the same time a controversy was raging in the Press as to whether the priests at the Congress in Kazan had passed a resolution calling upon the State to separate children from their Sectarian parents." There was no need to argue the matter at all, for the law was already in existence and was being enforced.

Kostromin, one of the early pioneers of the Baptist faith amongst the Cossacks of the Don, had his eight children taken away from him. The boys were placed in monastic schools and the girls in nunneries; no two in the same establishment; and until this present time the parents have failed to trace the whereabouts of three of them.

This form of persecution is defended on the ground that it is necessary to remove children from the pernicious influence of their Sectarian parents, and to give them an Orthodox education. This excuse is based on a circular of the Minister of the Interior, Gorevykin, who recommended the measure on the strength of the Article 39 before mentioned. Not alone in the Baltic provinces has this policy been ruthlessly carried out. Down in the Caucasus and in Poland we have records of similar tactics upon the part, not only of the "missionary" priests, but of the civil authorities acting in collusion with them.

The close and vital connection between Church and State has meant that the missionary activities of the Church have degenerated into a policy of Slavophile persecution.

To be Orthodox is to be a true Russian; to be a Sectarian is to be a traitor to the Fatherland.

ι

Religious persecution has always accompanied the attempts of the bureaucracy to Russify the people as quickly as possible by the suppression of the national languages. Attacks were first made on the schools, then against the Churches and local officials; everywhere the Russian tongue was made compulsory. The attack against the Churches was usually made in a veiled and indirect way, to prevent the intolerance of the priests and officials from creating too great a sensation in Western Europe, and too many protests from the fellow-believers of the persecuted ones.

Thus the "missionary" had somehow or other (the means of obtaining it was immaterial) to get a petition forwarded on behalf of a village or district, that the inhabitants were desirous of being received into the Orthodox Church, whereupon the whole population was officially declared to be admitted to the bosom of the Orthodox. This subtle method is still being pursued in the frontiér provinces of the Baltic, amongst Lutherans; in Poland, amongst Roman Catholics; and in the Caucasus, amongst Armenians. Not only were these tactics adopted against non-Russians, but whenever possible they were resorted to against the Sectarians, such as the Molokans, Doukhobors, and Baptists.

Prince Galitzen, Governor-General of the Caucasus in 1896, in a report sent to the Ministry of the Interior in St. Petersburg, expresses his alarm that the Armenians, living in the Caucasus (their home before the Russians seized their territory) show a distinct national spirit, and are thus a menace to the Government. He details his proofs of this spirit in the fact that they have such national institutions as charities, schools, and churches, which they have founded and maintained out of their own funds; and the best way of opposing this national spirit was to place all such institutions under the direct control of the Russian Government. For this reason he also depicted in glowing colours the effect of the decree of June 14, 1897, relating to the placing of all Armenian schools under the Ministry of Public Instruction, and reported that in conformity with this decree 320 Armenian schools had been closed on the ground of the priests' refusal to submit to the orders of the decree, whilst thirty-one remained open. "But," the report continues, "some of these we later closed, for all that, on the ground of the incompetence of the teachers." In the report of June 17, 1897, he petitioned the Tsar to sanction the transfer of the property of the closed schools to the Ministry of Public Instruction.

The Armenians were by this decree not only robbed of the administration and control of their schools, but of the property which they had acquired by their own industry and sacrifice.

In a marginal note upon Prince Galitzen's

report and recommendations, the Tsar wrote:
" This is the proper way of acting "; and upon
the suggestion that the invested charitable funds
for aged and infirm Armenians should be se-
questered, His Highness commented: " This deserves to be carefully considered."

Zilliacus, in *The Russian Revolution*, records
a phase of the " missionary activity " of the
Orthodox Church.

" One of the most brutal cases of proselytising
happened in the year 1893, at the little town
of Krozhe, on the frontier of Russian Poland,
where the community, although it had been announced by one of the ' missionary priests' as
about to embrace the Orthodox Church, refused to
leave the Roman Catholic Church. All the
admonitions of the Russian authorities remained unheeded. The community did not leave the Church,
in which service was regularly held by the Catholic
priests. A detachment of Cossacks was sent to
drive out the disobedient congregation, and the
command was carried out with such zeal that
twenty Catholics were killed on the spot, over a
hundred were more or less seriously wounded, and
a further considerable number drowned in an
adjoining river, into which the fugitives were
chased by the Cossacks."

That the higher clergy, at least, if not the
general body of parish priests, are at one with the
civil authorities in this policy of " missionary

activity" through persecution, may be gathered from the fact that in August, 1897, a Congress of more than two hundred priests was called to assemble in Kazan, under the auspices and authority of the Most Holy Synod. The subject for discussion was, "The best ways and means to be adopted to check the lamentable spread of Sectarianism."

From the official report of the discussions and resolutions of the Congress it appears:

Firstly, that the Baptists were still rapidly spreading.

Secondly, that the priests were prepared to go further than the Government in suppressing the same.

The Baptists, since it was forbidden to them to hold prayer-meetings, had begun to attend Lutheran (German) Churches wherever such were to be found, and the Lutheran clergy had assisted them by holding Divine service in the Russian tongue. The Congress consequently resolved that an order should be issued prohibiting the Lutheran clergy from rendering assistance of this kind, and to declare the Sectarian views on religion as blasphemy, thus enabling the village communes to banish, without trial, members of the obnoxious sect of Baptists, to Siberia; that Sectarians should be forbidden to employ any young people of the Orthodox faith; and that adult Sectarians should be placed under the special supervision of the parish priests.

L

The Congress also resolved that the punishment for *open* defence of Sectarian, i.e., Baptist,
doctrines, should be amended by the omission
of the word *open*, so that the law could be more
rigorously enforced.   All these resolutions were
carried unanimously.   It is perhaps unnecessary
to add that the Procurator of the Holy Synod,
Pobiedonosteff, was the soul and leading spirit
of the Congress, and that the result was that the
Sectarians were placed in an even worse position
than formerly.

In 1901 a similar Congress was held at Orel,
to devise means to suppress the Baptist heresy.
Mr. Stakhovitch was the official representative of
the Government for the nobles.   During the proceedings, Mr. Stakhovitch moved that the Congress should forward a petition to the Minister
of the Interior and to the Holy Synod "that
all punishments attached to 'offences and crimes'
against religion, i.e., the Orthodox Church, should
be abolished."

An incident connected with the district of
Trubchevsk, in the government of Orel, was related by him in support of his motion.

The civil authorities, with the knowledge and
approval of the local priests, arrested a number of
persons upon suspicion of being Baptists, and
imprisoned them in the Church.   A table, covered
with a clean cloth, was brought into the centre
of the Church, and on it was placed an Icon

of the Immaculate Virgin The Baptists were then brought one at a time to the table and ordered to kiss the Hóly Picture. Those who refused to do the bidding of the police and priests were scourged with the *nagaika*, even in the sacred (?) building. Some, whose faith could not stand such severe punishment, recanted, and were thereupon immediately received back again into the true fold. With some of the men it took four and five thrashings for them to yield to the " missionary."

Mr. Stakovitch questioned some of the priests as to the number of Baptists in their parishes. To one he said:

" You stated that a little while ago there were forty Baptist families in your village, and that now there are only about four or five. How do you account for the decrease? What has become of the others?" "Oh," was the naive reply, "by the grace of God they have been deported to Siberia and the Trans-Caspian district."

The Procurator of the Holy Synod, Pobiedonostseff, immediately after the accession of his former pupil, Nicolas, to the throne, moved His Majesty to give his approbation to fresh measures for the persecution of the Baptists, who were absolutely forbidden to assemble for worship in any form of their belief, their " sect " being regarded, according to a Ministerial circular, as a very dangerous one for the Church and State.

The Western European nations do not seem to know that they have next door to them a Power more intolerant in matters of religious liberty than Spain at her worst period, with more unprincipled and narrow-minded persecutors of all the Dissenting sects than were Alva and Torquemada.

How can they know it? Russia works in silence; her methods are occult, and the victims are mute. The Press rarely dares to publish and brand persecution and persecutors.

Trials against heretics are frequently held behind closed doors, and publicity is carefully excluded. I have talked with Russians sympathetically inclined towards religious liberty, and they do not know a tenth part of what is actually occurring. And if they did know, under the bureaucracy, they are practically helpless.

General Alexander Kirief, defending Russification by forcible conversion and persecution, says: "We are guided by two considerations:

"1. Our country being organically united with her Church—hence the name of Holy Russia —everything attacking the Church attacks the very essence of the country.

"2. Being absolutely convinced of possessing absolute Truth, all that attacks that Truth is an aggression we can never tolerate. Only indifference could allow Sectarian propaganda under such conditions. If the Twelve Apostles came we would receive them with open arms, because they would only strengthen us in our faith, and not shake it."

Following out this Slavophil programme, Pobiedonosteff and his henchmen tried to magnify religion as a bulwark against modern ideas. Undoubtedly for years there was room in Russia for a Church revival, and to a certain extent a real revival took place, but the Procurator would have none of it; he appointed to high office in the Church men who would be docile instruments of his policy. He surrounded himself with place-hunters, and through them intimidated the local clergy into being instruments of a political re-action.

But he did not see that the peasants, liberated from serfdom, meeting in the village *mir*, would begin to think for themselves in matters of religion. He did not realise that the coldness and mere ceremonialism of the Orthodox Church could not for ever satisfy the religious hunger of the people. He did not appreciate to the full that Orthodoxy, unless supported by genuine feeling and strong religious conviction, could not for ever hold the people in check.

Whilst the Russian Government and the priests are following their policy of Russification amongst the non-Russians of the West, and the forcible conversion of the Russian Sectarians of the Central Provinces, they do not altogether

L

neglect the pagan and semi-pagan peoples of the East. Paganism is not altogether extinct in European Russia, but in the Eastern Provinces there are many thousands of tribesmen, mainly nomads, who have yet to be brought under Christian influence. Surely in this work there should be sufficient scope for the missionary activity of the great Russian Church!

To set herself earnestly and zealously to this work would bring a breath of new life into the Church and would quicken her with the very Spirit of Jesus Christ. At present, however, as far as one can judge from personal observation and from current Russian literature, this great field is almost neglected, or if worked at all, it is in a most perfunctory spirit.

Stephen Graham, in his most interesting book, *Changing Russia*, records a conversation he had with a monk about the Abkhasian tribesmen:

"They are mostly Christian now, owing to our influence. We stand here as the most important institution in the world. These tribesmen used to be Mohammedans when the Turks were here, but now they are Christians.

"Still, they can't consummate the faith, that is the pity; they confess Christ and bow themselves a little, but they don't understand what it means. They know how to cross themselves, but they don't know why they do it. They stand before the pictures and make the sign, or come to Church and imitate other people, but it is only a new superstition."

Wherever Russia is extending her Empire, there this policy of Russification through religion is in progress. The priest accompanies the surveyor, the engineer, and the workmen on the new railways, with the soldiers in northern Persia, not necessarily for the spiritual benefit of the Russians themselves—many of them are too indifferent—but for the stated purpose of bringing the non-Russian inhabitants of the newly-acquired territories under the powerful influence of the Orthodox Church. Thus we have seen the "railway-car Church," with its gorgeously-apparelled priests initiating the tribesmen into the mysteries of the Christian religion.

Teaching there is none. The Bible can only be had in the Old Sclavonic. Like the Abkhasians before mentioned, the converts only acquire a new superstition. All that the clergy demand is that those who are within the pale of Orthodoxy should show the Church a certain nominal allegiance; and in this matter of allegiance they are by no means very exacting. So long as a member refrains from openly attacking the Church and from going over to another confession, he may entirely neglect all religious ordinances, and publicly profess scientific theories logically inconsistent with any kind of dogmatic belief, without the slightest danger of incurring ecclesiastical censure. The Govern-

L

ment vigilantly protects her from attack, and all discussions in the Press are rigorously censored, although here and there a stray article eludes the eagle eye of the censor.

RELIGIOUS LIBERTY

BIBLIOGRAPHY

KROSSNOGEON . . *Constructive Quarterly, Dec., 1913.*

VON DER BRUGGEN *Russia of To-day.*

MILYOUKOV . . . *Russia and its Crisis.*

LATIMER . . . . *Under Three Tsars.*

LATIMER . . . . *Life of Dr. Bædeker.*

BYFORD . . . . *Peasants and Prophets.*

"By lasting out the strokes of fate,
  In trials long they learned to feel
Their inborn strength; as hammer's weight
  Will splinter glass but temper steel"
                              Pushkin

RELIGIOUS LIBERTY

AS we have seen in the previous chapter, all
who have dared to dissent from the
doctrine, practice, and authority of the
Orthodox Church in Russia have had their full
meed of persecution and suffering. Whilst the
Church, as an ecclesiastical organisation, has not
been entirely free from the charge of persecuting those who have denied her authority, the
chief blame must undoubtedly rest upon the civil
government.

Wherever there has been an outburst of
fanatical intolerance, resulting in brutalities almost
unspeakable, the cause can almost always be
traced to the higher civil Authorities.

The Russian peasant is peculiarly tolerant of
other religious faiths (save perhaps amongst the
members of the "Union of the Russian People,"
commonly called the "Black Hundreds"), and he
takes quite a philosophic view of people who are
not Orthodox.

His general attitude is, "After all, we are
brothers." "The Tatars, when they are ill, send
for the witch doctor to drive away the bad devils;

l

when we are ill we send for the priest to pray
to the Mother of God." " For the Tatars the
witch-doctor beats a drum, and the illness goes;
we burn a candle to our saint, and the illness
goes."

"If he calls in the witch-doctor, that is his
business; if we have the 'pope,' that is our business. Never mind; when they are well they come
to our Church and worship our God. We are
brothers." " God made Christianity for me, and
Mohammedanism for the Tatars; and if the Tatar
finds that his witch-doctor cannot keep the devil
away he comes to our 'pope,' and if the witch-
doctor keeps him well, that is good. We are
brothers."

Christian Russian and Mohammedan Tatar
mutually respect each other's religion, they inter-
mingle socially, they are subjects of the one Tsar,
they live their ordinary life on terms of civic
and social equality, they enjoy the same privileges
and help to bear the same burdens.

Save in exceptional and rare circumstances
there. is neither racial nor religious animosity in
the nature of the Russian peasant; for bigotry
and intolerance one must turn to the higher priests
and the bureaucrats.

From the time of the Strigolnik heresy until
the present day, every movement away from the
Orthodox Church has passed through a time of
bitter sorrow and tribulation,

Whilst it is true that there is a full measure of religious liberty for those born outside the Orthodox fold, it is at the same time true that those who dare to forsake her courts and become Sectarians are laying themselves open to severe and lasting persecution. The point of view of the Orthodox Church has been ably presented by Professor Krossnogeon of Dorpat University. He lays down certain principles which guide the Church and Government in their attitude towards other religious bodies, principles which grant to the Sectarians born outside the fold of the Orthodox Church a fairly full measure of religious liberty, but which must inevitably lead to repression if not the persecution of all those who are compelled by conscience to leave the Orthodox Church.

He says, in an article in the *Constructive Quarterly* for December 1913:

"Every Church, considering that it is necessary to belong to it to be saved, cannot be indifferent towards other creeds, or allow indifference in the affairs of faith; still less can it tolerate their proselytising; yet it is its duty to spread its teaching amongst people not belonging to it.'

"No Church can remain indifferent if one of its members leaves it and joins another religious community.

"Every Church, considering that it is

L

necessary to belong to it in order to be saved, cannot allow its members to have any intercourse with the followers of other confessions, either in Sacraments, or religious rites, or prayers in general . . if it permitted the promiscuous meeting of various confessions in Church communion, it would bring destruction on itself."

These principles are based upon the absolute confidence with which the Orthodox Church identifies religious faith with the Church's creed and religious duty with the Church's requirements.

Professor Krossnogeon brings us back to the old battle ground of the Reformers of three centuries ago. The Reformation raised the question of the relation of the free individual to the religious society. Professor Oman, in *The Problem of Faith and Freedon*, says: " That the Reformers, as is so frequently asserted, ignored the Church . . . is not shown either by their principles or their practices. To Calvin, as to Augustine, the Church is our mother. At her breasts our religious life is nourished."

The Church is something higher than the organised society, and her true succour is something more than word and sacrament.

In Russia the Orthodox Church is considered to be the only true and salutary religion. It always has been the dominant religion. All the others are tolerated upon the strict condition that their adherents do not impugn the rights of the dominant Church, and do not lead Orthodox persons astray into their own confessions.

"In regions of personal religious judgment, the State must guarantee a complete freedom of conscience; in this region it cannot have recourse either to sword, prison, or deprivation of civic rights. But we must discern between freedom of personal confession and freedom of religious assembly in public worship and founding new religious communities. The unlimited and un-conditioned freedom of such assemblies passes the limits of the demands of religious toleration; the State cannot leave public religious communities of this kind without supervision and regulation."

The policy of the Russian Government towards all "alien" confessions for five centuries or more, at least until very recent times, has been very clear and decided.

In all lands conquered by Russian arms and incorporated into the Empire, the inhabitants have had granted to them, by Imperial Ukase, the right to retain their own faith and practice. Thus in the Crimea and the Caucasus one will frequently see Mohammedan Mosques, Armenian, Georgian and Greek Churches almost side by side, whilst in Siberia and Turkestan; Buriats, Kalmuks, Samoyedes retain their primeval forms of worship. True, in many places there is a veneer of Ortho-doxy over all, but it is only a veneer. So also we find in the Baltic provinces Lutheranism in

l

the ascendancy, whilst in Poland the Roman Catholics are supreme.

When Dorpat was surrendered to the victorious Russians, the following proclamation was issued to the inhabitants:

"The citizens of Dorpat shall keep their religion of the Augsberg confession without any changes, and they will not be compelled to give it up; their Churches with all their belongings remain as they were."

This proclamation, of course, has not prevented the Orthodox Church from pursuing a policy of vigorous propaganda amongst the people; again, when, after a long and severe struggle with Sweden, the latter country had to cede the Baltic provinces to the Tsar, the Russian Government decreed that:

"No violation of conscience shall be introduced in the lands that have been conceded; on the contrary, the Evangelical faith, its Churches and schools and all that belongs to them, will remain and shall be maintained on the same foundation as they were under the last Swedish Government, on condition, however, that in these lands the faith of the Greek confession shall be allowed henceforth to be practised fully and without impediment."

Under Catherine the Great the boundaries of the empire were greatly extended, and she followed the same broad spirit of tolerance to-

l

wards her new subjects. The Government of her day issued a proclamation.

"In such a great Empire, spreading its dominions over so many different peoples, to forbid them to have different religions would be a defect, very harmful for the peace and safety of the inhabitants."

And the Holy Synod followed with.

"As the Most High God tolerates on earth all religions, languages, and confessions, Her Majesty complying with His Holy Will, allows to all free action, desiring only that love and harmony should always reign among her subjects."

This policy of non-interference has been departed from in recent years, largely owing to the new watchword, "One Nation, One Tsar, One Church." Strong measures have been taken to win over whole villages and townships to the dominant faith, money has been poured forth constantly and liberally, and even the dreaded Cossacks have been called in as "missionaries."

The same policy of broad toleration was followed in connection with the settlement of the Mennonites and Hussites in South Russia. They were guaranteed religious liberty, the right to assemble for public worship, and even according to their religious principles, were granted exemption for ever from compulsory military service. In fact, during the reign of Peter the Great, "alien" confessions not only had freedom, but in a large measure enjoyed his personal approval, if not patronage, for he at times visited the Churches and joined in the worship.

Whether among the inhabitants of conquered territories, or settlers from other lands, religious toleration was granted upon the condition that the non-Orthodox should make no attempt to propagate their doctrines amongst the Orthodox, and that the Orthodox should have freedom to establish their Churches, and that priests and monks could carry on an active missionary work in the midst of the " aliens " from the true Church.

The Russian Government, in its attitude to non-Orthodox confessions, has always been guided by the two principles: The preservation of the dominant Orthodox faith, and non-interference with the inner religious life of the individual, leaving herself free to suppress public assemblies for public worship.

Whenever and wherever there has been any spread of " alien " confessions amongst the Russian Orthodox peasantry, then the strong arm of the Government has come down upon the propagandists swiftly and ruthlessly.

There are many, very many, black pages in recent Russian history dealing with the ' new methods " in the Baltic Provinces, Poland, Bessarabia, and amongst the Georgians and Armenians in the Caucasus. Whilst the policy of the Govern-

l

ment towards the non-Orthodox of non-Russian nationality has been one of broad toleration, limited by the restriction against spreading their distinctive doctrines, a different principle has prevailed concerning those born of Russian Orthodox parents, who, upon the compulsion of conscience, have seceded from the dominant Orthodox Church.

The fundamental law of Russia on the subject of religion is, " Every nation is free to believe its own religion." The Tsar, some time ago, when the matter of religious liberty was being agitated throughout the Empire, owing to the forcible conversion of Roman Catholics to the Orthodox faith, wrote: "Let the Poles worship God according to their Latin rite, but Russian people always were and will remain Orthodox; together with their Tsar and Tsarina they above all venerate and love the native Orthodox Church."

Whilst theoretically there is religious freedom, practically there is no such thing. A Russian Orthodox, or any other believer, is only free to adhere to the faith in which he was born. An exception to this rule is to be found in the fact that the Orthodox Church is free to receive converts into her borders from other religions. Legally a man born in the Orthodox faith cannot change it. He may be a heretic, a freethinker, a Sectarian; in law he is still Orthodox; he may be compelled to attend the confessional, to take Holy Communion at least once a year; if he

l

insists on his individual belief or want of belief, he does not cease to be Orthodox; he is an erring Orthodox; he is supposed to repent and then to be given over to his ' pope ' in order to learn better.   Strictly speaking, there is nothing in Russian law to countenance persecution for forsaking the Orthodox faith, no legal punishment for the change exists.   In law the convert is not held responsible; the responsibility rests with the converter.   He is the criminal   It is just here where persecution finds an entrance.   Not being able to chastise the converts, and according to the law being compelled to recognise the conversion as an accomplished fact, so far as the next generation is concerned (a man shall remain in the faith in which he is born), the law concentrates all its severity on the would-be converters.   Where there is a crime, there must be a criminal.   In cases where the sect is proclaimed as " particularly dangerous," as recently with the Baptists, then the punishment meted out to the converter may be stripes, hard labour, or banishment.

The principle that a Russian is always supposed to be an Orthodox   must inevitably lead to persecution and crying injustice.   One typical case came to my notice whilst travelling in the Eastern Provinces.   R—— was a worker in a mill.   He had beeen baptised four months.   Filled with enthusiasm for his new faith, he had spoken to some of his fellow-workmen. Three of them subsequently were baptised, with the result that they were interrogated by the police as to who had persuaded them to change their faith, during their severe cross-examination they mentioned the name of R——. He was arrested and brought before the judge. His defence was that the New Testament commanded him to " preach the Gospel to every creature." Instead of being committed to prison, he was ordered thirty strokes on the bare back.

Dostoiesfsky, in *The House of the Dead*, describes the feelings of one who had undergone the flogging.

" I questioned my companion often in reference to this pain, that I might know to what kind of suffering it might be compared. It was no idle curiosity which urged me. I repeat that I was moved and frightened; but it was in vain; I could get no satisfaction. 'It burns like fire,' was the general answer; they all said the same thing.

"First I tried to question M . . . 'It burns like fire; like Hell. It seems as if one's back were in a furnace.'"

That Carl Joubert was right when he described the Manifesto of 1905 as " Liberty in Matters of Faith " as a "Stock Exchange Ukase, has been proved by subsequent events.

On November 24, 1912, the Council of Empire

L

in Russia adopted the first paragraph of the Bill regulating conversion from one belief to another. According to this clause, no one can be transferred from one sect to another unless he has attained his majority, and has given forty days' notice to the police of his intention. Further, transfer is only allowed from one Christian Church to another, or from a non-Christian to a Christian religion. The Duma wished for a wider liberty, and proposed that an adult should have the right to choose his Church freely, but this proposal was rejected by the Council.

In October of that year the Minister of the Interior published regulations forbidding the formation of Young Men's Societies and the holding of Sunday Schools in connection with the Baptists. He has also forbidden the practice of baptism in the open air, save where special permission can be obtained direct from the Minister of the Interior. Anyone at all acquainted with the difficulties in the way of receiving permission for anything at all contrary to the wishes of the Orthodox Church, will recognise that the primitive practice of baptism in river and stream is practically forbidden.

Strenuous efforts are being continually made to bring about the abrogation of the limited amount of religious freedom granted by the Ukase of 1905. The Government is engaged in an active campaign against this right, especially as it refers to the growing body of Baptists. All manner of charges are trumped up against the leaders of the sect.

Take what happened in Odessa during 1913 as a typical instance; Pavlov, one of the early pioneers of the Baptist faith, writes:

"During the last four months I have had on four occasions to attend in the Law Courts to answer false accusations. Twice I was acquitted, in the third I was sentenced to one month's imprisonment, and one charge is still pending. In all these cases I have not violated the Law, the charges against me being dictated by animosity. The last case occupied the Court for three days, about sixty witnesses being summoned. Three other ministers were accused with me of blasphemy concerning the Lord Jesus Christ, His Mother, His Church, the Holy Cross, Holy Icons, and Holy Relics. The accusing witnesses confirmed on oath their depositions, but their falsehood soon became manifest through their contradictions among each other and the testimonies of our witnesses. The accusers had, during three years, in four different places of worship, gathered from our sermons separate phrases and sentences to prove their case, but now they were confounded.

"The Public Prosecutor, finding that his accusation of blasphemy might be rejected by the jury, added a further charge of unlawful propa-

L

ganda of our faith. After protracted hearing the jury declared one of the ministers 'not guilty,' and the other three, Shamkov, Kramshenko, and myself, guilty of propaganda, and we were sentenced to one month's imprisonment."

This is but an illustration of what is going on all through Russia. "Persecution rages throughout the Empire" writes another worker, and he gives instances of heavy punishments being inflicted upon the Sectarians for propaganda and blasphemy. Blasphemy, it should be remembered, does not necessarily mean the use of insulting language. It is blasphemy to refer to the Icon as an idol, and the penalty is as much as three years' imprisonment.

Prayer-meetings were recently prohibited by the Police of Poltava, on the ground that they were "directed against the State," though the congregation was legalised. After a long protest, the Baptists got the prohibition cancelled. Then the police refused to allow the meetings to proceed because the application contained the words, "To meet for reading the Word of God," while the permit was only for "singing and praying." Eventually they were permitted to meet on condition that they did nothing but pray and sing.

These are but typical instances of what is going on all over Russia, and reveal the spirit and the attitude of the authorities towards all Dissenters from the Orthodox Church,

The following proclamation issued in Moscow three years ago, on the opening of a Baptist Church there, speaks for itself:

" Orthodox Christians, what is being done in our Holy Russia? What is happening in our Mother Moscow, the white-stoned city? From far-off lands, from seas of the enemy, an unseen army has come upon us to make war against our holy faith. . . . The enemy remembers that in the twelfth year of last century, i.e., the Napoleonic invasion, he could not break the Russian might, but was himself broken on the Rock Christ, that is, the Holy Orthodox Church. And the enemy knows he cannot break the Russian might if in the future also our people will have strong faith in Christ, if Moscow, the heart of Russia, in the coming years also will be faithful to the Holy Orthodox Church.

" See, then, on the street Pokroff, which is so called from the Pokroff shrine of the Most Holy Mother of God, is an inimical camp. Baptists have laid siege. But why have they come to the heart of Russia, to Moscow? Take notice. They desire to teach the Orthodox Russian people what it is to believe in Christ. Wonder of wonders! For a thousand years the Holy Orthodox Church of Christ has been known in Russia; tens of millions of the Russian people, together with their Tsar, love Christ and His Holy Church. And now Fetler cries aloud that the Orthodox Church do not

14

believe in Christ, and offers to show them Christ
and to instruct them in the faith of Christ. Is
this not to mock the Russian people. . . . Ah,
you see, it is not faith that Fetler is after. He
wants to break in pieces in Orthodox people their
faith in Christ in order that after that he may
destroy the Russian land itself. . . . Wake up,
then, O ye Orthodox, from your perilous dream.
Quench these diabolic arrows. . . . Think well
into what an abyss you are being drawn by
these servants of Antichrist. Be not deceived
when they quote Gospel texts: Satan also, when
tempting Christ, quoted Holy Scripture. But the
Lord replied, 'Go thou behind me Satan.' Oh,
brethren, preserve the Holy faith and the Orthodox Church above everything."

Nothing more pernicious to the health of the
nation can be thought of than this violent sub-
jugation of the national soul which cries for air
and freedom. Nothing will touch the fibre of
this Russian people so much as the unfettering
of the conscience by the liberation of the religious
instinct. Nothing that the Government can do
in the way of further facilities for education, for
agrarian relief, or the almost innumerable quack
remedies proposed from the various Ministries for
the remedy of the people's wrongs, will have a
tithe of the effect upon the soul of Russia and
its fuller development, of a bold policy of free
and unfettered right to worship God according

to the peasant's own religious instinct. The
Russian peasant is a curious mixture   He lets
himself be almost ill-treated even to death's door;
he suffers everything almost without complaint;
physically, spiritually, and morally he shows an
enviable strength to bear and to suffer, to be
and to do; and wherever the Bible penetrates
amongst this people and they surrender their lives
to Jesus Christ, there the effect of the new faith
is seen at once.   It is such as the best Government
in the world could not effect by worldly means
alone.

FROM THE *Petersburg Herald*. SEPT. 22, 1913.
AN OFFICIAL DECLARATION CONCERNING
THE BAPTISTS.

The "Information Bureau" notifies as under :

"In a number of papers rumours have been
circulated of late to the effect that the Ministry
of the Interior has taken up the question of declaring the Baptist sect as 'illegal' and their influence injurious.

"For this reason it appears necessary to make
the following statement:

"The existing law provides the possibility of
a restriction of the liberty of the creeds only
with respect to such sects as are of a fanatical
and openly immoral character, in which cases the
adherence to such sects involves criminal proceedings.

l

"In the creed professed by the Russian Baptists hitherto there are no indications of elements which would evidence such fanatical or immoral characteristics. From the standpoint of the law referred to, there are not, therefore, at present, sufficient grounds for declaring the Baptists criminally punishable or their teaching as not to be tolerated.

"However, the study of the present position of the Baptists in Russia leads to the undoubted conclusion that the efforts of the leaders of this sect are directed towards the farthest-reaching proselytising, not only among other denominations of the population, but principally among the masses of the purely Orthodox population. Closely connected as they are with foreign Baptist organisations, and receiving from the latter directions as to their activities, the Russian Baptists enjoy far-reaching material support from foreign Baptist leaders, as evidenced in financial reports of Baptist Congresses and from other data, the said foreign leaders frankly stating that they have found in Russia the most favourable field for the work of their religious mission. It is obvious that these special conditions of Baptist activity, in view of the depreciative attitude of our Legislature towards the propagation of foreign creeds, imposes upon the Ministry of the Interior the duty of carefully controlling this sect, and call for energetic measures being taken to combat these tendencies, within the limits of the present laws, since such manifestations can in no wise be founded upon the religious privileges conferred upon Sectarians by the most high Ukase of April 17, 1905."

THE RASKOLNIKS

BIBLIOGRAPHY

MOURAVIEFF   .   *History of the Russian Church.*

STANLEY . . .   *Lectures on the Eastern Church.*

UROSSOV . . .   *Memoirs of a Russian Governor.*

WALLACE . . .   *Russia.*

MILYOUKOV . .   *The Crisis in Russia.*

              Free Russia, 1897.

l

i

THE RASKOLNIKS

(OLD BELIEVERS.)

THE beginning of "the great Schism" in Russia can be traced back to the middle of the fifteenth century. The Orthodox Church was until then under the Patriarch of Constantinople. There was continual correspondence between learned Greek prelates and the Russian ecclesiastical authorities, the service-books were carefully preserved from unauthorised innovations, and mistakes in copying were regularly corrected; but with the fall of Constantinople and the consequent involuntary separation of Russia from the headship of the Eastern Orthodox Church, inaccuracies crept little by little into the Slavonic books of Divine Service and into some of the ceremonies, and as they could no longer be compared with the Greek books and ceremonies, they gradually took deep root amongst the people.

In 1551, the Tsar, John IV., being aware of the errors which had crept into the performance of Divine Service, and the disorders which

l

resulted therefrom, convoked a great Council of the Russian Bishops, under the Metropolitan Macarius, and opened the proceedings himself in a speech which deserves to be placed on record for its strength and simplicity.

" My father, pastors, and teachers, see now every one of you what counsel or discernment is in him, and pray God at the same time for His merciful aid; stir up your understandings, and enlighten yourselves with sound knowledge as to all the Divinely-inspired ordinances, so as to discern in what way the Lord hath delivered them; and me, your son, enlighten and instruct to all godliness, as it ought to be with religious Kings, in all righteous laws for the Kingdom, in all soundness of faith and purity; and be ye not slack to establish the whole of Orthodox Christianity, that we may keep the law of Christ in all its truth, perfect and inviolate. I for my part shall always be ready, as with one soul, to join and support you either in correcting what is amiss, or confirming what is well established, according as the Holy Ghost shall show you; if so be I should ever oppose you contrary to the letter or spirit of the Divine Canons, do not ye hold your peace at it, but rebuke me; if I should still be disobedient, inhibit me without any fear; so shall my soul live, and the souls of all my subjects."

The Tsar went on to desire the Council to

L

find a solution of the many questions relating to the Church courts, ceremonies, chants, Icons, the making of the sign of the Cross, the correction of the Service-books, the eradication of super-stitions, etc.

The Council spent many months over its labours, and at last sent forth an authoritative answer to all the questions in a document of one hundred chapters, thus earning for itself the name of the Hundred Chapter Council.

The Council, however, instead of reforming abuses and rectifying mistakes, gave their countenance to certain superstitions and local errors, which, ultimately, under the reforming zeal of Peter the Great and the Patriarch Nikon, produced the great schism of the " Raskolniks."

In our study of Russian Dissent, we must not confound the Raskolniki, Starabradski, or Staraveri with the " Sectarians," for the Dissenters, as such, are more Orthodox than the official Orthodox. They are conservatives in the social as well as in the religious sense.

Many factors led to "the great Schism"; the abolition of the Patriarchate and the substitution in place thereof of the Holy Synod, the new customs introduced by Nikon from the South, and finally, the new spirit brought into the Church by Peter the Great, consequent upon his travels in the West.

The external causes seem to have been very

L

trivial. They objected to the change in the way of spelling the name of Jesus, from Isus to Iesus; to them it was a mortal sin to say the name in two syllables instead of three; they objected to the clergy giving the benediction with three fingers instead of two; and to sing the Hallelujah thrice instead of once was a sin against the Holy Ghost.

Their form of the Cross has three transverse beams instead of the Greek two and the Latin one, whilst they held that the course of the sun demonstrated to all true believers that processions should proceed from left to right, instead of right to left. The introduction of passports was the mark of the beast, for to them the ancient habit of the Russians to wander where they will was the outward evidence of true Christianity. Huge bonfires were lit, and passports, which more or less confined a man to his own village, were publicly burned as a protest against this negation of Christianity. They objected to the use of modern Russian in the services and any alteration in the service-books or revision of the Scriptures.

The zeal of the Tsar Peter also led to violent protests upon the part of the Old Believers. To them it was a mortal sin to introduce into the Churches religious pictures painted by Western artists, or men outside the pale of the Orthodox Church. All such pictures were an abomination in the eyes of the ancient Russians. To listen to chants, sung in the sweeter and purer notes of the Greek deacons, and those imported by Peter from Germany and Catherine II. from Italy, was to be in danger of eternal torment To smoke tobacco was anathema. Had not the Tsar and Patriarchs threatened to tear out the nostrils of such offenders? They declared that "it has been said that it is not that which goeth into a man defileth him, but that which cometh out."

Until quite recently it was a sin to eat the potato, for was it not that accursed apple, the very fruit of the devil, which led to the driving out of their fathers from Paradise?

The alteration of the beginning of the New Year from September—the time of the creation of the world—to January was one of the signs of Antichrist. Could there be any truth in the year beginning in January when the ground was covered in snow, whilst in September the corn was ready for the sickle and the orchard fruits were fully ripe?

Peter's command that the Russians should shave their beards was denounced in no unmeasured terms. "To shave the beard was a sin which even the blood of martyrs could not expiate." "Man was made in the image of God; was the image of God to be defaced?" Many, when compelled to shave, kept their beards to be buried with them, fearing lest without them they would not be recognised at the gates of heaven.

In 1714 toleration was permitted on condition that the Dissenters paid double poll-tax, and upon their paying certain fines. Many of them who had been harried and hunted through the forests and in almost wild and inaccessible places, settled along the banks of the Volga and Don, where they have large villages, neat and orderly— a striking contrast to the ordinary village of the Russian peasant. Under Catherine II. further measures of religious liberty were granted, and the faithful returned in their thousands to Moscow and adjacent towns, and quickly became prosperous merchants.

These Dissenters have suffered the knout; exile, and even execution, for their convictions, and largely because of their persecutions they became a militant Church, and now are some of the most moral, energetic, and prosperous of all the subjects of the Emperor.

Prince Urossov, in his *Memoirs of a Russian Governor*, refers to the Dissenters in the following glowing terms:

" I had had ever since childhood a strong sympathy for the Raskolniks, who in our vicinity were distinguished from the rest of the population by sobriety, industry, and a certain sense of personal dignity. Consequently I was convinced that among the Russian Christian population

Orthodox (which, as a matter of fact, so far as ritualistic forms and in part also the confession of faith are concerned, came near to idolatry) the Raskolniks and Sectarians must be considered the most active, and, in religious respects, the least indifferent element, since they hold to their belief and to their ritual, although sometimes they seek new paths for their religious ideals. I had come to have an unconquerable prejudice against the great mass of the Greek Orthodox clergy, who can hardly find a defender outside of their own number. Hence, I used every opportunity to accede to the modest request which they laid before me."

Over against the testimony of the liberal prince we have the fulmination of Gorboonov, who, with unmistakable prejudice, describes them as " enclosed in strong walls which effectually shut him in from the outside world and prevent his eyes seeing, or his ears hearing. Ancient tradition, of which he knows only the ceremonial, constitutes his faith; remove the walls, and the sect stands exposed a hollow sham. The ignorance of the peasantry alone maintains it. Illumine this nest of obscurity with the light of truth, and it stands exposed to all and each as the essence of frivolity and meaningless emptiness—total darkness. Let the light of God shine and expose all the emptiness, all the lawlessness. Outside restraints, what strong walls surround this fortress

L

of religion! inside, nothing but emptiness.   Hence,
light, more light!"

Under toleration, strong differences of opinion
set in, and the Old Believers separated into parties
and sects.   One section retained all the sacraments
and ceremonial observances in the older form.
As the original priests died, others were not
ordained in their places, and so the services were
necessarily emasculated.   However, in 1844 the
Austrian Government sanctioned a Bishopric of the
Orthodox in Galicia, and since that time priests
have been regularly ordained there for the fuller
services of the Dissenters.   This sect is called
the Staraobradski, and the Government has sought
to incorporate them in the Holy Orthodox Church
by making certain concessions to them in matters
of ritual, and has even allowed to them a regular
priest of the Establishment, whilst they have the
use of several Churches in and near to Moscow.

"Of all the sects, the 'Old Ritualists' stand
nearest to the official Church.   They hold the
same dogmas, practise the same rites, and differ
only in trifling ceremonial observances, which few
people consider essential.   In the hope of inducing
them to return to the official fold, the Government created at the beginning of the last century
special Churches, in which they were allowed to
retain their ceremonial peculiarities on condition
of accepting regularly consecrated priests and submitting to ecclesiastical jurisdiction.   As yet the

design has not met with much success   The great
majority of the 'Old Ritualists' regard it as
a trap, and assert that the Church, in making this
concession, has been guilty of self-contradiction.
'The Ecclesiastical Council of Moscow,' they say,
'anathematised our forefathers for holding to the
old ritual, and declared that the whole course of
nature would be changed sooner than the curse
be withdrawn.   The course of nature has not
changed, but the anathema has been cancelled."*
This argument ought to have a certain weight
with those who believe in the infallibility of
Ecclesiastical Councils.

A fine diplomatic stroke was made by the
Government when, at the Coronation of the Tsar,
a number of prominent "Old Believers" were
invited to take part in some of the ceremonies
and rejoicings.   But the hope that they will ultimately fuse with the National Church is a futile
one.   The roots of antagonism are too deeply
fixed in them for the "Old Believers" lightly to
renounce the position which they have inherited
from their fathers.

The larger number of the "Raskolniks," however, when the original Dissenting priests died,
refused to accept others, on the ground that those
ordained by the National Church had not sacramental grace, and refrained from all ceremonial
observances, arguing that there could be no real

* (Wallace, *Russia*.)

priesthood without valid ordination. They are known as the Bezpopoftsi or "priestless ones."

"The Old Ritualists" are mainly ceremonial conservatives; they have a profound repugnance to all manner of innovations, theirs is mainly a *non-possumus* attitude towards the official Church, and they have been a solid, compact body from early days; on the other hand, the "priestless ones" have been pioneers, seeking out new paths, trying to discover some way of salvation, a means of reaching the final goal of Truth. Consequently they have split into many different bodies, their number being almost beyond reckoning. We deal with a few of the more lasting and important ones here, relegating the more fanatical and *bizarre* to the chapter headed "The Russian Sects."

The "priestless ones" divided into two bodies—the "Pomortsi" and the "Theodosians."

The "Pomortsi" preserved intact the religious ideas of the Schism, but they came to a compromise with the Government, paid their taxes, found scriptural authority for submitting to the civil power, and became more or less reconciled to their position under the local authorities. They commenced to render unto Caesar the things which belonged to Caesar, to pray for the "Little Father" (the Tsar), and to accept military service. Gradually they settled down as law-abiding citizens, the question of marriage largely influencing them in their decision. Being without priests, they could not have a valid marriage ceremony (according to them marriage was a sacrament), and although they nominally resorted to celibacy, children were born of their irregular unions, and a class of "orphans" arose.

In addition, celibacy was an "economic" failure, as the peasant needed a housewife who would attend to the domestic side of his nature, and at times help him with his agricultural pursuits. After a Council of leaders, held at Moscow, many accepted the doctrine of the necessity for marriage, and although such a union is not recognised by the State law, or valid in the eyes of the Orthodox Church, yet in all other respects it makes for purity in the relation of the sexes.

When the "Pomortsi" effected a partial reconciliation with the civil authorities, a number of their adherents followed a leader named Theodosi (hence they are called "Theodosians"). These absolutely refused to recognise the authority of the State, and maintained that the Tsar was Antichrist. At first they stood aloof from all save their fellow-believers.

Gradually the necessities of trade and living brought them into closer touch with their fellow-men, and much of their exclusiveness was broken down. Under Catherine II. they were allowed to build a semi-monastic establishment near to Moscow. The Superior was a man of much native shrewdness, and became on very good terms with

L

many of the officials   " His name and fame were
spoken of in Moscow, Astrakhan, Riga, St. Petersburg, Riazan, and beyond the frontiers." He did
much to soften the character of his " flock,"
and they began to live in the cities, engage in
trade, and generally to mingle on equal terms
with their fellow-men. They gradually forgot
their wild and extravagant ideas concerning the
" Reign of Antichrist," " The time of trouble for
the faithful," " The Day of Judgment," and other
Apocalyptic studies, and accommodated themselves to the ordinary routine of the daily lives
of ordinary men.

The Theodosians coming into touch with the
civil authorities led to another " split." The " marriage " question was the centre round which the
storm raged. Some few of the sect had striven
to conceal the origin of the " orphan " class, but
after the sanction of the Council that regular
unions could place place and be approved of,
boldly declared that the irregular cohabitation between the sexes was a religious necessity, " because in order to be saved from sin men must
confess and repent, and in order to repent men
must sin." Their leader was a peasant, known
as Philip, hence their name of Philipists. They
reverted to the old doctrines that the Tsar is
Antichrist, that Imperial and local authorities are
the servants of Satan. However, they do not
openly resist the authorities of Church and

L

State, but they do not attempt to hide their opinions.

They are severe in their aspect, Puritanical in many of their views, and Pharisaical in their horror and detestation of anything which could be called heretical and unclean. Wallace says of them " that they sometimes carry their Pharisaical fastidiousness to such an extent that they will throw away the handle of a door if it has been touched by a heretic."

In the second half of the eighteenth century, Euphemius revived the old doctrines, repudiated the " truce with the civil authorities," denounced both " Theodosians " and " Philipists," and founded a new sect, called the Christoviye or Christ's People. He formulated anew the doctrine that the Tsar is Antichrist, that landed property was invented by Peter the Great to tie people to the soil, and thus contaminate the faithful with the world by causing them to live in the midst of heretics.

He brought about a complete rupture with the civil authorities, with the State and its law, with the Church and its ordinances, with Society and its traditional morals.

They are known to-day variously as " Stranniki " (Wanderers) or " Beguny " (Fugitives). According to their creed, all who wish to escape from the " Wrath to Come " must have no settled home; they must sever all ties; they should wander

L

about from place to place. The true Christian is a pilgrim and a stranger, and to be associated with any given locality means that in the Day of Judgment, being of the world, he will perish with the world.

The practical needs of life, however, have led to compromises in the past few years. The nomadic life is still lived by hundreds of the sect; they wander from place to place, and they are not infrequently met with in the State railways as "hares" (Russian term for stowaways). There are many, however, who belong to the sect who live in villages, follow mainly agricultural pursuits, hold their passports from the authorities, pay their dues to the taxgatherer, and generally act as the villagers around them. They are liberal in their gifts to their more thorough brethren, and never refuse food or shelter to the "pilgrim." When they feel death approaching, they will go into the forests and woods—or into a garden, if there be no more secluded spot near—and in the open air their soul will leave its tenement and bid farewell to an apostate world.

There are many minor bodies, differing on many points of minor doctrine. Every village has representatives of them, especially in the Caucasus and amongst the Cossacks of the Don and Ural—men who are lineal descendants of the early fugitives.

The spread of the Scriptures, however, is

modifying many of the extravagances of the various bodies of Dissenters, as this extract from *Free Russia* will show.

The speaker is an Old Believer.

"The Scriptures which came to us from England have been the mainstay, not of our religion only, but of our national life."

"Then they have been much read?"

"In thousands, in tens of thousands of pious homes. The true Russian likes his Bible, yes, even better than his dram, for the Bible tells him of his world beyond his daily toil, a world of angels and of spirits, in which he believes with a nearer faith than he puts in the wood and water about his feet. In every second house of Great Russia—the true old Russia, in which we speak the same language and have the same God—you will find a copy of the Bible, and men who have the promise in their hearts.

"I am an old man now," continued the priest, "but my veins still throb with the fervour of that day when we first received, in our native speech, the Word that was to bring us eternal life. The books were instantly bought up and read; friends lent them to each other; family meetings were held, in which the Promise was read aloud. The Popes explained the text, the elders gave out chapter and verse; even in parties which met to drink vodka and play cards, some neighbour would produce his Bible, when the

ı

company gave up their games to listen while an aged man read out the story of the Passion and of the Cross. That story spoke to the Russian heart, for the Russ, when left alone, has something of the Galilean in his nature; a something soft and feminine, almost sacrificial; helping him to feel, with a force which he could never reach by reasoning, the patient beauty of his Redeemer's life and death."

l

THE UNIATS

BIBLIOGRAPHY.

MOURAVIEFF . *History of the Russian Church.*

WADDINGTON . *History of the Church.*

LESCŒUR . . . *L'Eglise Catholique in Pologne.*

MEAKIN . . . *Russian Studies.*

L

THE UNIATS

D URING the latter part of the fourteenth century, strong attempts were made upon the part of prelates of the Eastern and Western Churches for union.

The menace of the Turk, the fall of Constantinople, the pressure of the Lithuanians upon Muscovy, led the Emperor John in 1430 to respond to the invitation of Pope Eugenius IV. to hold a conference with a view to the union of the two Churches.

Eugenius was an experienced and politic old man, and in proposing to John the calling of a Council, promised that if the union of the Churches was agreed to, then the forces of Western Christendom would be used to rescue Constantinople from the Turks.

Isidore, Metropolitan of Moscow, one time Bishop of Illyria, a friend of the Pope, a man of distinguished talents and eloquence, was chosen to attend the Council on behalf of the Russian Church, the Prince beseeching him to stand firm in defence of the doctrines of orthodoxy

Platon, writing of the embassy, says, " The Pope, the most artful of men, seeing that Russia

L

was the most powerful country which professed the Greek faith, persuaded Isidore, whose sentiments he knew, to get himself consecrated and sent as Metropolitan to Moscow, that he might assist at the Council about to be held at Florence in subjecting both the Greek and Russian Churches to His Holiness's slippers."

Isidore, accompanied by a numerous suite, travelled, by way of Riga and Lübeck, to Ferrara, where the Emperor, the Pope, and other dignitaries were awaiting his arrival to open the Council.

The controversies were long and bitter concerning the procession of the Holy Spirit, purgatory, the use of unleavened bread, and, not least of all, the temporal and ecclesiastical power of the Pope. The Council was transferred to Florence, where Eugenius gained the mastery, and declared beforehand the union of the Churches on terms favourable to Rome. The controversy broke out afresh, the Council was dissolved, but Isidore was decorated with the Roman purple, and had the title of "Cardinal Legate of the Apostolic See in Russia" conferred upon him.

He returned to Moscow in triumph, bearing friendly letters from the Pope to Prince Basil, but the first time he was called upon to perform Divine Service in the Cathedral of the Assumption, he was about to name the Roman Pontiff, when the Prince indignantly rebuked the Primate, denounced him as a traitor to orthodoxy, and charged him with being a false pastor. Bishops and Boyars were summoned to meet and pass judgment on the new doctrines. Not one of the delegates would consent to acknowledge the Pope as Vicar of Christ; and all rejected the Western doctrine respecting the procession of the Holy Spirit, that it is not only from the Father, but also from the Son, in contradiction to the ancient creed.

Isidore was confined in the Choudoff monastery; escaped, and fled to Rome; was consecrated Patriarch of Constantinople; and through a disciple of his, he succeeded in having a number of Latin Bishops consecrated to the See of Kieff; but despite the powerful influence of Casimir, sovereign of Lithuania and Poland, the attempt to subject Russia to Rome failed.

A century and a half later the whole country was to feel the effects of this ecclesiastical intrigue between the Pope and Isidore in the fearful wars and massacres between Catholic, Orthodox, and Uniate.

In 1467, Sophia, heiress of the Greek Emperors, was, through the instrumentality of the Pope, Paul, betrothed to the Tsar John, in the hope that such a union would lead the two Churches to unite in a general crusade against the Turks for the recovery of Constantinople and the holy places. Sophia had been brought up in the doctrines of the famous Council of Florence,

l

but the expectations of Rome were doomed to frustration, for no sooner had Sophia crossed the frontier into Russia than she embraced the Orthodox faith.

Anthony, the Papal legate who accompanied her, desired to make his public entry into Moscow, with the Cross borne before him after the Latin fashion, and whilst the Tsar hesitated, the Metropolitan of Moscow, Philip, insisted upon the supremacy of the Holy Orthodox Church in his own country. "Whoever," declared he to the Tsar, "praises and honours a foreign faith, that man degrades his own. If the legate enters with his Cross at one gate of the city, I shall go out of it by the other." The Metropolitan won the day, and after the celebration of the marriage, he had several discussions with Anthony concerning the faith and practice of Rome, but the wily Roman legate avoided entering into any detailed controversy, excusing himself upon the grounds that he had not brought his books with him. Thus the second attempt upon the part of Rome for union or absorption failed, and the Orthodox Church emerged triumphant.

Towards the end of the sixteenth century the continual 'wars between Russia, Poland, and Sweden led Gregory XIII., then Pontiff of Rome, to intervene. He sent as his envoy the Jesuit, Anthony Possevin, who, in his capacity as mediator, passed from one camp to another, negotiating an armistice, and at the same time seeking to gain the adherence of the Tsar to the decisions of the Council of Florence.

In every discussion with John upon political matters the priest sought to introduce the question of the union of the Churches, until, exasperated and enraged, the Tsar expressed himself strongly on the ambition and tyranny of the Romish Pontiffs and their greed for temporal power.

The work of Anthony produced practically no effect in Moscow and the then central parts of Russia, yet his zealous exhortations and wily policy resulted ultimately in the founding of the Uniats in the western districts. The propaganda of Possevin resulted in the adhesion of various isolated and scattered communities to Rome upon the granting of certain privileges. Thus, whilst they would submit to papal authority, marriage should be granted to the priesthood, communion in both elements should be given to the laity, each Church should retain its own peculiar customs and liturgy, the Latin tongue should not be demanded in the services, and the Slavonic should not only be tolerated, but approved. This compromise was confirmed under Jagellon, Prince of Lithuania, conqueror of the White Russians. The Orthodox peasants of White Russia, though they had learnt the habit of subjection, yet, in spite of persecutions upon the part of the Poles, held closely to their re-

L

ligion, and accepted the purely nominal headship of the Pope in return for the promise of toleration and the aforementioned privileges.

Following upon the compromise, a conference of Uniats and Romans was held, and after solemnly confirming their agreement for a union, which was sealed by a joint celebration of the liturgy in the same Church, they pronounced a sentence of excommunication against the Orthodox, and thus the Church of Russia was divided into Uniat and Orthodox, both preserving, however, the same form, not only of external rite in the celebration of Divine service, but even of doctrine; for Rome allowed the Creed without alteration, and required nothing but the one capital point of submission to the Pope.

The internal troubles of Russia in the early years of the seventeenth century led to a bold attempt on the part of Rome to make a fresh effort to subjugate the Orthodox to the papal authority. The Pretender Demetrius, who claimed the Imperial throne, was supported by the Jesuits and by the papal nuncio, Rangoni, who selected him as their instrument for the purpose of obtaining the submission of the Orthodox in the very centre of the Empire—Moscow. Every expedient seemed lawful for such an end. Riot and rebellion followed in quick succession. The Patriarch Job denounced the attempt. Whilst he was celebrating the liturgy a band of insurgents rushed into the Church of the Assumption and tore from him his ecclesiastical robes. He was dragged from the altar to the Staritsky monastery, but before leaving he declared, " Here, before this sacred Icon, was I consecrated to my office, and for nineteen years have I preserved the purity of the faith: I now see that misery is coming upon the Kingdom, that fraud and heresy are to triumph. Oh, Mother of God, do thou preserve orthodoxy!" The plot of the Jesuits for a time prevailed. Roman priests not only performed services in the Kremlin, but began openly to condemn the Orthodox religion, held correspondence with the Pope, who urged them to bring about a union between the Churches, counselled them to maintain the closest relations between the nuncio Rangoni and the Jesuits. The murder of Demetrius and the firmness of the Orthodox Bishops and priests brought this, the third attempt, to an inglorious end.

In the year 1620 there followed a renewal of the intrigues of Rome, and the Government, through the boyars, recommenced the persecution of the Orthodox Bishops, whose legitimate titles to the office were not recognised by the papacy. The Cossacks, who had embraced orthodoxy, came to the help of their brethren, and the Jesuits and Uniats ceased their attempts to gain the ascendancy.

The next move upon the part of Rome was during the visit of Peter the Great to Paris. Whilst

16

L

he was there the celebrated Academy of the Sorbonne took advantage of the personal presence of the Russian Monarch to make proposals to him for the union of the Western with the Eastern Church; but he declined taking upon himself so weighty a matter, and only promised that he would command the Russian prelates to return an answer to the document which had been presented to him by the Sorbonne.

Upon his return home Peter delivered to the guardian of the patriarchal throne and the Bishops who were with him the memorial which he had received from the Sorbonne.

It was a document of some length, in which the Parisian doctors enlarged upon the agreement of the two Churches, in their doctrines, sacraments, and traditions, in their reverencing of holy relics and Icons, in invocation of the saints, and ecclesiastical discipline. They touched superficially on the doctrine of the procession of the Holy Spirit, endeavouring to interpret the correct Greek expression of the mission of the Holy Spirit from the Father through the Son, by the incorrect Latin addition to the Creed concerning the Procession being "also from the Son"; and in testimony of their desire for peace, proposed the example of the Uniats, with whom the Greek Creed had remained unaltered by the permission of the Pope.

Still more slightly did the Sorbonne doctors

speak of the Pope, dwelling on all the liberties
of the Gallican Church, and calling him only the
first according to seniority among other Bishops his
equals, according to the testimony of the ancient
fathers, and rejecting his infallibility, made him
subject to the authority of the Catholic Church
as expressed by a general Council.

However plausible this request for unity might
be in appearance, the Russian Bishops were
cautious; they expressed for themselves the wish
for unity, but they replied that in a matter of
such great importance the decision could not rest
with a conclave of divines, but that the whole
Western Church, together with the whole Eastern,
must take part in one common agreement, and
they could not endanger their ancient unity with
the four Œcumenical and Orthodox thrones by
forming a new league with a foreign Church. The
activities of Peter in ecclesiastical as well as civil
matters finally scattered all proposals for union,
as by the establishment of the Most Holy Synod
he placed the Orthodox Church upon a stable
State foundation, impregnable against the attacks
of Rome.

With the consolidation of the empire and
the Church, the intrigues of Rome ceased, and
gradually an outward semblance of peace was
maintained between the Orthodox and the Uniats.
With the growing power of the State, and the
spread of orthodoxy, the Uniats began to suffer

persecution in their turn. They lay at the mercy of the State.

In 1773 Catherine made a treaty with the Poles, which guaranteed the maintenance of the *status quo* and full religious liberty to the Polish Catholics · it was hardly signed when over 1,200 Churches were forcibly taken from the Greek Uniats, and their priests, with their flocks, compelled to join the Russian Church. This move on the part of Catherine was purely political, although her action was clothed with an assumed zeal for religious toleration and liberty.

" What political advantage will be gained by Russia if she undertakes the defence of the Uniats and Orthodox believers? " she asked of her representative in Warsaw.

" Madam, four hundred miles of rich territory, and a large Orthodox population, can be seized from Poland and become part of the Russian Empire."

. Catherine made it perfectly plain that her interests were purely political, and the Most Holy Synod, in supporting her, shaped her views. For fuller details of the struggles between Roman Catholicism and Russian orthodoxy see *L'Eglise Catholique en Pologne,* by Lescœur.

In 1839 a petition was presented to the Emperor from a number of Uniats, asking for readmission to the Orthodox Church. The Tsar, by a stroke of the pen, made all the Uniats

l

Orthodox; 1,600,000 men were affected They were called upon to denounce their allegiance to the Sovereign Pontiff. Russian priests were sent to officiate in their Churches. In a few districts they were welcomed, but as a rule they found the Churches closed against them and the people hostile. Forcible conversion was the order of the day. Police and Cossacks were sent for, and a period of rigorous persecution set in which has continued until this present time. Under Pobie-donotseff it was vigorous and continuous. In the first Duma was a peasant member whose family for three generations had suffered bitter persecution.

No one who knows Russia well could ever dream of the Roman and Greek Churches uniting. Never would the Russians submit themselves to a foreign Pontiff.

The peasantry are wedded to the Orthodox faith, and where they break away, it is always along lines peculiar to their own temperament and national genius.

" Le principe qui admet le pape comme chef visible de l'Eglise, comme vicaire du Christ, est antipathique aux sentiments du peuple russe," wrote Turgeniev in 1847, and he went on to say that " the fate of Italy alone would be a sufficient warning—of Italy, so beautiful and so unfortunate." *

* A. M. Meakin.

L

For a full and complete history of the re-union of the Uniats with the Holy Orthodox Church see "An account of the re-union of the Uniats with the Orthodox Church in the Russian Empire." St. Petersburg Synodal Press, 1839. Printed by the direction of the Most Holy Synod. In general it is a biassed account from the Holy Orthodox point of view, but the historical documents are of great value.

Waddington, in the *History of the Church*, shows that the most important part of the Creed allowed to the Uniats was in the following confession: "In the name of the Holy Trinity, of the Father, the Son, and the Holy Ghost, we Latins and Greeks agree in the Holy Union of these two Churches, and confess that all true Christians ought to receive this genuine doctrine. That the Holy Spirit is eternally of the Father and the Son, and that from all eternity. It (He) proceeds from the One and the Other as from a single principle, and by a single production, which we call *spiration*. We also declare that what some of the Holy Fathers have said, viz., that the Holy Spirit proceeds from the Father through the Son, should be taken in such manner as to signify that the Son as well as the Father, and conjointly with Him, is the principle of the Holy Spirit; and since whatsoever the Father hath, that He communicates to His Son, excepting the paternity, which distinguishes Him from the

Son and the Holy Spirit, so is it from the Father
that the Son has received from all eternity that
productive virtue, through which the Holy Spirit
proceeds from the Son as well as from the
Father."

L

l

RUSSIAN SECTS

BIBLIOGRAPHY.

MILYOUKOV . . *The Russian Crisis.*

POBIEDONOSTSEFF *Reflections of a Russian States-man.*

MOURAVIEFF . . *History of the Russian Church*

WALLACE . . . *Russia.*

BARING . . . . *The Russian People.*

LATIMER . . . . *Under Three Tsars.*

THE EXILES' BEGGING SONG

Have pity on us, O our fathers,
Don't forget the unwilling travellers,
Don't forget the long imprisoned.
Feed us O our fathers—help us
Feed and help the poor and needy.
Have compassion O our fathers,
Have compassion O our mothers;
For the sake of Christ have mercy
On the prisoners—the shut up ones.
Behind walls of stone and gratings,
Behind oaken doors and padlocks,
Behind bars and locks of iron,
We are held in close confinement;
We have parted from our fathers,
From our mothers;
We from all our kin have parted;
We are prisoners.
Pity us, O our fathers.

ι

RUSSIAN SECTS

RUSSIA is the largest and most prolific breeding-ground of religious sects in Europe, or even the world, to-day. The great majority of Russian people will always believe in God; their religion is based on common sense and experience. In order to express it and to practise it, they will either be satisfied with what the Orthodox Church gives them, or they will express their dissatisfaction with their Church by founding or belonging to a sect.

From the middle of the fourteenth century, when the deacon Nicetas formed the sect of the Strigolniks (forerunners in doctrine of the modern Baptists), until the present day, there has been one continual struggle between the Orthodox Church and those who have sought soul-satisfaction outside her borders. The ordinary Russian of the people has, and will always have, a religion of his own, based, not on a theory, but on experience which proceeds from his life, and which is the working hypothesis of his existence.

As we have already seen, the Russian is intensely religious by nature, and the majority

are content with the National Church. They are
simply Orthodox, but to them Orthodoxy merely
means to be baptised, to wear a cross round the
neck, to pray to the Virgin, to reverence the Holy
Icon, to abstain from work on the holy days, to
fast rigorously twice a week, and through Lent,
to attend the Church services and generally to
follow the customs and traditions made venerable
by long sanction and usage.

Whilst the nation as a whole is claimed by
the Bureaucrats and the Most Holy Synod as
Orthodox, only sixty-two per cent. of the people
are even nominally within the pale of the Establishment.

Professor Milyoukov, in *The Russian Crisis*,
devotes a lecture to " The Religious Crisis," and,
dealing with the national type of religion, says:

" Orthodoxy is one of the most distinctive
features of the Russian national type.   Such is
at least the common belief of Russian nationalistic
politicians.   This belief necessarily implied that
Orthodoxy has remained unchanged, as befitted
a distinctive feature of an immutable national
type.   It seems particularly fitting to choose for
such a distinctive feature the Orthodox creed, just
because immutability was thought to be an inherent quality of Christianity in general and the
Eastern form of the Christian creed especially.
As a matter of fact, Russia is no exception to
the general rule of religious change and evolu-

tion. There, as everywhere, Christianity suffered change; it took as many different shapes as there were consecutive stages of culture, and these stages were the same in Russia as everywhere else. First, there was a long stage of transition from paganism to ritualism. Then followed the stage of transition from ritualism to evangelical and spiritual Christianity. Peculiar to Russia was the particular circumstance that the Established Church refused to take any active part in aid of this religious evolution, but was very active in its repression. Owing to the non-interference of the Established Church, the whole process in Russia took a somewhat incidental character. The religious movement was deprived of its natural leaders, and thus a regular evolution of doctrine was made impossible. Moreover, the natural growth of religious thought was branded schism and heresy, and thus exposed to the persecution of the authorities and doomed to popular disgrace. This, of course, could not prevent the final triumph of new religious ideas, but it helped greatly to retard the movement. Yet, in spite of all these obstacles, the movement went its natural way, and has long broken all ties of tradition. Religious feeling was not unchangeable in Russia, and if Orthodoxy was, so much the worse for it. The pale of the Established Church was therefore forsaken by everybody who wanted any kind of living religion. If everything remained

unchanged inside the true fold it was because
there was no life. Accordingly we come to the
conclusion that religious immutability is not a
national distinction of Russia, because there was
no religious immutability, perhaps not even
within the precincts of the Established Church."

The non-Orthodox in Russia are divided into
a bewildering variety of religious bodies, ranging
from the intensely evangelical, through the
"spiritualistic," to the neurotic and basely de-
praved. So long as the Orthodox Church remains
cold and lifeless, so long will the peasants "find
their soul" in other forms, if not according to
the New Testament and primitive Christianity, then
according to their own wayward will.   There is
a strong tendency in the Russian character towards
freedom of thought in matters appertaining to
religion, and it is useless for Pobiedonostseff
to fulminate against this tendency as he does
in his *Reflections of a Russian Statesman.*

"Meantime, from the day of its foundation,
the proud and impatient have not ceased to seek
outside the Church, and in opposition to it, new
gospels to regenerate humanity, to fulfil the law
of love and justice, to realise the ideal of peace
and prosperity upon earth.   Struck by the
monstrous inconsistencies between the teachings
of Christ and the lives of Christians, they impeach
the Church and its works; abjuring an institution
established since the foundation of Christianity,

they aspire to replace it by a Church of Christ, in their opinion purified, severed from the universal Church, and based on their own interpretation of single precepts of the Gospel.

"It is a strange error. Here are men subject to the passion and the sin to which all their fellow-creatures are given, condemned to will what they cannot do, and to do what they do not will, priding themselves on unity of spirit, and taking up the unappointed work of the teacher and the prophet. While all the world, and they together with it, turn around, they delude themselves that they stand upon an immovable point. They begin with the destruction of the law, yet they are unable to establish a new law from the scraps which they reject. They deny the Church, yet they must needs build a Church for themselves, with their own preachers and ministers, repeating among themselves that which they condemned and rebelled against, with the added faults of falsehood and hypocrisy, and an insensate pride which lifts them above the world. The pride of intellect and contempt for men of their own flesh and blood impel them to destroy the old law and to establish the new. They forget that the Divine Master whose name they invoke, being meek and humble of heart, would not change a single word of the law, but inspired each with the spirit of love and charity which He found concealed there.

" While condemning dogma and ceremony, they themselves end as narrow and masterful dogmatics; revolting against fanaticism and intolerance, they become the fiercest fanatics and persecutors. Unconsciously they themselves are corrupted by malice and passion. Blinded by pride, they know not the scandal they bear to the Faith, destroying its simplicity and completeness in the souls of those simple ones whom the Church has not yet enlightened and taught to know it well.

" It is easy—but how mad, how iniquitous it is! —to seduce a simple soul in which there is a pure, clear field of religious feeling—a soul uncultured, and virgin to the influence of belief. It is sad to think that such souls are approached with confident denial of the Church, and persuaded that the Church, with its doctrine and mysteries, its symbols, its ceremonies, and its traditions, with its poetry which has inspired from generation to generation a multitude of Christians, is a false and execrable institution. These souls are in themselves humble; sectarianism leads them to the heights of pride, while faith decays in the narrow prison of sectarian formulas. The fruits of this pride in its ultimate development are known. They are, first, hypocrisy in the pretence of righteousness; then, malice and intolerance of all other faiths; and, lastly, a passionate desire to lead astray from the Church its scattered flock, to attain which end all means are allowable. Whatever the aim, the end of the religious reformer is—the wilderness, where a hundred sinuous paths diverge, but no straight road is found."

The intensely religious nature of the Russian people, added to their illiteracy, has tended to make them, in matters of independent religious activity (i.e., away from the Orthodox Church), separatist and fissiparous.

Thus, as we have seen, the " Old Believers " have divided into many separate and distinct bodies, under two main divisions, the " Priestly " and the " No Priests."

While dealing with sects in Russia, we must not overlook the broad distinction made by the Government between " Dissenters " and " Sectarians."

The Dissenters are the descendants of the " Old Believers " who revolted against the reforms of Peter the Great and Nicon, and who in large measure have retained the doctrines, rites, and ceremonies of the ancient Church and are wedded to the old ways.

The Sectarians are those who have broken from the Orthodox Church and have forged a creed and a practice for themselves, sometimes from the New Testament, and at others as followers of some reformer or fanatic who has led them into strange expressions of faith.

17

Sectarianism is no modern development in Russia, for in the late fourteenth century we have records of several bodies who started to think and worship independently of the ruling Church.

Georg Brandes, in his lectures on " Mysticism," refers to the Slavic religious temperament. " There is no obstacle to singularity, individual peculiarity, and absurdity, which not infrequently becomes merged into mysticism, a Slavic peculiarity, but one which with the Russians is wonderfully united to realism."

It is this mysticism which is outwardly shown in the numerous sects which are found in Russia. The membership of the sects amounts to from fourteen to fifteen millions of males, divided among some fifty or sixty different moral and religious systems.

Curiously enough, the first record of sectarianism in Russia describes a sect very closely akin to the modern Baptists in faith and polity.

SECT OF STRIGOLNIKS

THE first appearance of the sect of the Strigolniks is in the year A.D. 1371. The founders were Karp (from whose trade the sect derived its name) and a deacon named Nicetas.

They began their crusade against clerical disorders and extortions first in the city of Pskoff, and gradually reached Novgorod, where they met with great success in their propaganda. They

commenced by denouncing and rejecting the
clergy, not only in Pskoff and Novgorod, but
throughout the whole Church. From the denunciation of the clergy for alleged disorders and
rapacity, they went on to deny the necessity
of confession, declaring that it was sufficient for
the penitent to make confession alone to God
and to prostrate oneself before Him. With further
study of the Scriptures they evolved the doctrine
that no man, priest or layman, had the power
to bind and unloose, that every man, according
to St. Paul, had the right to interpret the Scriptures, and they therefore elected their teachers
(pastors) from amongst themselves; instead of
episcopal ordination they substituted a " call " from
their own local society or community.

Denying that the clergy in a peculiar and
priestly sense had the power, by virtue of their
office, to impart the Grace of the Holy Ghost to
members of the Church, they claimed that,
according to the Scriptures, each member, godly
in life and character, indwelt by the Holy Ghost,
could impart such grace.

They refused Baptism and the ordinance of
the Lord's Supper as being the peculiar prerogatives of the priestly caste, and observed those
commandments of the Lord amongst themselves,
the Sacraments being administered by the leader,
or teacher, chosen by themselves, and grounded
their faith and practice upon the doctrine of the

priesthood of all believers, maintaining that all Christians are "priests" unto the Lord.

With the development of the sect came the rejection of oblations for the dead, as an invention of clerical covetousness, an artifice whereby the corrupt clergy could substantially augment their incomes; and in practice they went further still, for they put on one side the force and efficacy of all the customary acts of piety or affection for the benefit of the dead. They taught, "It is not fitting or proper to sing over the dead, nor to make commemorations, nor to celebrate mass for them, nor to bring oblations for the dead into the Church, nor to give away victuals or alms for the soul of the deceased."

Partisan historians of the Holy Orthodox Church dismiss the whole movement as being merely a veiled attack upon the clergy, instead of an attempt to attain some measure of purity and scripturalness in religion, but this almost first attempt at reformation met with the bitter hostility of the officers of the Church State, and Nicetas was degraded, and finally imprisoned for life in the Solovief Monastery, his followers were excommunicated and scattered, whilst Karp was thrown into the river Volkoff, at Novgorod, and drowned.

Despite these rigorous measures, the sect, in small numbers, spread over Russia and maintained their doctrines, until they were merged into larger Reform movements.

In the following century a sect arose called the "Judaizers," a body who combined Jewish tendencies with rationalism. They denied the Divinity of Jesus, and rejected the worship of Icons. The movement apparently commenced in Novgorod, spread to Moscow, and for a time achieved considerable success, obtaining adherents even at Court. In 1505, however, the sect was practically crushed in Northern Russia Some of the leaders were burnt to death; others were imprisoned. Those who escaped made their way through the forests to Western lands and Southern Russia. The "Soubbotruki (Sabbatarians) are a small remnant of lineal descendants, and are to be found in small communities in Eastern and Southern Russia. There are good historical grounds for connecting the "Judaizers" with the strong, flourishing communities of Unitarians amongst the Slav population of Transylvania (Hungary).

In the year 1505 a Council was held in Moscow to condemn the new heresy that had sprung up, and which had been spoken of as adopting in some points the tenets of the Strigolniks, though its leading feature was rather that of a disposition to inculcate Judaical tenets and practices. It did not indeed preach circumcision, but it rejected in reality all the doctrines of Christianity.

Many were found guilty, and according to

L

some accounts, delivered over to the civil arm, and burned as heretics. This Platon condemns as being altogether abhorrent from the spirit of Christianity. He says: "they ought to have been banished and removed from the society of other men, that they might not infect them with their opinions."

He declares also that "these severe measures are not to be attributed to the clergy, but to the civil authorities, who may have had other reasons for proceeding to such extremities."

In 1517 Luther nailed his thesis to the door of the Church in Wittenburg. Six years later we find Reformed Churches in Riga and other Baltic towns, and by 1547, or thirty years later, there were Churches in Kieff, Podalia, and other towns of Central Russia. The effect of Protestantism in strengthening and encouraging Russian dissent is a constant, though never a very prominent, factor. Milyoukov, in *The Russian Crisis*, mentions the Reformation and its part in the development of religious faith in the Empire.

The influence of Protestant ideas on Russian belief appears very early; it is contemporary with the first attempts at a religious reformation in Europe itself. The religious movement in the Balkans, which spread over mediæval Europe, and found its final expression in the building of such sects as the Albigenses in France and the Lollards in England in the thirteenth and fourteenth cen-

turies, had a remote reverberation in Russia also.
This influence of 'Paulikianism,' further developed
by other mystical teachings and rationalistic
heresies, came to Russia in the fifteenth century,
through the Orthodox channel of the Greek monasteries at Mount Athos, and through the immediate intervention of the Karaite Jews—they
being also a kind of Jewish Paulinists. But
until the period of the unification of Russia, at
the end of the fifteenth century, the influence
of those heretical doctrines was limited to the
most civilised parts of the Russia of those times,
to the rich merchant republics of Pskoff
and Novgorod. From this last city the heretical
teachings found their way to Moscow, just at the
time of the political unification, at the end of
the fifteenth century. But here, just then, a
nationalistic type of religion was being formed,
entirely opposed to the new currents. The
nationalistic religion was growing ritualistic,
formal, and subject to State influence. The tendencies of the rationalistic and mystic currents
were spiritualistic, critical, and bent on independence, moral and spiritual. Thus no other
relation was possible between the old and the
new types of religious thought than struggle.
The struggle set in indeed, and after half a
century, as was to be expected, it resulted in
the triumph of the nationalistic type. The new
'heresies' were completely vanquished and driven

L

out of Russia; they found their refuge in the neighbouring countries of Lithuania and Poland. Every spark of the pre-Reformation ideas in Russia seemed herewith entirely extinguished.

" But now the immediate action of the Reformation began to be felt. In Moscow, where there was a large foreign element, this new current of religious ideas succeeded the former one, almost without interruption, as early as the middle of the sixteenth century. The old heresy, imported from the Orthodox East, from Constantinople and Mount Athos, here came into contact with the new heresy coming from the German West. The German religion was then supposed, in Moscow, to be still Roman Catholic, because little or nothing was known as yet about the Reformation."

In the year 1550 we have the beginnings of a new movement of a rationalistic type, under Bashkin, and one of the first to identify himself with it was Kassian, Bishop of Kazan.

One day, at confession, Bashkin expressed a wish to have a reasonable knowledge of religion, and that the holy faith might, in the persons of its appointed servants, produce fruit amongst the people. "In matters of religion, words are not sufficient; deeds are required: the whole law is summed· up in the saying, 'Thou shalt love thy neighbour as thyself.'" Puzzled how to deal with a penitent of this kind, the priest reported him to the higher authorities.

ι

Bashkin did not consider Jesus to be God
equal with the Father. He did not hold the
bread and wine in the Eucharist to be truly the
flesh and blood of Christ. Icons of the Virgin
and of the saints he called idols. Confession to a
priest he looked upon as useless, saying that if a
man ceases to sin, he will be free from sin, even
though he has confessed to no priest. He did
not consider the traditions of the Church binding.
The lives of the saints he held to be fabulous.
He rejected the authority of the Councils. Of the
Bible he did not accept what was not included
in the Gospels and the Epistles. Prayer for the
dead he thought useless, and all prayer, apart
from conduct corresponding thereto, futile.

In 1552 the Metropolitan Macarius laid in-
formation of this new heresy before Ivan the
Terrible, and a Council of the Church condemned
Bashkin and some of his followers to imprisonment.

Bashkin's teaching was followed by Kosoy,
a Moscow man by birth, who had been a servant
at Court, but had run away from his master and
had entered the Byelo Lake Monastery as a monk.
There he heard of, and adopted, the doctrines of
Bashkin.

Kosoy denied the doctrines of the Trinity,
and said that Jesus was not God, but simply a
man. He rejected the theory of Redemption,
pointing out that it had not done away with death,
as it should have done had it really redeemed us

ι

from the effects of Adam's sin. Rejecting Icons, he also refused to believe in miracles performed by them. He thought it wrong to pray to the saints, and considered that their relics ought to be buried, and not indecently exposed in Churches. The prayers, fasts, and ceremonies of the Church, Kosoy considered to be ordained merely by human traditions. He rejected monasticism, reproached the Church with lack of unanimity, and said that the Bishops, by rejecting heretics and not accepting their repentance, broke the law of the Lord which commands us to forgive sinners even if they repeat their sin. In general, he adopted the teachings of Bashkin, and carried them to further conclusions. In 1555 Kosoy was condemned to confinement in a monastery, but escaped, and made his way into Lithuania. ·

None of these doctrines found any further echo in Moscow. This new conception of religion was incomprehensible to the Russians of the sixteenth century. The European Reformation failed to strike root in Moscow at this time. Platon refers to this Synod as the first occasion in which the Reformation, or Protestant doctrines of Western Europe, came into contact with the Russian Church.

The "great Schism" of the seventeenth century gave a tremendous impetus to the Sectarian movement. The "priestless" section of the "Old Believers" were fatally led into the most wild and fantastic extravagances; whilst the emancipation of the serfs led to more or less searchıng of .hearts as to the foundations of the faıth as revealed in the New Testament. Along with a social and political revolution as profound as the French, is going on a popular religious Reformation comparable only to the peasants' movements of Luther's time. The peasants have created systems of religious belief on an entirely independent basis. A recent traveller in Russia, John Foster Fraser, has called it a " religious revolutıon." It is more far-reaching in its scope and effect than the Reformation inseparably connected with the names of Luther, Melancthon, Knox, and Calvın. The subtlety, simplicity, and dignıty of these beliefs, the morality and prosperity of their adherents, have charmed, and even won, many of their impartial observers. Though these sects are still in progress of growth and development, their adherents are numbered by millions.

The Government, of course, is at present straining every nerve and using almost any resource to repress and conceal these schısms from the Orthodox Church, and to strengthen in every possible way the National Instıtution of Religion. Persecutions relaxed for a year or two after the Tsar's Manifesto are beıng renewed. The warfare between the peasants' genuine religious ınstinct and the State Church is bound to go on.

The Sectarians may be roughly described as:

ι

1. Those who take the Scriptures as the basis of their faith and order, and use them as their sole guide in doctrine and practice. They ·are closely akin to the great Protestant Evangelical bodies of the rest of Europe, and received their initial impulse from Western preachers and teachers. The main sects, answering, to this de-scription, are the Molokans, Baptists, and Evangelicals (the two former are described in separate chapters).

2. Sects which take the Scriptures as the basis of their belief, but interpret and complete the doctrines therein contained by means of occasional inspiration or internal enlightenment of their leading members. The most prominent body coming under this description is the Doukhobors (see separate chapter).

3. Sects which reject the spiritual interpretation of Scripture and insist upon certain chosen passages being taken in the literal sense. Under this description we find the Skoptsi, Castrates, Hleests, and Nazarenes.

4. Sects which believe in the continual reincarnation of Christ, and are occasionally led away to find the millennium in some distant part of the Empire. They are mainly bodies of people, confined to one or two villages, who follow some "miracle-working" monk. They usually have a very brief and troubled existence.

5. Sects which confuse religion with nervous

excitement, and are more or less erotic in their character. Amongst these we find communities which address their fellow-members as "Christs," "Saviours," "Mothers of God," "Redeemers," and even go to the length of praying to each other as to real "Gods," "Madonnas" and living "Christs."

6. Sects in which bestial orgies are the resultant feature of their worship. Many of these are nearly akin to the whirling dervishes of Mohammedanism. Amongst these we place the Shakuni and the Jumpers.

Some of the sects are exceedingly difficult to place, as their meetings are jealously guarded and they are very reticent as to their dogmas and practices. Again, some of them are the offspring of the "Old Believers," and came into being through the personality of one man, many of them having but comparatively few members, and by the very extravagances of their practices being but short-lived.

In addition to the above are a number of sects which are peculiar to Russia alone, and are named after some striking peculiarity in their doctrine or morals.

Thus we find the

Nemolyaki or the "do not pray" sect, who in their revolt against Icon worship and invocation of the saints, went to the other extreme, and abolished prayer in public and private worship.

L

The Vozdy Rhateli or "sighers." One who was privileged to meet with a small community of this sect in Eastern Russia described them as melancholy of countenance, and finding the world an extremely unhappy place and but little comfort in their religion.

The Dietoubitsi or "Slayers of Children," now no more, who considered it their duty to send the souls of the innocent newly-born children direct to Heaven and to God.

The Molchalniks or "Silent Ones," who, like some of the Fakirs of India, vow never to break silence. They literally believe that the tongue, like money, is the root of all evil, a member which can only be tamed by complete suppression.

The Ne Nastrinik or "Not ours," who taught, not only community of land and goods, but also of wives.

The Ne Platelshchiki or "Non-tax-payers," who entirely repudiated the civil authorities. They were Anarchists, but without the violence usually connected with Anarchistic propaganda.

The Dushilschiknik or Suffocaters, who held that it was their bounden duty to save parents and friends from a natural death, and in cases of serious illness to bring about that end by suffocation. This is an instance of a sect taking literally one text of Scripture, "And from the days of John the Baptist until now the Kingdom of Heaven suffereth violence, and the violent take it by force,"

L

The "Fire Baptists" had a brief but inglorious existence. Whole villages of them
gathered together, and after locking themselves in
a building, would set fire to it and perish gladly
in the flames. Strahl says, "It is probably the
most signal instance of martyrdom in the cause,
not even of a corrupt practice, or a corrupt
doctrine, but of a corrupt reading of a text—
'There is one baptism *by fire* for the remission of
sins.'"

The Samoibesnik or Sect of Suicide. This sect
usually springs into being through the fanaticism
of one man. A ragged pilgrim will appear in
the village. Even if not wearing them at the time,
he evidently has worn manacles and chains; he has
all the appearance of an ascetic: his topic is
usually the imminence of the last judgment, when
all those left alive will be cast into hell. One
such, a few years ago, persuaded many of the
peasants to commit suicide by throwing themselves into the river, whilst he himself deliberately
hung himself from the branch of a pine-tree on
the eve of the "Day of Judgment."

Devil possession is also held tenaciously by
many of the peasants. In a village in Samara a
woman confessed to her neighbours that she was
Antichrist, and that Satan was using her to seduce
the faithful from the service of the true Christ. A
whole day was spent in prayer, an improvised altar
was erected just outside the village, the holy Icons

l

were placed in position, and five men slew her with axes in front of the altar.

The doctrine of Antichrist accounts for many child murders amongst the peasantry. Any abnormal child is likely to be charged with being Antichrist, and some meet with a violent end. In one case a girl was chained for eight years to a staple in the room, until death mercifully released her.

The foregoing, however, whilst revealing the innate religious fanaticism of the Russian, must not be taken as being typical examples of the sects in Russia. They are usually small communities, easily led away by some one man of strong personality.

The Hleests were the first Russian sect of Spiritual Christians of more modern times. They were a direct product of the stirring times of the end of the seventeenth century, when all over Russia men were daily expecting the Second Advent, the end of the world, or the " Day of Judgment." The " Priestless ones " had been hunted and persecuted, through forests, across the steppes, and beyond the rivers, and as a result, the doctrine of voluntary martyrdom had found a place in their beliefs; suicide and self-immolation was not only practised in isolated cases and amongst villagers as a whole, but an ardent propaganda to this end was carried on. As a result of the extravagances of religious emotion,

L

prophetism appeared. Men fell into trances and had "Divine" revelations. They called themselves "Men of God," then "Redeemers," "Saviours," then "Christs"; later on they were called Hleests, by reason of their self-floggings, the wearing of manacles and voluntary instruments of torture. They trace their beginnings to a legend concerning the founder of the sect, one Daniel Philipovitch.

He was reputed to be an old and wise man, well versed in religious truth, and was continually debating the question as to which contained the real truth, the "old," i.e., Pre-Nicon books, or the "new," i.e., the revised versions

This question Philipovitch resolved in a radical way. There was no need of either the "old" or the "new" books The only book necessary for salvation was a "living one," the Holy Ghost Himself. Coming to this conclusion, he collected all the books possible and within his reach, and finally disposed of them by throwing them into a river.

His followers then gathered themselves together and resolved to wait and pray that God Himself, by His Spirit, might come again to earth and teach men the right "way." Whilst they were praying, a chariot of fire rolled down from the clouds; God was in it, and, according to one version, He entered the body of Philipovitch *through his ear*. Philipovitch then became a "Christ," although the doctrine of inspiration was

L 18

of a very crude and unsatisfactory character. As may be assumed, the "teaching" is a queer mixture. "Old" and "new" are strangely blended.

To become inspired, a very peculiar method is adopted. It is almost entirely physiological and outward in its manifestation. The community meet in a large private room and sit in circles. As the service proceeds they rise, remove the forms, and begin to dance to the tune of their own special hymns. The time of the song grows gradually faster, whilst the singers quicken their movements in the dance. Some of the "disciples," possibly being more in tune for inspiration, begin to turn like dervishes in the midst of the circles, dancing the while, until they fall from sheer exhaustion upon the floor, when they begin to give utterance to incoherent words and wild phrases, which are seized upon by the others as a prophecy. Such of their number as can "turn the circle" are possessed by the "Spirit"; they are admitted to the higher ranks of the community; they are the "prophets" and "prophetesses" of the faith. The ordinary members are in a lower stage of preparation. At the head of every community, or "ship," as it is called, is a "Christ," and by his side a "Mother of God."

Many of the Hleests are of Finnish origin, and the old tribal customs of Communism, not in goods only, but also in women, may help to explain some of the most remarkable peculiarities of the sect. The sex question plays a prominent part in their religion, but every phase of opinion, from the advocacy of complete chastity and celibacy to the practice of promiscuous debauchery, finds a place in their religious services, and may be met with amongst the varieties of the sect.

It is common in the sect to look upon monogamy as a selfish and wicked monopolisation, and to consider regular marital relations as filthy and disgusting, whilst casual sexual intercourse is regarded with tolerance and even with approval. "Married life is impurity before men and impiety before God" is one of their sayings. They are an example of the lack of moderation and balance, and the readiness to "go the whole hog" so often met with amongst the Russian people.

Towards the middle of the nineteenth century there began a new development of doctrine and practice amongst the Hleests, partly through their coming into close contact with more evangelical bodies, and partly through dissensions in their own community. There was an attempt, successful on the whole, to purify their rites and ceremonies, to heighten the quality of inspiration, and to deepen the mystical sense. They desisted largely from the practice of ending their inspirational dances with fleshly orgies, and they regulated, in a certain measure, their habits of "spiritual love."

ι

Some communities have ceased altogether from using any artificial means whatever for receiving the "voice of the Spirit" in the soul. To them, the Spirit was to be received by a long series of spiritual exercises, such as "self-abnegation," a "surrender of self to the will of God," a "self-burial" in Christ. Only after complete mortification of the flesh and the suppression of fleshly desires, can the "voice of the Spirit" be heard. In this we have the doctrine of the "mysterious death," followed by the "mysterious resurrection."

The Skoptsi or Castrates are a sect founded as a reaction against the lust orgies of the Hleests. They are "ascetic" rather than "spiritualistic," and have gone a long way further than the Hleests in the development of doctrine and belief. Among them, men and women alike are recognised as "teachers" and "prophets," and in this character they lead a strictly moral and even ascetic life. Denying themselves even ordinary and harmless recreations and pleasures, they frequently exhaust themselves by long and rigorous fasts, and when gathered together for service, give way to wild, ecstatic religious exercises. Under the stimulus of religious excitement they call one another "Christ," "God," "Madonna," and will even pray to one another as to God Himself. It is commonly reported that many, if not all, of the Russian jewellers in Moscow belong to this sect. Whilst travelling through Roumania in 1910 I came across several communities of the sect who had been exiled from their homes in Russia. In Bucarest there are about two hundred and fifty men, besides women, the men being mostly cab-drivers. They are easily recognised by their hairless faces, high-pitched voices, and the development of the secondary mammalian characteristics.

The men generally submit to castration, usually after the birth of the second child (why then, I have not been able to discover), and the women, in their eagerness to escape sexual desire, frequently have part of their breasts cut away

In conversation with one member of the sect, he based the practice of self-mutilation upon the text, "There be eunuchs which have made themselves eunuchs for the kingdom of heaven's sake."

The Pretschoki or ·Jumpers are another offshoot of the Hleests, and, if anything, their practices are more disagreeable than those of the parent community. Wallace, in *Russia*, describes one meeting held in the forest in the summer time.

"After due preparation, prayers are read by the chief teacher, dressed in a white robe, standing in the midst of the congregation. At first he reads in an ordinary tone of voice, and then passes gradually to a merry chant. When he remarks that the chanting has sufficiently acted on the hearers, he begins to jump. The hearers, singing likewise, follow his example. Their ever-

L

increasing excitement finds expression in the highest possible jumps This they continue as long as they can—men and women alike yelling like enraged savages. When all are thoroughly exhausted, the leader declares that he hears the angels singing "—and then begins a scene which cannot be here described.

The Adamites, who are to be found in scattered communities along the shores of the Black Sea, are a recrudescence of the Gnostics of North Africa of the second century. They profess to return to the innocence of Eden, abstain from marriage, and in their nocturnal services discard clothing. I came across a small community of them in Croatia—not more than seventeen in number. Their chief argument is: "Clothing is the outward and visible sign of sin; without sin there is no shame; without shame there is no need of clothing. Paul teaches that 'if any man is in Christ he is without sin'; therefore, being without sin and without shame, we have no need of clothing in our worship, but in the world we wear clothing to prevent shame in others." It is interesting to notice that the Berghards or Brethren of the Free Spirit held the same doctrine and practices in the fourteenth century, and that the Doukhobors in Canada went on a nude pilgrimage in September, 1903.

New sects of an erotic kind are continually arising in Russia, symptoms of the general social unrest, of dissatisfaction with the lifelessness of the Orthodox Church, and an attempt on .the part of the people to find their " soul."

The three great spiritual and evangelical bodies, the Molokans, Doukhobors, and Baptists, I deal with in separate chapters.

There are a number of " foreign " sects in Russia, but they have had but little influence, generally speaking, upon the Russian people as a whole.

The Lutherans, whose Russian strongholds are in the Baltic provinces, are to be found in every large city, but as their sevices are mainly in the German or Lettish languages, they only appeal to the non-Russian nationalities.

The Mennonites, who originally settled in South Russia on the invitation of Catherine II , have become prosperous agriculturists, and their villages are a marked contrast to those of the Russians even in close proximity to them. Their houses are well arranged, their farms are large, their gardens are well stocked with fruit-trees and vegetables, and there is a general air of prosperity about them.

We need to remember in this connection that they are exempt from conscription, and almost entirely exempt from other than purely local taxes. The Government has recently tried to incorporate them into the Russian nationality and to break down their extreme exclusiveness. They

L

have resented this move on the part of the autocracy, for they rightly feel that if the barriers
which separate them from the rest of the popula-
lation are broken down, they will no longer be
able to maintain their stern Puritanical discipline.
Despite many subsequent concessions on the part
of the Government, thousands of them have
emigrated to the United States and Canada.

They are practically Baptist in doctrine and
practice, but have the ceremony of "feet washing" by one another at the close of the Lord's
Supper on Sunday mornings. It was amongst
the Mennonites that the great revival of the
"eighties" commenced which led to the Stundist
and Baptist movements.

The "Moravian Brethren," or "Hussites," as
they are sometimes called, settled in Russia in
the year 1765, and there is a large colony of
them on the banks of the Volga, in the district
of Sarepta. Many of the younger members are
sent to Hernhutt in Germany for more advanced
education than can be given to them in their
own villages. Like the Mennonites, they are
exempt from conscription and the more oppres-
sive taxation under which the Orthodox peasant
groans.

In 1803, Alexander I. granted a charter to
the Presbyterian Church of Scotland, allowing a
band of missionaries to labour amongst the Tcherkisses of the South, and they received from him a

large grant of land on what was then the frontier. Here they founded their mission, but quickly discovered that work amongst the Mohammedans was exceedingly difficult.

The mission was suppressed in the year 1835 under ukase by Tsar Nicholas I., and all the missionaries save two returned home. Many of the converts married daughters of German (Protestant) settlers, and have scattered to various parts of the "black earth" belt, but their corporate life has been effectually dissolved.

The Brethren have for nearly half a century had an active propaganda in the country, and Mr. S. H. Broadbent has done splendid pioneering work, especially in the Eastern Provinces For occasional reports of this work the reader is referred to the monthly publication, *Echoes of Service*. The Brethren in Russia are closely allied to the Baptists. There is no clear line of demarcation between them, and they are of mutual service to one another

The Christian Disciples have also been greatly blessed in their evangelical testimony, and differing, as they do, from the Baptists almost solely upon the question of the "paid ministry," there is good hope that in the near future they will fuse with the older and stronger body. At present (1914) they are considering the advisability of establishing a preachers' school for the training of evangelists.

The "Mildmay Mission to the Jews," which commenced work in Vilna in 1887, has been greatly blessed of God in its labours amongst the dwellers in the Ghetto. In Theodosia and Odessa, on the Black Sea, I had the privilege of meeting with their workers, and saw something of their Christ-like generosity and kindness to the "pogrom-hunted" ones during the black year of 1905.

The Methodist Episcopal Church of the United States has a preaching station in St. Petersburg, but its work is mainly in the Duchy of Finland, and can hardly be counted amongst the forces leading Russia to find her "Soul."

In the *Baptist Missionary Herald* for April 1825 there is an interesting letter from a correspondent in Leipsic, showing that nearly ninety years ago there were streaks in the sky, heralding the new day.

"I do not know whether you have already heard of that truly evangelical preacher, the Rev. John Gossner, a native of Bavaria, and member of the Catholic Church, though a decided enemy of Rome and its impostures.

"This highly-gifted man, by whose preaching hundreds have been snatched from the world and converted to Christ, after having suffered perse-cution and imprisonment in his own country, was called to St. Petersburg, by the special wish of the Emperor. This is now about five years ago. In St. Petersburg his preaching was uncommonly blessed, and a large congregation gathered, who assembled in a hired hall for the purpose.

"The enemies of the Gospel were not a little disappointed by his success, and used all means they could to destroy his work, and at length they also succeeded so far that last summer Mr. Gossner was suddenly sent out of the country, by command of the Emperor. His enemies, among whom were many of the Greek and Roman clergy, had insinuated that, in a work which he had written —a kind of commentary on the New Testament— he had spoken against the Virgin Mary and the Saints, and preached rebellion against the Emperor. The falsehood and wickedness of these assertions, especially of the last, is known to every one who has read the book, which tends only to practical godliness, and has done already much good in Germany. After Mr. Gossner's return to Germany, he first went to Altona, and for the last four months has been in Leipsic. He is very far from anything Roman Catholic, and would long ago have joined the Protestant Church if he did not see it so full of unbelief, and estranged from the truth of the Gospel."

l

THE DOUKHOBORS

BIBLIOGRAPHY.

MAUDE . . . . *A Peculiar People.*

MILYOUKOV . . . *The Russian Crisis.*

HARLAMOV . . . *Rousskaya Misl. 1884.*

TCHERKOFF . . . *Christian Martyrdom in Russia.*

HAXTHAUSEN . . *Studien uber die inneren Zustande das Volkleben, und insbesondere die landichen Einrichtungen Russlands.*

LIVANOF . . . . *Raskolniki i Ostrozhniki.*

NOVITSKY . . . *Doukhobortsi i Istoria i Veroutcheni.*

HEARD . . . . *The Russian Church and Dissent.*

BIRUKOV . . . . *Tolstoi et les Doukhobors.*

ι

"There is no denying that the people are morally ill, with a grave, although not a mortal, malady, one to which it is difficult to assign a name. May we call it 'An unsatisfied thirst for truth?' The people are seeking eagerly and untiringly for truth and for the ways that lead to it, but hitherto they have failed in their search. . . There is a clamouring for a new Gospel; new ideas and feelings are manifest. . . ."

Dostoieffski.

THE DOUKHOBORS

THE sect of the Doukhobors (wrestlers with the spirit) is a typical product of the peculiar Russian religious temperament. In the early days it was a protest against the gross materialism and spiritual deadness of the Orthodox Church.

The official religious life of the nation was at a very low ebb; with few exceptions, neither the priests nor the general body of the peasantry paid much heed to the teaching of the Russian Church. For one thing, the priests were in many cases too ignorant to be able to read the Service, whilst in many parishes there was no priest at all. In their religious zeal the villagers would build a Church, but they waited in vain for a pastor to shepherd them and to conduct Divine worship. The moral standard of the priests had sunk very low indeed, drunkenness and immorality being rife amongst them. In addition, the foreign influences at Court tended to debase the whole clergy. Bishops, priests, and monks who offended Peter the Great's foreign favourites were disfrocked,

L

punished, tortured, many of them being sent into Siberia as exiles.

As a natural corollary to the lowness of the spiritual forces of the nation, the social life was also in a bad way. Serfdom was being rigorously enforced in its most debased form. The evils of the system almost beggar description. The wealthy landowners and proprietors held the wives and daughters of their serfs at their mercy. Profligacy was rampant; there was practically no effective check upon the evil passions of the masters. Serfs ran away from the estates, and when caught, were sometimes drowned, or expeditiously done away with, to save the trouble and expense of restoring them to their owners. Cases are on record where they were even presented as a gift, or bribe, to rapacious officials.

In the palace, court intrigues were afoot for the deposition of the monarch, there were a series of revolutions led by ambitious men; the general disorder of the times affected even the clergy, for monks in the monasteries and priests in their parishes openly entered into league with brigands and robbers.

In the midst of this social, political, and religious anarchy we discover the source of Doukhoborism, although it is impossible, without access to State papers, to give an exact date for its rise amongst the peasantry.

No definite information concerning the sect

can be found earlier than the second half of the eighteenth century, the name being first met with in authentic documents in 1785.

Two theories are current as to the significance of the name. By the Orthodox they are Doukhobors because they "wrestle against the Holy Spirit," whilst they themselves claim that they "wrestle against evil, not with carnal weapons, but with the armour of the Spirit." Of recent years they have called themselves "the Universal Community of the Christian Brotherhood."

Aylmer Maude says: "A very plausible conjecture represents them as being spiritual descendants of the so-called Judaizers (see p. 259), who, rejecting the doctrine of the Trinity and the worship of. Icons and of saints, played a prominent part in the latter part of the fifteenth century: and yet again, they may be traced back to the Paulicians of the seventh to the eleventh century, and to the Bogomilites of the twelfth century."

According to the Doukhobors themselves, their sect was founded by a German officer—certainly a foreigner—who for a time lived at the village of Okhotch in the Government of Kharkoff, about the years 1735-1740. He was the general friend of the villagers, and acted as their adviser and teacher; he arbitrated in their disputes, and was one with them in their labour and toil; he had no settled place or home, but, like the "pilgrims," went from house to house.

L

His teaching was closely parallel to much of Tolstoi's of one hundred and fifty years later. He taught that "Governments are not necessary; all men are equal; the hierarchy and the priesthood are a human invention; the Church and its ceremonies are superfluous; monasticism is a perversion of human nature; the conspiracy of the proprietors is a disgrace to mankind; and the Tsar and Archbishops are just like other people." The seed sown in the midst of such a people, at such a time, was sure to germinate and ultimately to bring forth fruit many fold; for the unknown leader was evidently a man of integrity, of good character, and deeply devoted to the welfare of his fellowmen.

Over against the wickedness and wretchedness of serfdom was the doctrine of the essential equality of all men; over against the corruption and extortionate practices of the officials of all grades, the doctrine that the sons of the Living God need no rule but His; and the rites and ceremonies of the Church, performed by immoral priests and monks, led to the denunciation of the externals of religion and the prerogatives of the religious caste and the insistence upon the doctrine of the "Light within."

Unlike some of the other Russian sects, the Doukhobors have been mainly recruited from the peasantry, from those who have suffered under the exactions of landlordism, the tyranny of militarism, and the rapacity of ecclesiasticism. The adherents of the sect have been just those in the nation upon whom the crushing burden of the bureaucracy has fallen, who have been ground under the iron heel of a bitter and relentless despotism.

Following the " Unknown one," the first leader of note was Sylvan Kolesnikov of the village of Nikolsk, in the Government of Ekaterinoslav. He was a man of a generous and kindly nature, tactful and prudent, with a natural eloquence which won the hearts and sympathies of his hearers. From all available sources it is not possible to discover whether he intentionally founded a new sect. " He taught his followers that, as the externalities of religion are unimportant, they might conform to the ceremonial religion of whatever province or country they happened to be in, behaving as Catholics in Poland, Orthodox in Russia, or Mohammedans in Turkey and Persia."

With Kolesnikov there emerged the doctrine of the "Christ" within, probably at the beginning a modification of the doctrine of the Hleests (see p. 270). He taught, "Let us bow to the God in one another, for we are the image of God on earth"; and again, "In whose hearts the Sun of eternal truth has risen in midday brightness, there moon and stars have no more light. For the children of God, Tsars and authorities and every human law are truly superfluous. Through Jesus Christ their will is made free from any law; no

l

law is given for the righteous"; and again, "By the cleansing of repentance, and the enlightenment of spiritual instruction, men reach the sweetness of union with God."

Kolesnikov lived to a ripe old age, and during his life and activities he never came into conflict with the authorities, although his doctrines were calculated to undermine their prestige and power.

Skovoroda, a son of Cossacks living in the Kiev province, was in early life a chorister at the Court of the Empress Elizabeth, and later became a student in Kiev, where he studied Latin, Greek, and Hebrew, in addition to philosophy, natural history, and theology.

Declining to enter the Russian Church, he travelled in Hungary and Austria, where he mastered the German language and came into close contact with scholars of repute. Afterwards he visited Poland, Prussia, Germany, and Italy, thus enlarging his views and deepening his knowledge. Returning home, he became a wanderer, and with flute and Hebrew Bible would wander from town to town, accepting the hospitality of the common people and imparting to them something from his stores of knowledge. He was not a member of the sect, but he came into close contact with it, and undoubtedly had great influence with the Doukhobors with whom he occasionally lodged.

He it was who drew up for the Government

the Doukhobor confession of faith, and evidently, considering the paucity of learning amongst the members of the community, had no little hand in formulating their doctrines.

With the advent of Ilarion Pobirohin to the leadership, a new era commenced for the Doukhobors. He was a wool dealer in Tambov, and business necessitated his travelling from village to village and coming into contact with many places and people. He adopted the Doukhobor faith, became the recognised leader, and by his powerful personality diverted the current of their religious doctrines into a new channel

He taught that "truth is not in books but in the Spirit, not in the Bible but in the Living Book." Not content with being recognised as a Son of God like unto his fellow-worshippers, he made the stupendous claim to be Christ Himself. His pretensions were not repudiated by his followers, but rather accepted by them, with the result that he established a theocratic despotism. He chose twelve "apostles" from amongst his adherents, and twelve "death-bearing angels," who were set apart to punish all who fell away from the true faith and became "apostates." He also promulgated the doctrine of the infallibility of the Doukhobor Church. He it was who first introduced communism amongst the sect. His son-in-law, Ouklein, was his chief and ablest assistant, but Ouklein, being well versed in the knowledge

L

of the Bible, and not rejecting its authorty, finally broke with Pobirohin, and joined the Molokans, where his ability and personality soon secured for him the leadership.

Pobirohin became filled with self-assurance, and possessed unbounded confidence in his powers, so much so that he came into conflict with the Government, was arrested, tried, and with his children and some of his "apostles," was exiled to Siberia, his activities in the Tambov district ending about 1785

Savely Kapoustin now became the head of the community, and he was easily the most remarkable of the Doukhobor leaders.

Aylmer Maude says that, "according to some accounts he was a son of Pobirohin, and was taken as a recruit as a punishment for being a Doukhobor."

He served in the regiment of the Guards, and left the army with the rank of corporal. He assumed the leadership about 1790.

"He was a tall man, well built, had an imposing gait and appearance, an amazing memory, great ability, and remarkable eloquence. His ascendency over the Doukhobors who came under his influence seems to have been complete."

In the early years of the reign of Alexander I. (1801-1825) a period of religious toleration set in, and the Doukhobors, partly to prevent their proselytizing amongst their Orthodox neighbours,

were granted territory in the fertile valley of
Milky Waters, where they founded a colony, and
being free from taxation for five years, they pros-
pered exceedingly.

The migration commenced in 1801, when
thirty families were transported thither from the
Ekaterinoslav province, and the community gradually increased by other families going there   In
1805 many Tambov Doukhobors migrated thither,
amongst them Kapoustin, the leader.   By 1816
there were nine villages, and in them 1,459 "souls,'
or about three thousand inhabitants.   They were
easily the most compact body of Doukhobors in
Russia, and much of their prosperity and the
good order maintained in their villages was undoubtedly due to the personal influence of their
leader, Kapoustin.

Haxthausen says of them:

"All subjected themselves willingly to him
(Kapoustin), and he ruled like a king, or rather,
a prophet.   He expounded the tenets of the
Doukhobors in a manner to turn them to
his own peculiar profit and advantage.   He
attached peculiar importance to the doctrine of
the transmigration of souls, which was already
known among them, he also taught that Christ
is born again in every believer: that God is in
every one, for when the Word became flesh it
became this (i.e., man in the world) for all time,
like everything Divine.   But each human soul,

L

at least as long as the created world exists, remains a distinct individual. Now, when God
descended into the individuality of Jesus as Christ,
He sought out the purest and most perfect of
all human souls. God, since the time when He
first revealed Himself in Jesus, has always remained
in the human race, and dwells and reveals Himself
in every believer. But the individual soul of Jesus,
where has it been? By virtue of the law of the
transmigration of souls, it must necessarily have
animated another human body! Jesus himself said,
'I am with you always, until the end of the
world.' Thus the soul of Jesus, favoured by God
above all human souls, has from generation to
generation continually animated new bodies; and
by virtue of its higher qualities, and by the
peculiar and absolute command of God, it has
invariably retained a semblance of its previous conditions. Every man, therefore, in whom it
resided, knew that the soul of Jesus was in him
In the first centuries after Christ this was so
universally acknowledged among believers that
every one recognised the new Jesus, who
was the guide and ruler of Christendom, and
decided all disputes respecting the Faith. The
Jesus thus always born again was called Pope.
False Popes, however, soon obtained possession
of the throne of Jesus; but the true Jesus only
retained a small band of believers about Him;
as He predicted in the New Testament, 'many

l

are called, but few chosen ' These believers are
the Doukhobors, among whom Jesus constantly
dwells, his soul animating one of them 'Thus
Sylvan Kolesnikov, of Nikolsk,' said Kapoustin,
'whom the older among you knew was Jesus;
but now, as truly as the heaven is above me and
the earth under my feet, I am the true Jesus
Christ your Lord."

Kapoustin introduced communism; the fields
were ploughed in common; common barns were
built in which to store grain against time of
famine; and the community flourished and made
good progress. He used every means possible
to retain the allegiance of the villagers as a
whole.

For the government of the community he
appointed thirty elders and twelve apostles. The
members were not encouraged to learn to read
or write, and they were discouraged from trade
and commerce, as they might imbibe the opinions
of the " Gentiles " or " Chaldeans," and thus receive harmful teachings

He was their representative before the civil
authorities, and paid taxes for the whole colony.
He required absolute and implicit obedience from
all the members, and held that at any time he,
as leader, was free to dispose of property or
person.

Maude says, "The result of Kapoustin's influence was to convert what had been an ultra-

L

democratic, anti-governmental sect into a society in which he was an autocrat controlling not only the persons and property, but even the very thoughts of his subjects."

Prosperity was the indirect means which brought adversity to the community. Seeing their flourishing condition, Orthodox peasants began to join the community at the Milky Waters, with the result that the Doukhobors were open to the charge of proselytizing, and several men who had been expelled from the community brought accusations against the sect. Some of the leaders were arrested, and after long confinement in prison, were at last released.

In February, 1816, a priest was sent to convert them, but Father Nalimski, on the night of his arrival, got drunk, misbehaved himself, and started fighting, for which missionary labours, or rather, the result of them, he was confined in a monastery for four months.

On July 19 of the same year Kapoustin was arrested on the charge of perverting the Orthodox. Although he was seventy-three years of age, he was kept in prison for some months awaiting trial, and was at last released on bail, and died about November 7, 1817, although many accounts are current as to the date and place of his death.

In 1819, William Allen and Stephen Grellet, the Quakers, visited the Milky Waters, and made

inquiries into the tenets and life of the Doukhobors.
It is interesting to compare their impressions of
the Doukhobors with those they formed of the
Molokans (see p. 328).

William Allen writes in his diary:

"In the evening . . we visited a village,
Terpenie, where there is a settlement of one of
the sects of the Doukhobors. We crossed the
Milky Waters, and on our arrival were conducted
to the house where they are in the practice of
meeting on public occasions, and where we found
several of the fraternity. They were well dressed
according to the custom of the country, but there
was something in their countenance which I did
not quite like. We had some conversation, and
informed them that we had heard in England
of the persecution they had endured, and also
of the humane interposition of the Emperor on
their behalf; that while we had felt sympathy
for them in their sufferings, we wished to know
from themselves what were their religious principles. It soon appeared, however, that they
have no fixed principles. There was a studied
evasion in their answers, and though they
readily quoted texts, it is plain that they do
not acknowledge the authority of Scripture,
and have some very erroneous notions. I
was anxious to ascertain their belief respecting our Saviour, but could learn nothing satisfactory. Stephen (Grellet) endeavoured to con-

L

vince them of their errors on some points, but they appear in a very dark state; they have driven out from among them all those who receive Scriptural truth and who are of the class with whom we were so much pleased at Ekaterinoslav (Molokans). My spirit was greatly affected, and I came away from them much depressed."

Stephen Grellet writes:

"The following morning was also spent with the Doukhobors; a considerable number attended what they called their worship, but some of their ceremonies were painful to witness. They manifested great ignorance on the subject of religion, and the interview did not prove more satisfactory than that on the preceding day.

"This afternoon we went to the principal village of the Doukhobors. We went to the abode of the chief man among them. He is ninety years old, nearly blind, but very active in body and mind. He appears to be a robust, strong man. Fourteen others of their elders or chief men were with him We had a long conference with them. He was the chief speaker. We found him very evasive in several of his answers to our inquiries. They, however, stated unequivocally that they do not believe in the authority of the Scriptures. They look upon Jesus Christ in no other light than that of a good man. They therefore have no confidence in Him as a Saviour from sin. They say that they

L

believe that there is a spirit in man to teach
and lead him in the right way, and in support
of this they were fluent in the quotation of Scripture texts, which they teach to their children;
but they will not allow any of their people to have
a Bible among them. We inquired about their
mode of worship. They said they met together
to sing some of the Psalms of David. Respecting
their manner of solemnising their marriages, they
declined giving an answer; but a very favourite
reply to some of our questions was: 'The letter
killeth, but the Spirit giveth Life.' We found,
however, that they have no stated times for their
meetings for worship; but that to-morrow, which
is First Day, they intend to have one, and this
they said we might attend, and see for ourselves.
We left them with heavy hearts.

"I had a sleepless night; my mind being
under great weight of exercise for the Doukhobors. I felt much for these people, thus darkened
by their leaders, and I did not apprehend that
I should stand acquitted in the Divine sight without seeking for an opportunity to expostulate with
them, and to proclaim that salvation which comes
by Jesus Christ. . . . We rode again to their
village in the morning. . . . The Doukhobors collected on a spacious spot of ground out of doors.
They all stood, forming a large circle; all the
men on the left hand of the old man, and the
women on his right; the children of both sexes

l

formed the opposite side of the circle; they were all cleanly dressed; an old woman was next to the old man; she began by singing what they call a psalm; the other women joined in it; then the man next the old man, taking him by the hand, stepped in front of him, each bowed down very low to one another three times, and then twice to the women, who returned the salute; that man resuming his place, the one next to him performed the same ceremony to the old man and to the women; then, by turns, all the others, even the boys, came and kissed three times the one in the circle above him, instead of bowing. When the men and boys had accomplished this, the women did the same to each other; then the girls; the singing continuing the whole time. It took them nearly an hour to perform this round of bowing and kissing; then the old woman, in a fluent manner, uttered what they called a prayer, and their worship concluded, but no seriousness appeared over them at any time. Oh, how was my soul bowed before the Lord, earnestly craving that he would touch their hearts by His power and love! I felt also much towards the young people. I embraced the opportunity to preach the Lord Jesus Christ, and that salvation which is through faith in Him. . . . We then went into the house with the old men; they had a few things to say, but not to any more satisfaction than yesterday. We left them with heavy hearts."

Again, "One of the Molokans saying that he was formerly among the Doukhobors, I inquired of him how he had become convinced of his errors. He answered with great energy, 'I had the Bible put into my hands; I read it, and is it possible to read the Bible and not be convinced of the great errors under which I was?'"

With the death of Kapoustin a day of darkness and evil dawned for the settlers of the Milky Waters.

Haxthausen reports the events as follows:

"After the death of Kapoustin, the office of Christ passed to his son. He (Kapoustin) is said to have assured his people that the soul of Christ had the power of uniting itself with any human body it pleased, and that it would establish itself in the body of his son."

"The son and heir of Kapoustin was Vasilli Kalmikof, and his son was Ilarion Kalmikof Neither of them inherited Kapoustin's genius. They fell into evil practices and became drunkards

"The elders and apostles now assumed the authority, acting nominally in Vasilli's name

"The Council of the Elders constituted itself a terrible inquisitional tribunal. The principle, 'Whoso denies his God shall perish by the sword,' was interpreted according to their caprice, the Justice Hall was called 'Paradise and Torture'; the place of execution was at the mouth of the river. A mere suspicion of treachery was punish-

L

able with death.   Within a few years some four
hundred people disappeared, leaving no trace behind " (see Aylmer Maude's note).   The authorities
intervened, and discovered bodies mutilated, whilst
some had evidently been buried alive.

In 1839 the order came for the whole sect,
then at the Milky Waters, to be transported to
the Caucasus, save such as joined the Orthodox
Church.

The order was given by proclamation of the
Governor-general in these terms:

"In the name of your religion, and by the
command of your pretended teachers, you put
men to death, treating them cruelly . . . Conceal-
ing crimes committed by your brethren, everywhere opposing disobedience and contempt to the
Government.   These things, contrary to all the
laws of God and man, many of your brethren
knew, and, instead of giving information of them
to the Government, they endeavoured to conceal
them.   Many are still in custody for their conduct,
awaiting the just punishment of their misdeeds."

In 1841 eight hundred were transported,
including Ilarion Kalmikov and his family.   In
1842 eight hundred more were transported, and
in 1843 a further nine hundred.   In all, more
than four thousand were sent to the South-East.

"Ilarion Kalmikov died soon after the migration.   It is said that after Kapoustin's death, the
Doukhobors were in such a hurry to raise up

l

seed to inherit his divinity, that they supplied
Ilarion, when he was scarcely sixteen, with a
succession of six young women by whom he might
have offspring. He left two young sons, on one
of whom, at the age of thirty, the Doukhobors
hoped the soul of Jesus would descend. Meanwhile, after the death of Ilarion, an Elder called
Lyonuskha directed affairs for a time. He also
got into trouble with the authorities, and was
banished to Siberia."

One of Ilarion's sons, Peter, became leader,
and the sect flourished under his rule. He died
in 1864, whilst still a young man. He nominated
his wife as leader. "I leave you to my cuckoo
here; she will take my place, but after her the
Holy Spirit will abide with you no more."

During the "reign" of the latter the sect
spread to Tiflis, Kars, and Elizabetpol, and
numbered about 21,000 in the Caucasus.

Loukeriya died in 1886, and the sect were
apparently left without a leader. The prophecy
of Peter seemed to be likely of fulfilment

Under Loukeriya's leadership the Elders had
taken a large share of the management of the
colonies into their hands, and had been the official
channels of intercourse with the Imperial and civic
authorities. They were prosperous, had a larger
vision than the men who came from the Milky
Waters, and had discovered that their salvation
no longer depended on keeping the Doukhobors

20

l

entirely secluded from other men and communities.

They looked upon themselves as the "Chosen Ones," a race superior to all others—"God's Elect."

Their property was of considerable value, and as Loukeriya had no direct descendant, it seemed that there was little likelihood of a successor to Kalmikov's authority appearing; when, to the surprise of all concerned, a claimant appeared in the person of Peter Verigin

Aylmer Maude quotes from the "Confidential Report" from Prince Shervashidze, dated October 7, 1895.

"Under the circumstances described, the said Verigin, quite a young Doukhobor, literate, unprincipled, and unusually handsome, had, during the last years of Loukeriya Kalmikov's life, been constantly in attendance upon her; and by his turbulent character, arrogance, and efforts to raise himself above others, had provoked against himself the relations and *entourage* of Loukeriya, as well as the influential members of the village of Goreloe, where the Orphans' Home was situated, and where the head of the sect dwelt. In other words, Peter Verigin provoked against himself the most influential members of the sect. But, in the villages at a distance, amid the ignorant mass of the Doukhobors, educated in the absurd traditional belief in the supernatural power of the Kalmikovs, rumours began to circulate, even during Loukeriya's

life, which gave the managers of the Orphans'
Home cause for uneasiness, and which were to
the effect that this well-built, handsome young
man was of no common origin, but was the son
of the late Peter Kalmikov, the fruit of a visit he
paid, not long before his death, to Verigin's family,
and that this was the explanation of his peculiar
nearness to Loukeriya, who kept him in attendance, not as a courtier, but as an heir, preparing
him by frequent conversations and directions for
the exalted position due to his race, to the joy
and happiness of all true believing Doukhobors,
who, as a result of their education and the
traditions of their sect, could not conceive of the
possibility of doing without having a God-man
at the head of the sect; and who, therefore,
accepted with credulity a rumour which flattered
their imagination. As a result of this, the conviction of the exalted, divine destiny of Peter
Verigin had become so confirmed in the hearts
of the sectarians towards the end of 1896 that,
soon after the death of Loukeriya, it was quite
possible for him to advance his pretensions.

"Meeting with strong opposition from the influential men of the sect, who knew him well, and
with the object of breaking down their resistance
and definitely dispelling doubts that might arise
as to the justice of his cause, Verigin set out for
his native village. Here, in solemn gathering,
before all the people, his mother submissively

L

announced that her son Peter was begotten, not by her husband, but by Peter Kalmikov, who, to the great joy of all her family, had honoured her by his holy attentions at the time of his last visit to the village; and that this great secret was well known to Loukeriya, who had only awaited Peter's coming of age in order, during her own lifetime, to hand over to him the inheritance of his ancestors. After these words, both she and her husband fell at Peter's feet, and when they had done so, all the people imitated them. Next followed the administration of the oath of allegiance to Verigin, and the signing of the attestations of allegiance. In this way the new leader's right of succession and connection with the holy race were established, so that it was unnecessary for him to prove his Divine origin by miracles, his title being acknowledged on the strength of his birth."

Afterwards about seven-tenths of the Doukhobors signed attestation papers, and, with invincible faith in the infallibility of their leader, blindly submitted their fate into his hands. The sect, after a period of turmoil and violent altercation, split in twain, and the minority appealed to the law for a decision concerning the leadership and control of the property. The judges decided in favour of Peter's rival, the brother of Loukeriya, Michael Goubanov. The contention was so severe and bitter between the two parties that they refused to acknowledge one another, and even families were broken up, taking sides upon the question of leadership.

In 1887 Verigin was banished to the province of Archangel, in the far North, for five years, and at the end of that time, instead of being released, he was sent to Siberia. Whilst in exile he read largely in Tolstoi's works and imbibed much of his teaching, with the result that, owing to his frequent correspondence with his followers, he modified their doctrines considerably, and even induced them to change their name to that of "The Christian Community of Universal Brotherhood." The strife and contention between the two factions was so bitter and severe, and the fanaticism of Verigin's followers was of such a nature, that at last the Government interfered in a most brutal way (letting loose the Cossacks upon them), and Christian Europe was horror-stricken, funds were raised in England and America, and for the third time in their history the Doukhobors had perforce to find a new home. They were settled in Canada, largely by the help and sagacity of Mr. Maude, the well-known translator of Tolstoi, and in 1902, Peter Verigin, being freed from exile in Siberia, joined them in their new home, and is there their leader and guide.

Some thousands of them are still in Russia, but the troublous times through which they have passed, the disillusionment they have gone through in respect to their God-man, have considerably modi-

L

fied their doctrine of the incarnate Christ, and they are rapidly becoming more akin to other sectarians, who have been compelled to live with them "by administrative order."

With the story of the Doukhobors before us the question naturally arises, "What did they believe?" and "How did they act?"

With reference to their conduct the testimony varies considerably. In some cases the writers are violently prejudiced against the sect on religious grounds, whilst in others, humanitarianism has led the writers, moved to compassion for a severely persecuted people, to gloss over many of their faults—faults inherent in their system.

Novitski says of them, although he is opposed to their belief and religious practices, that·

"To the credit of the Doukhobors, one must say that they are sober, laborious, and frugal; that in their houses and clothing they are careful to be clean and tidy; that they are attentive to their agriculture and cattle breeding, occupations which have been and still are their chief employment."

He refers to their superstitions, to their quarrels amongst one another, and to their quick anger. "The distinguishing trait in their character is obstinacy in their doctrine, insubordination to the authorities, insults and slanders towards those who differ from them. The dissensions and agitations whereby they formerly disturbed the

l

public order have ceased, but the sect itself has seethed and surged with many passions."

Novitski was of the opinion that, taken as a community, there was, compared with other Russians in the same stage of development, less crime, vice, poverty, luxury, and superstition; that although there was a gulf fixed between their faith and practice, it was no wider or deeper than that amongst their neighbours Professor Milyoukov says of them:

"The high moral tone which these sectarians exhibit in their family life and social intercourse, by the strict observance of their pledged word, by the rigid keeping of their obligations toward their fellow-men, by their readiness to help and sympathise both with outsiders and with their brethren in the faith, they present exactly the opposite to the average Russian type. Theirs is a higher social type—the type of the Russian of the future."

That at times they have committed excesses and done strange things under the stress of great religious excitement, cannot be denied, but on the whole they have been a law-abiding, quiet, prosperous people, and like the vast majority of sectarians in Russia, their homes and villages present a marked contrast to the squalid and ofttimes filthy *izbas* of the Orthodox.

Aylmer Maude says of them:

"With all their limitations and deficiencies, with their history for nearly a century before us,

l

one may fairly say of the Doukhobors that, without any Government founded on force, they have managed their affairs better than their neighbours have done: with no army or police, they have suffered little from crimes of violence; and without priests or ministers, they have had more practical religion, and more intelligible guidance for their spiritual life. . . . Without political economists, wealth among them has been better distributed, and they have suffered far less from extremes of wealth and poverty. Without lawyers or written laws, they have settled their disputes (save in the case of the great dispute concerning the leadership of Peter Verigin). Without books, they have educated their children to be industrious, useful, peaceable, and God-fearing men and women, have instructed them in the tenets of their religion, and taught them to produce food, clothing, and shelter needed for themselves and for others."

It is now more than fourteen years since more than seven thousand of the sect settled in the Great North-West of Canada, and impartial observers report that they are clean, industrious, honest, and frugal; that there is every prospect of their becoming good citizens and valuable colonists.

THE DOUKHOBOR BELIEF AND DOCTRINE. NOVITSKI, in his book on the Doukhobors, compares their doctrines with the

l

(1) Gnostics, in their opinion of the Holy Spirit;

(2) Manicheans, in their belief in an inward light, in their opinion of Jesus Christ, and in their belief in the pre-existence, fall, and future state of man's soul.

(3) Paulicians, in many matters, and especially in their rejection of bishops, priests, and deacons, and, in general, of the authority of a visible Church.

(4) Anabaptists, in their Theocratic aspirations and their dislike of mundane governments; also in their repudiation of infant baptism.

(5) Early Quakers, especially in their belief in the Christ within, and their non-resistant principles.

THE CREED.

(1) There is one God. The Holy Trinity is a being beyond comprehension; the Father is light, the Son life, and the Holy Spirit is peace; it is affirmed in man, the Father by memory, the Son by reason, the Holy Spirit by will; the One God in Trinity.

(2) Our souls existed and fell before the creation of the material universe; they are sent here as to a prison—as a punishment, and for their reformation. The sin of Adam is like the rest of the Bible stories, figurative. His sin does not pass to his descendants, but each man has sinned for himself.

l

(3) The Divinity of Jesus Christ, our Saviour, as shown in the Old Testament, was nothing but wisdom revealed in nature; but in the New Testament He was the spirit of piety, purity, etc., incarnate. He is born, preaches, suffers, dies, and rises again spiritually in the heart of each believer.

Another view of Jesus Christ is: He is the Son of God, but in the same sense in which we also are sons of God. Our elders know even more than Christ did; go and hear them. Of miracles they said, We believe that He performed miracles; we ourselves were dead in sin, blind and deaf, and He has raised us up, pardoned our sins, and given us His commandment; but of bodily miracles we know nothing.

(4) For our salvation it is not essential to have external knowledge of Jesus Christ; for there is the inward word which reveals Him in the depths of our souls. It existed in all ages, and enlightens all who are ready to receive it, whether they be nominally Christians or not.

(5) Those enlightened by the Spirit of God will after death rise again—what will become of other people is uncertain. It is the soul and not the body that will rise—a new heavenly body. Desires reaching man through his senses of hearing, seeing, smelling, tasting, or touching, including sexual desire, sow the seeds of future torment. The craving for honours now torments the ambitious man, and the craving for drink, the

drunkard, but much more will those who have sown the seeds of such desires be tormented in the future life, when they will not be able to gratify the passions, which will nevertheless grow stronger and stronger.

The fire of abuse and contempt will burn and torment those who have striven for honours; the fire of aversion, shame, and loathing will be the consequence of impure love; and the flames of fury, enmity, revenge, rancour, and implacability will punish anger.

If this is the result of sowing evil passions in this life, on the other hand, the result of sowing good seed will be continued growth towards perfection till the purified souls become like God Himself.

(6) Our bodies are cages restraining and confining our souls, and as the passions sow the seeds of evil, we should deny our lower selves, and forego what pleases our senses, and thus weaken their power over our souls. "If the desire for fame is condemned among them, yet more is luxury in food or dress, because luxury, indulging the flesh, strengthens it to stifle the inward light coming from above."

(7) Inasmuch as all men are equal, and the children of God do good willingly, without coercion, they do not require any government or authority over them. Government, if needed at all, is needed only for the wicked.

l

To go to war, to carry arms, and to take oaths, is forbidden. "Regarding war as a forbidden thing, they say they have set themselves a rule not to carry arms."

(8) The Church is a society selected by God Himself. It is invisible and scattered over the whole world; it is not marked externally by any common creed. Not Christians only, but Jews, Mohammedans, and others may be members of it, if only they hearken to the inward word; and therefore—

(9) The Holy Scriptures, or the outer word, are not essential for the sons of God. It is, however, of use to them because in the Scriptures, as in nature and in ourselves, they read the decrees and the acts of the Lord. But the Scriptures must be understood symbolically to represent things that are inward and spiritual. It must all be understood to relate in a mystical manner to the Christ within.

(10) The Christ within is the only True Hierarch and Priest. Therefore, no external priest is necessary. In whomever Christ lives, he is Christ's heir, and is himself a priest unto himself. The priests of temples made with hands are appointed externally, and can perform only what is external: they are not what they are usually esteemed to be. The sons of God should worship God in Spirit and in Truth, and, therefore, need no external worship of God. The external sacra-

ments have no efficacy; they should be understood in a spiritual sense. To baptise a child with
water is unbecoming for a Christian; an adult
baptises himself with the word of truth, and is
then baptised, indeed, by the true priest, Christ,
with spirit and with fire.

True Confession is heartfelt contrition before
God, though we may also confess our sins to
one another when occasion presents itself.

The external sacraments of the Church are
offensive to God, for Christ desires not signs but
realities; the real communion comes by the word,
by thought, and by faith.

Marriage should be accomplished without any
ceremonies; it needs only the will of those who
have come of age and who are united in love
to one another, the consent of the parents, and
an inward oath and vow before all-seeing God
in the souls of those who are marrying, that they
will to the end of their days remain faithful and
inseparable. An external marriage ceremony, apart
from the inward marriage, has no meaning, it
has at most this effect, that, being performed
before witnesses, it maintains the bond between
the spouses by the fear of shame should
they break the promise of fidelity they have
given.

The priesthood is not an office reserved
specially for selected people. Each real Christian,
enlightened by the word, may and should pray

L

to God for himself, and should spread the truth that has been entrusted to him.

What am I then ? A temple to the Lord most high.
The Altar and the Priest, the Sacrifice am I.
Our Hearts the Altars are; ours Wills the Offering,
Our Souls they are the Priests, our Sacrifice to bring

The forms of worship of all the external Churches in the world, their various institutions, all the ranks and orders of their servants, their costumes and movements, were invented after the time of the Apostles—those men of Holy Wisdom —and are in themselves naught but dead signs, mere figures and letters, externally representing that sacred, invisible, living, and wise power of God, which (like the sun's rays) enlightens and pervades the souls of the elect, and lives and acts in them, purifying them, and uniting them to God. To pray in temples made with hands is contrary to the injunction of the Saviour: " When thou prayest, enter into thine inner chamber, and having shut the door, pray to thy Father which is in secret." Yet a son of God need not fear to enter any temples—Papal, Greek, Lutheran, Calvinist, or other: to him they are all indifferent.

Later the addition was made: All the ceremonies of the Churches, being useless, were much better left alone.

(11) Icons they do not respect or worship, but consider as idols. The saints may be re-

spected for their virtues, but should not be prayed to. Fasting should consist in fleeing from lusts and refraining from superfluities. The Decrees of the Churches and the Councils should not be accepted

(12) The Church has no right to judge or to sentence any one, for it cannot know all man's inward, secret motives.

L

THE MOLOKANS

BIBLIOGRAPHY.

MILYOUKOV . . . . . . *The Crisis in Russia.*

TSAKNI . . . . *La Russie Sectaire.*

LATIMER . . . . *Under Three Tsars.*

WALLACE . . . . *Russia.*

L

L

THE MOLOKANS

THE "Molokans," or "Milk drinkers," are so called because, contrary to the practice of the "Orthodox," they drink milk on the "holy" or "fast" days of the Russian Church.

In a statement of their faith, printed at Geneva, and written by members of the sect exiled from home, they attribute their origin to the reign of Ivan the Terrible. Ivan employed at Court an "English" physician; the common people, in their ignorance, regarded him as Antichrist, and closed their gates and doors against him. However, at the Court of Ivan he made the acquaintance of a boyar (a wealthy landed proprietor) whose estates were in the province of Tambov

Physician and boyar had much conversation about the Bible, which at that time, in Russia, the people were not allowed to possess. This landowner had a favourite servant, named Matthew Semenof, who understood Bible truths more readily than his master, and soon began to neglect the services of the Russian Church and to abandon the worship of Icons.

Semenof obtained a copy of the Sclavonic Bible, and commenced teaching those about him

l

the truth concerning the pure worship of God, of God who would be worshipped in spirit and in truth.

But in those days it was dangerous to say anything against the Church services, and finally Semenof was arrested, tried, and sentenced to death. He was martyred by being broken upon the wheel. Some of his disciples, serfs of his master, returning home from Moscow with the Bible, secretly spread the doctrine, as they called it, "of the true and pure worship of God." These too were at last discovered, tried, flogged, imprisoned, and ultimately sent to convict labour for life. Despite all the efforts of the priests, the teaching spread secretly amongst the peasants of Tambov, and reached even to the neighbouring Province of Saratov.

Later, the movement received a great impetus from the influence of Tveritinov, who was a doctor in Moscow during the reign of Peter the Great. He had been brought into touch with German Calvinists and Protestants, of whom there were very many in Russia at that time. They had settled mainly in Moscow, upon the invitation of Peter, who was intent upon introducing some of the arts, sciences, and industries of the West into his own country.

The effect of Peter's reforms, of the favour he showed to foreigners, of his unceremonious treatment of old traditions, made it possible, for a

L

while at least, to speak with considerable freedom on religious matters. Tveritinov's practice as a doctor brought him into touch with people of all classes, and he appears to have omitted no opportunity of denouncing the superstitions of the Church. While adopting the attitude of Bashkin and Kosoy towards Icons, prayers for the dead, transubstantiation, and Church Councils, he accepted the Divinity of Jesus, and took the Bible as the Rock on which to base his criticism of the Holy Orthodox Church.

Tveritinov's premier position was due, not to the originality of his views, but to the fact that he could state his views clearly and pithily, and he thus reached a wide audience. He carefully circulated manuscript booklets containing the Scripture texts upon which his followers based their indictment of the Holy Orthodox Church.

These books carried his teaching far afield amongst the peasants, and many of his aphorisms, as well as his favourite texts, are still habitually quoted among the Molokans.

God, he taught, should be worshipped in spirit; an Icon is only a board, which burns if thrown into the fire. He questioned the sanctity of many of the saints, and especially of St. Nicolas the Wonder Worker (the favourite saint in Russia). Nicolas, he declared, was only an ordinary peasant, whom people took to worshipping when they had forgotten God. He called in question the canonisa-

l

tion of saints, on the ground that no one has conversed with God, or can know saint from sinner until the Day of Judgment of the dead; and as to prayers for them, he quoted Paul, "each shall receive his own reward according to his own labour"; and added that priests, for their own profit, invented prayers for the dead He held that what is written in the Bible should be believed, but that there is no need to believe what the Church has added thereto.   Monasticism he called a senile contrivance.

Ultimately he was brought to account.   The last Council of the Russian Church was held in 1714, and by it he was anathematised, and escaped by abjuring his heresies.

His cousin, Thomas Ivanof, a barber, was confined in the Tchoudof Monastery.   There he chopped to pieces a sculptural figure of Alexis (Metropolitan of Kiev and All Russia, 1348-78), in consequence of which conduct he was burnt to death.

The next figure of importance in the Molokan movement was Grigoriev Skovoroda (1750-1790). He travelled the country after the fashion of the Russian pilgrims, clad only in rags.   Being a man of some education, he had with him copies of the Scriptures in the original tongues as well as in the Sclavonic.   He went from village to village, playing upon his flute, talking to the people concerning the things of God, expounding to them the Scriptures, and teaching them to sing simple hymns to simple tunes of his own composing. He thus led many to accept the evangelical doctrine of the sect.

These men represented the Russian School, which bases itself on the Bible: man is free to think, provided he thinks what is in the Bible, and does not think that which runs counter to the Bible.

Under Catherine the Second, a peasant tailor, named Uklein, resident in the province of Tambov, was brought into touch with the itinerant evangelist, Skovoroda. He seceded fom the Doukhobors because he could not hold their doctrine that God dwells in the human soul, that the individual is a continual reincarnation of Christ, and that consequently the chief source of religious truth was to be found in internal enlightenment. To Uklein, religious truth was to be found only in the Scriptures. With this doctrine he soon made many converts, and within a few months, more than seventy of them were arrested and imprisoned at Tambov, handed over to the ecclesiastical courts, and in the event of their remaining obdurate they were to be tried by the civil judges.

Most of them stood by their faith and were imprisoned, but on their release they continued their propaganda. At the time of his death, Uklein had more than five thousand followers in Tambov alone.

Persecution, bitter and severe, has been brought to bear upon them, and by the exile system they have been scattered all over the Empire, but to-day they still number about one hundred and twenty thousand.

The severe trials through which they were called upon to pass aroused the sympathies of the Society of Friends in England, and in the year 1819 William Allen and Stephen Grellet were sent as "messengers" from the "Committee of Sufferings" to visit the Molokans and seek the help of the Tsar to modify their tribulations at the hands of the priests and civil authorities.

The two Friends sent the following report to His Imperial Majesty the Tsar:

" The Molokans believe in the Divine authority of the Holy Scriptures, in the deity of our Lord and Saviour, and in the influence of the Holy Spirit, as fully as any Christians whom we ever met with. They believe it their duty to abstain from all ceremonies, and think that the only acceptable worship is that performed 'in spirit and in truth.' They collect their families two or three times a day to hear the Scriptures read, and abstain from secular employment on the first day of the week, called Sunday, considering it their duty to appropriate this day to religious exercises. Their marriages are performed with solemnity in their public meetings, and the parties promise to be faithful to each other

during life. They believe that the only true
baptism is that of Christ with the Spirit,
and that the water baptism of John is not now
necessary; and they consider that the true communion is altogether of a spiritual nature, and
make use of no outward ceremony. In their meetings for worship they sing Psalms, and several
of those who are esteemed by the rest as more
pious, read to the others in turn. They have no
appointed preachers, but anyone who feels himself
properly qualified, through the power of the Divine
Influence upon the mind, may expound and speak
to edification; they, however, consider that it
should never be done for hire, or from any worldly
motive.

"They believe that a true Christian can never
harbour revenge, and they think it their duty
rather to suffer wrong than to seek to avenge it;
if any differences arise, they are settled amongst
themselves, and not brought to the tribunals

"Some among them are considered as elders,
and though it does not appear that they are
regularly appointed, yet those who are most
eminent for their piety are regarded as such,
and it is their duty, when any of the fraternity
are ill, to visit them, and if able to do so, to offer
them advice, or afford them comfort. . . . No
particular ceremony is observed at their burial,
but they sing a psalm.

"If the moral conduct of anyone does not

L

correspond with his profession, he is tenderly exhorted, and much labour is bestowed upon him; but if they judge that he cannot be reclaimed, he is dismissed from the Society. With respect to the poor among them, they deem it Christian duty to take care of and support each other. It appears that they have no instance among them of children acting irreverently towards their parents, and they are very careful to have them instructed in reading and writing."

In the interesting *Memoirs of Stephen Grellet* an extended reference to the faith and practice of the Molokans is to be found. He writes

"Previous to our going to the meeting with the Spiritual Christians we prepared a list of the principal subjects respecting which we wished to inquire of them. They were very free to give us every information we asked for, and they did it in few words, accompanied, generally, with some Scripture quotations as their reasons for believing or acting as they did; these were so much to the purpose that one acquainted with Friends' writings might conclude that they had selected from them the most clear and appropriate passages to support their several testimonies. On all the cardinal points of the Christian religion, the fall of man, salvation through Christ by faith, the meritorious death of Christ, His resurrection, ascension, etc., their views are very clear; also respecting the influence of the Holy Spirit, wor-

ship, ministry, baptism, the supper, oaths, etc,
etc., we might suppose that they were thoroughly
acquainted with our Society, but they had never
heard of us, nor of any people that profess as we
do.   Respecting war, however, their views are
not entirely clear, and yet many among us may
learn from them.   They said, " War is a subject
that we have not yet been able fully to understand,
so as to reconcile Scripture with Scripture; we
are commanded to obey our rulers, magistrates,
etc., for conscience sake, and again, we are
enjoined to love our enemies, not to avenge ourselves; to render good for evil; therefore we cannot see fully how we can refuse obedience to
the laws that require our young people to join
the army; but in all matters respecting ourselves,
we endeavour to act faithfully as the Gospel requires.   We have never any lawsuits; for if any-
body smites us on the one cheek, we turn to him
the other; if he takes away any part of our
property, we bear it patiently; we give to him
that asketh, and lend to him that borrows, not
asking it back again; and in all these things the
Lord blesses us.   The Lord is very good to our
young men, for though several of them have been
taken to the army, not one of them has actually
borne arms; for, our principles being known, they
have very soon been placed in offices of trust,
such as attending to the provisions of the army,
or something of that sort.   Their ministers are

L

acknowledged in much the same way as ours, and, like us, that their only and best reward is the dear Saviour's approval; therefore, they receive no kind of salary. They use the Slavonian Bible; few of them, however, can read, but those who can, read to the others, and these, from memory, teach the children, so that their young people are very ready in quoting the Scriptures correctly. They pointed out to us the great distinction there is between them and the Doukhobors. The latter deny the divinity of Our Lord Jesus Christ, the offering up of Himself a sacrifice for sin on Calvary, and salvation by faith in Him."

Since the days of Stephen Grellet, however, there have been marked changes in the Molokans. Outside influences have exercised sway over them, and the rise of the Evangelical Baptists has helped them considerably. The ability to read is, in contradistinction to the Russian people, so widely spread amongst them that hardly a member lacks it. They are undoubtedly better housed, better clad, more punctual in the payment of their taxes, more prosperous than their neighbours. They impress one as a quiet, decent, sober people. Again and again in conversation with them I have tried to get them to speak freely about their religious beliefs, but long years of persecution on the part of the Government and much suffering at the hands of local officials and priests, have made them reticent in the presence of a stranger.

Quite accidentally I discovered their repugnance to pork. My friend, Vassily Stepanov, had accepted an invitation to have a meal with me, and amongst the viands on the table were some ham sandwiches. I offered the dish to him, and he declined, with the information that as a Molokan he did not eat pork. Their knowledge of Scripture leaves little to be desired. I have met men and women who have practically memorised the four Gospels, and numbers who have committed to memory the greater part of the Epistles. Their love for the Word of God is deep and true.

As a community they are very loosely organised, and have practically no Church polity. Two or three meet together and claim the blessing of the presence of Christ. Consequently they have little or no means of developing their fundamental principles and of forming their vague religious beliefs into a clearly defined and logical system. With many, their theology is in a more or less fluid state. Their principles allow great latitude for individual and local differences of opinion. Thus many "false prophets" have arisen amongst them.

In 1835, a peasant from Melitopol, named Bêlozborov, announced, amidst great excitement, that the Second Advent was at hand. He declared himself to be Elijah, and that on a given day he would ascend into heaven in a chariot of fire.

L

The - day came; crowds gathered around the
" prophet "; all was expectancy; but the chariots
delayed, and the impostor was handed over to
the police for punishment.

The year following, a peasant in Tambov
Province persuaded many to dress themselves in
their best clothes and journey with him to the
Caucasus, where, upon a given day, the Millennium
was to be inaugurated.

As recently as 1904 a man named Grigorieff,
travelling with an American passport, urged community of goods, free love, abolition of personal
and private property, and then proclaimed himself to be the Messiah. He had no real religious
enthusiasm, and from what we can learn concerning him, his teaching, and his methods, he was
a strange blend of the visionary, prophet, social
reformer, and cunning impostor. He ultimately
landed in gaol, and his dupes returned to
their previous mode of life, sadder, if wiser,
men.

But these movements, common to all religious bodies in Russia, are perhaps fewer amongst
the Molokans and other evangelical sects than
with the Orthodox.

Generally speaking, the Molokans take as
their model the early Apostolic Church, as depicted
in the New Testament, and uncompromisingly reject all later authorities. Their services are very
simple. A few meet together, sometimes con-

trary to the decrees of the local police, and spend two or three hours in psalm-singing, Scripture-reading, prayer, and conversation.

If one of the brethren has a doctrinal difficulty he will state it to the assembly, and there will be a great searching of Scripture in an attempt to solve the same with texts.

Tsakni, in *La Russie Sectaire*, writes concerning them:

"The Molokans, in private as in public life, avoid all formalities and ceremonies. They have no Churches; a house, an open yard, or, better still, a field, serves the believer. When the leader appears they all bow to him; he takes his place, and begins to read aloud. After the reading, hymns are sung, whereupon follows discussion upon the subject read. Every Molokan enjoys complete freedom with regard to religious ceremonies. No general dogma of form or ceremony exists, so that, for instance, the celebration of a marriage with them is limited to the civil formality, a mutual agreement, which, with the consent of both parties, can be rendered void, for which the wish of any one of the parties is sufficient. The initiative in matrimonial affairs is left to the young people. 'When the parents want to compel their children to marry against their will, they commit an act against the Will of God.' A marriage can only take place before the whole of the community, who decide whether the marriage candidates are

l

in a position to support a family in a spiritual as well as in a material sense, and investigate whether the proposed marriage is made of their own free will and without compulsion from any side whatever."

There is severe moral supervision. Drunkenness means exclusion from the Society for a longer or shorter period. Tobacco-smoking, or the use of tobacco in any form, is an offence against the community. If one should be in monetary difficulties the others will render him mutual assistance. As a general rule they are more prosperous than their Orthodox neighbours, for they are intelligent and alert, industrious and thrifty, and very conscientious in business and trade.

In common with all the Russian sects, they have had their full meed of persecution and suffering. From the earliest days the Government has sought to suppress them, but every attempt has been in vain. Their leaders have been banished to Siberia and the Caucasus, but far from diminishing their zeal, it has but made them cling closer to their faith and doctrine. Wherever they have been driven to, their patience, humility, industry, modest habits, and simplicity of life have but increased their numbers.

Martyrdom has had as little effect upon them as the suppression of their meetings.

In 1805, Tsar Alexander I. gave to the sect the right "to perform their worship in whatever

ι

way their conscience and their interpretation of the Word of God directed."

In 1905 the sect held a centenary congress in commemoration of the coming of religious liberty—a congress with representatives from fifteen Russian provinces, besides those who came from Sweden, Germany, Finland, and the United States.

At present, Zachary Feodor Zacharov is the President of the Committee of Molokans, or Evangelical Christians, as they prefer to be called, and, as a member of the State's Duma, he is able to place their position before the Parliament of the Empire and to seek for them a fuller measure of religious freedom.

A description of the Molokans, published in 1874, and quoted by R S. Latimer in *Under Three Tsars*:

" There may be some two millions of Molokans at the present day in Russia. They live in the provinces of Kaluga, Samara, Saratov, Astrakhan, Tauria, and the Caucasus. To the last-named two provinces, as well as to Siberia, they were banished in the reign of the Emperor Nicholas.

" This sect is not only free from all adoration of images, but rejects all visible means of grace, so that even baptism and the Lord's Supper are only used spiritually by them. They also abstain from pork. They have a more intimate

L 22

acquaintance with the Word of God than may be found in almost any Protestant Church. Every one of them knows many of the most beautiful psalms, and the most important chapters from the New Testament and prophets, by heart. Their service principally consists in reading the Word of God, with a few explanations. Their hymn-book, too, is the Bible. To a monotonous tune they sing for hours a chapter, then pray a chapter kneeling, then again sing a chapter. Thus they usually sing nine chapters standing, and pray nine chapters kneeling, all in chorus and by memory.

"At the close, they have the holy kiss. Thus, every one bows down before the other three times, and kisses twice, men and women promiscuously. This is hard labour, and they become very warm with the exertion. I have seen this myself in Odessa; but in some parts they have some variation to this service, and less kissing. Our rhythmical singing and extempore praying they call 'adding to, and taking from, the Word of God.'"

l

BAPTISTS AND STUNDISTS

BIBLIOGRAPHY.

LEHMANN . . . *Geschichte der deutschen Baptisten.*

STEPNIAK . . . *King Stork and King Log.*

PRELOOKER . . *Russian Flashlights.*

LATIMER . . . *Under Three Tsars.*

   ,, . . . *With Christ in Russia.*

   ,, . . . *Life of Dr. Baedeker.*

GREGORIEV . . *Friends of Russian Freedom. May, 1892.*

SAVARIEF . . . *Free Russia.*

MILYOUKOV . . *The Crisis in Russia.*

WALLACE . . . *Russia.*

BYFORD . . . *Peasants and Prophets.*

.

ι

THE CURSED STUNDIST

Roar, ye Church thunders,
Arise, ye cursers of the Holy Councils,
Strike with eternal anathema
The outcast Stundist's progeny.

The Stundist destroys the Dogmas,
The Stundist rejects tradition,
The Stundist scoffs at the ceremonies,
He is an Apostate—the cursed Stundist.

The Lord has bestowed His honours
Upon our Holy Russian Church,
But this, our dear Mother,
Is insulted by the cursed Stundist.

Like stars in the firmament of heaven
So shine in our native land
God's Holy Temples everywhere,
Shunned only by the cursed Stundist.

Prayers go up in the Temples,
Church hymns are resounding
And Holy Sacraments performed,
All blamed by the cursed Stundist.

All our great saints,
The intercessors of the Russian land,
And all our spiritual leaders,
Are dishonoured by the cursed Stundist.

Whether we offer thanksgiving in the fields,
Or bless the sources of the water,
Or kiss the Cross of our Lord,
We are mocked by the cursed Stundist.

He is stern and gloomy, like a demon,
Shunning the sight of the faithful Orthodox,
He hides in dark haunts,
This enemy of God, the cursed Stundist.

But as soon as the simple minded
Looks into the den of this crafty beast,
By blasphemy, insinuation or flattery,
Entraps him, the cursed Stundist.

ARCHBISHOP AMBROSIUS,
TRANSLATED BY JAAKOFF PRELOOKER IN
Russian Flashlights.

l

BAPTISTS AND STUNDISTS

THE phenomenal rise, growth, and influence of the Baptists in Russia may be largely attributed to three great events in Russian religious development:

First: The settlement of German and Dutch Mennonites in Russia. Persecuted for their religious views in the sixteenth century, a large number of them accepted an invitation to settle in West Prussia, where they helped to drain and cultivate the extensive marshes between Dantzic, Elbing, and Marienburg. Here, in course of time, they forgot their native language, and became identified with the Prussians. An attempt was made by the Prussian Government to impose military service upon them, contrary to their religious views and terms of settlement in the country, with the result that they once more left their homes and accepted an invitation from Catherine II. (1789) to settle in south-eastern Russia. Here they founded flourishing communities, mainly agricultural, and lived in comparative peace.

Their immigration into Russia was upon the

L

distinct understanding that they and their sons should be exempted from military service, which compact has been observed by the Russian Government, at least, until very recent years. At present, as Mennonites, they number, male and female, about 50,000 souls, living in 160 colonies or settlements, and between them possess about 800,000 acres of land. Travelling through their villages, a sharp contrast is noticed between their orderliness, cleanliness, and general air of prosperity, and the reverse of these things in the purely Russian villages.

In the middle of the nineteenth century a company of German Baptists from the Fatherland visited these Mennonite Communities in the South of Russia, and a revival of religion began amongst them which speedily spread to their Russian employees and neighbours. The missionary zeal of J. G. Oncken, of Hamburg, led him to visit the brethren, and amongst his many arduous labours he not only encouraged them, counselled them in matters of organisation, but joyfully baptised converts upon profession of faith.

Although the modern Baptist movement sprang from the Mennonites, the Baptists from amongst the latter remain in what is called the Russo-German Union, and their services are conducted in the German language. As non-Russians they enjoy certain political and religious privileges denied to those of pure Russian nationality.

Secondly: This religious revival synchronised with the abolition of serfdom. The peasants were no longer as slaves under a master, but were free, holding their land on the communal system, having to meet periodically in the *mir* to discuss matters concerning the welfare of the local community and the distribution of land. For the first time in their lives they had to think for themselves in matters appertaining to their civic welfare, and from the discussion of political rights to religious duties was but a short remove.

Politically, a wider horizon opened before the one-time serf, and his new outlook upon life affected his old-time relationship to the Orthodox Church.

Thirdly: Whilst the religious revival was in full swing amongst the Mennonites, and the serfs were beginning to realise their newly-found independence, the British and Foreign Bible Society received permission to circulate the Scriptures broadcast throughout the Empire.

The Russian peasant, being of an essentially religious nature, greedily received the Word of God from the hands of the colporteurs, and frequently the meeting of the village *mir* resolved itself into an informal Bible-class. Thus the ground was prepared in a threefold manner for a widely-spread acceptance of the new evangelical doctrine.

Meanwhile, in St. Petersburg, an unexpected development was taking place. During the visit of J. G. Oncken to the capital, in 1864, we learn

l

from his diary, and the Geschichte-der-deutschen Baptisten, von J. Lehmann, that eight persons had expressed their desire to be baptised upon profession of faith in Christ. During his five weeks' stay Oncken became fully acquainted with them, and on December 3, between twelve and one o'clock in the night, he administered the ordinance. As far as one can trace the Baptist history in Russia, this was the first administration of the ordinance of believer's baptism in the capital city of Russia.

Lord Radstock, during the Crimean war, where he served with the besieging forces, had come into touch with some members of the Russian nobility, and in 1874-7 he held a series of evangelistic services, in the first instance in the American Church, and afterwards in the home of the Princess Lieven, close to the Winter Palace.

His influence was uncompromisingly evangelical, and many well-known Russian nobles felt the stirring of a new religious life within them. Foremost amongst these were the Prince and Princess Lieven, Count Korff, Count Brobinsky, and Colonel Paschoff, of the Imperial Guards (who died in Paris, an exile from his home, in 1902).

Colonel Paschoff opened his home to all and sundry; he resigned his colonelcy in the Guards, distributed his riches amongst the poor, established charitable institutions, and not only preached the Gospel, but translated it into everyday life. Nobles and crossing-sweepers, ladies and laundresses,

.   l

officers and soldiers, colonels and cabmen pressed into his home to hear the glad new tidings. Substantially, at the beginning it was a revival of religion from the dead ritual and ceremony of the Orthodox Church, but opposition on the part of the higher clergy, and subsequent persecution on the part of the Government, speedily led the scattered and fugitive members to form a new community and a new sect. By some they were called Radstockites, and by others Pashchovists, but of recent years they have adopted the official title of Russian Evangelical Christians (Baptists). The central doctrine of the Evangelicals is "justification by faith," with the immersion of the believer as the outward and visible expression of that faith.

Under the leadership of Ivan Prokhanoff (one time student in Bristol Baptist College) they are coming into closer touch with the other Baptist bodies in Russia. They are already federated with the Baptist World Alliance, and the day is not far distant when they will be in organic union with all the Baptists in Russia. Owing to the persecuting policy of the Government, they have spread to Siberia, Transcaucasia, Kashgaria, and the Transcaspian provinces, whilst their propaganda has reached France, Switzerland, and Austria.

Reverting to the main stream of Baptists in the South, the first peasant converts from Orthodoxy were Ratushny, Lassotsky, and Rjabos-

chapa, the two former being ordinary farm workers,
and the latter a blacksmith, serf to the great landed
proprietor, Schibeks, of the village of Lubomika.
After their baptism by Abraham Unger, a German
Baptist in Alt Danzic, they commenced work
amongst their fellow-peasants.

Great success attended their labours, but the
Government stepped in   Ratushny was sent to
Siberia, Lassotsky to Transcaucasia, and Rjabos-
chapka to Erivan, near to Mount Ararat, later
he was allowed to proceed to Bulgaria, where
he continued his preaching and missionary propaganda.

The New Testáment, and this alone, constitutes
the religious handbook of the Baptists.   Theoretically they hold both the Old and New Testaments
to be of equal value, but in practice the latter
is their sole guide to life and faith.   They hold
the doctrine that everyone has the right to interpret the Scriptures according to his enlightenment
by the Holy Ghost.   They reject the authority of
Church, or Council, or commentator to interpret
the Scriptures for them.   Their love for the Word
of God is phenomenal, and I have frequently found
numbers of men and women who have memorised
the Gospels.

Persecutions bitter and severe broke out
against the members of the scattered Churches.
They were robbed of their Bibles and hymn-books,
were forbidden to assemble for worship at one

l

another's houses; their leaders were prohibited from leaving their own villages to carry the message to neighbouring districts; goods were confiscated; they were turned off their farms; scourging, imprisonment, and exile were resorted to by the State officials to suppress the movement; but the pioneers survived all these and similar reactionary measures, and they continually increased in numbers.

Stepniak, in *King Stork and King Log*, has a long chapter upon the Stundists (Baptists) and their persecutions. We quote fully from his work, as he is an unbiassed and independent witness.

" The new sectarianism evidently springs from the direct influence of the Gospel, and it is remarkable for its uniformity. It is a return to the simple creed of the early Christians, for which the Stundists are striving, so that one can say that this religious sect represents the type of the religious aspirations of modern reformers. The religious doctrine of the Stundists is much akin to that of the Baptists and Anabaptists of the time of the Reformation. They baptise only grown-up people, rebaptising those to whom this sacrament was administered in babyhood. Instead of the communion they have simply the ' breaking of bread,' accompanied with the singing of hymns. The wedding ceremony exists, but it is a very plain one.

" Both communion and baptism are viewed by

the Stundists, not as sacraments, but 'as rites performed in commemoration of Christ, and for a closer union with Him.' They consider the Icons as no better than pictures, and do not keep them in their houses. They recognise only the Lord's Prayer. At their meetings they sing hymns of their own composition, and psalms. As to prayers, they are left to the personal inspiration of the believers.

"As regards their moral code, suffice it to say that it is prohibited among them to ill-use even dumb creatures. An observer says that once he saw a girl of eight—a Stundist—who rushed into the house, saying, with an appearance of great distress, that she could not restrain her little brother, a boy of three, from throwing stones at a dog."

The Stundists, like all Ruthenians, or Southern Russians, hold land as private property, not in common, like the Great Russians. Among them there is no conscious leaning towards collective ownership of land. According to their tenets, all earthly goods are not given, but, so to say, *lent* by God to men, who will be held responsible before Him for the use they have made of their worldly possessions. To prove faithful debtors, men are bound to come to the assistance of their neighbours when they are in need, sickness, or affliction. It is well known that this doctrine is in no contradiction with their life, but on the contrary their lives are a confirmation and illustration of their doctrine.

One of their peculiarities is the perfect absence of national and religious intolerance. During the Anti-Jewish riots, they used all their influence to restrain the Orthodox from committing any outrage. There were no Anti-Jewish riots in the villages where the Stundists formed even one-third of the population. Rjasboschapka (see my *Peasants and Prophets*) delivered several sermons upon the subject. In one of them he said to his congregation: "The Jews have received from God a law for their guidance. When they transgressed it He punished them. Perhaps they are suffering now for their own sins. You have heard how they are beaten, ruined, plundered, murdered. But God preserve you, brothers and sisters, from participating, even in thought, in such deeds. The Jews are the eldest sons of God. He punishes them more severely than the others. Woe to the man who will take upon himself to be the instrument of God's wrath. God preserve you from wishing it, and still more from taking part in these violences."

With regard to politics, the views of the Baptists are easily formulated; they teach that one must obey the authorities in everything, save in matters pertaining to religion. At the close of every meeting they pray for the Tsar. A few years ago I accompanied a deputation of Baptist pastors to interview the Minister of the Interior in St. Petersburg. After the formal introductions were accomplished, the President of the Russian Baptist Union led in prayer, beseeching the blessing of Almighty God upon His Imperial Majesty the Tsar and his Ministers of State. On another occasion I went with a company to a high official of State, in reference to libellous statements made concerning the politics of the Baptists, and again, before the discussion commenced, there was perfectly free and natural prayer for the Tsar, the Empire, and the State officials. The Baptists are absolutely loyal to constituted authority. They are too good New Testament Christians to be otherwise.

The Autocracy are attempting Russification by means of the Orthodox Church and forcible conversions thereto, but the Baptists are accomplishing the same end by means of their propaganda. Turn where one will throughout the whole Empire, and each nationality has its Baptist Church and witness. Letts and Poles, Ests and Finns, Tatars and Tcherkesses, Gypsies and Jews, Great Russians and Little Russians, all are susceptible to the plain, simple preaching of the Gospel. The writer of the article on Russia in the *Encyclopædia Britannica* testifies that the Baptists are the only Christian body in the Empire winning converts amongst all the diverse races which go to the make-up of modern Russia.

The rapid growth of the Baptists during the Reign of Alexander II. aroused the animosity of the priests and higher clergy, and wherever possible, attempts were made to suppress them. The regular courts, when called upon to judge the "sectarians," frequently acquitted them, but there was a sinister influence at work which moved the authorities to arrest the leaders again and again, throw them into prison, and keep them there long, weary months, waiting for trial, imposing heavy and even ruinous fines upon them, and at last sending them in hundreds to Siberia and Transcaucasia, or, when leniently disposed, exiling them to Roumania, Bulgaria, and Turkey—in Europe. In the bitter persecutions of the eighties and nineties one sinister figure comes prominently into notice.

Pobiedonosteff, the Procurator of the Holy Synod, the confidential adviser of the Tsar, was a militant upholder of Orthodoxy and a violent hater of "sectarianism." To account for his violent antipathy to the Baptists we need to peep behind the scenes. Stepniak, in *King Stork and King Log*, deals at length with this phase of his character.

"It is known that in 1887 K. Pobiedonosteff was on the point of falling into disgrace. This was due to two circumstances. We will not dwell upon the first, as it is strictly private. Suffice it to say that, thanks to a court intrigue, the Tsar was shown an authentic letter from the Procurator, in which the latter boasted that he could make his master sign anything he wished. At the same time the Tsar was much incensed against Pobiedonostseff through his being worsted in polemics by the Evangelical Society."

The severe persecutions of the Lutherans in the Baltic provinces caused the Evangelical Society to write an address to the Russian Holy Synod. The Procurator replied, but so poorly that he exposed himself to a crushing rejoinder from the Evangelicals. It was rumoured at this time that K. Pobiedonostseff would be dismissed altogether. He got a two months' furlough instead, to compose at his leisure a reply to the Evangelical pamphlet. He made no reply, but he got out of the difficulty by resorting to a trick very often practised in Russian official circles. Everything is forgiven there, and condoned, for some zeal in the cause of Autocracy. Pobiedonostseff contrived to make a show of this zeal at the expense of the Stundists. With the assistance of a South Russian Bishop, Nicanor, he concocted against these inoffensive people the accusation of being traitors to the Russian Tsar and emissaries of Prince Bismarck and the German Lutherans. Such was the purport of the famous "Letter from Simferopol," published in the *Moscow Gazette*, his own organ, after the death of Katkoff.

The grounds for these sweeping accusations were as follows:

(1) This sect was founded by German Lutherans residing in Southern Russia.

(2) They had in their houses portraits of the German Emperor and of Prince Bismarck, instead of the Tsar.

(3) They shaved their beards in order to look like Germans.

In reply to the "Letter from Simferopol," the Baptists held a General Council, and sent to the Holy Synod a petition expressing their wish to be officially recognised as Baptists and to be fully tolerated in Russia. As was to be expected, it was the Procurator himself who replied to the petition. His answer was rough and peremptory. He begins by declaring that there is nothing in common between them, and warns them not to trouble their superiors in future.

Under the malign influence of the Procurator, persecutions broke upon the Baptists with severity and virulence. That the higher clergy were involved in the incitements to plunder, arson, and rape may be gathered from the "Poem" by Ambrosius, the Bishop of Kharkov, printed at the beginning of this chapter, entitled:

THE DAMNED STUNDIST.

Boom ye Church thunders!
Flash forth ye curses of the Councils,
Crush with eternal anathemas
The outcast race of Stundists, etc.

L   23

This tirade from the Archbishop was nailed to the Church doors, scattered in the "traktirs" (taverns), and spread broadcast throughout Russia, and, as we shall see, led to persecution bitter and severe.

A copy of this poem came into the hands of Prince Dmitri A. Khilkoff, of Pavlovka, in the diocese of Kharkov. Some of his peasants had been flogged, others imprisoned, and the wives of some, as we shall see later, were grossly outraged. The Prince thereupon forwarded the following open letter to His Grace the Archbishop:

"Your Grace,—Everybody sees with pleasure the result of your labours . . Your Grace can now see clearly what fruit your activity has yielded. The repeated warnings of your Grace and other similar shepherds, as you will find in the tenth chapter of John, have found an echo in the hearts of the rural police of the Kieff government; it will give your Grace pleasure to hear this· The proclamations which, ordered by you, were nailed on the walls of the Churches, to incite to hatred one part of the people against the other, such writings as 'The Accursed Stundist,' which were distributed with so much zeal; your sermons and those of your followers, which incite to hatred and intolerance; all these have had at last the desired effect. The new champions of Orthodoxy have found a new method to force women to make the sign of the Cross. Infamy and baseness. If an inquiry were to be made, the subordinate tools would probably be found guilty; but who incited these subordinate tools?"

For daring to come between the persecutor and the persecuted, for having the audacity to stand up for the peasants' right, for himself "apostasising" from the Holy Orthodox Church, the Prince himself, with his wife, have been exiled to the Caucasus, and their children kidnapped "by order of the Tsar."

Two priests were sent down to Pavlovka by the Archbishop to "confound the heretics," but their chief argument was free vodka before and during the disputation, and the result can be better imagined than described   The peasants sided with their peaceable neighbours, even though they were sectarians, and the "missionaries" returned to their superior utterly defeated.

In 1882 the central administration gave to the chiefs of the local police the right to condemn on their own initiative and authority any peasants who, in spite of warnings, continued to attend meetings of the hated Baptists, and to inflict upon them fines to almost any amount.   Two years later, seeing that the previous measures had proved useless as a deterrent to the propaganda, a further step was taken.

The leaders were condemned to long years of imprisonment in the company of common criminals, banished to Siberia and the Caucasus

L

(to which they had to travel on foot at all seasons of the year), and driven beyond the frontiers. But even this restriction had no effect. Where-ever these men went

> "They took the stamp of foreign friendships
> In a foreign land;
> And learnt to love the music of strange tongues"

"Now they which were scattered abroad owing to the persecutions" under the Tsar of all the Russias, "went as far as" Siberia and Trans-caucasia, Moldavia and Wallachia, Bulgaria and Turkey, "preaching the Word." "And the hand of the Lord was upon them, and a great number believed and turned unto the Lord."

In the places where they were incarcerated and banished, men were converted, baptised, and Churches were formed.

Leaders were imprisoned and exiled, and fresh ones sprang up in their place. Many; thousands were banished to the penal and free colonies of the east and south-east, but thousands remained faithful in the villages. In 1888 sterner measures were taken by the Government, not only against the leaders, but against the members generally.

Every country policeman, village magistrate, or even Orthodox priest could maltreat or arrest the Sectarians with impunity, and use against them violence of every kind.

The most usual way of rendering life unbearable to them was to impose upon them compulsory labour—the construction of bridges, the repairing of roads, to compel them to keep guard at night time in their own and even distant villages, inciting people to deeds of violence against them and their homes; and further, to coerce them into Orthodox baptism, or to flog them until they made the sign of the Cross or kissed the Holy Icon.

An endless number of disgraceful outrages were practised upon them, some of them incredible in their bestial coarseness and their impurity, many of these indignities being so infamous that it is impossible to allude to them even in veiled words.

The record of the writer to the Hebrews leaps to one's mind as one reads the story of the heroic pioneers of the Baptist faith in Russia:

"And what shall we more say! for the time would fail me to tell of *Pavloff* and *Makaroff*, of *Ivanoff* and *Kostromin*, of *Stepanoff* and *Erstratenko*, who, through faith wrought righteousness, escaped the edge of the sword, knew the interior of the dungeon, out of weakness were made strong, waxed valiant in their fight for truth.

"They had trials of cruel mockings and scourgings, yea, moreover of bonds and imprisonment; they were stoned, were slain with the knout; they wandered about in sheepskins, in goatskins; being destitute, afflicted, tormented (of whom the world was not worthy); they wandered in the deserts of *Siberia*, and in the mountains of the *Caucasus*, making their homes in dens and caves of the earth."

R. S. Latimer, in *The Life of Dr. Baedeker*, writes:

"In August, 1891, M. Pobiedonosteff called a great Conference in Moscow of Orthodox ecclesiastics from all the forty-one Russian Episcopates, to consider the burning question of the best methods of preventing the spread of sectarianism in the Empire. Great alarm was expressed at the rapid growth of the Baptist, Stundist, and Pashkovist heresies. Statistics were presented to the delegates proving that twenty-eight out of the forty-one dioceses were badly 'infected,' and that the 'virulence of the infection' was such that it was entirely beyond the control of the clergy. One of the delegates declared that, under the stress of persecution, a few Protestants were returning to the fold, but, alas! they were exactly those persons whom the Protestant communities were too glad to get rid of.

"What are we to do," he asked, "to win back to our midst those earnest and God-fearing men who have left us and despise us."

The answer of M. Pobiedonosteff to this question was a determination to employ severe measures.

"The rapid increase of these sects is a serious danger to the State.   Let all sectarians be forbidden to leave their own villages   Let all offenders against the faith be tried, not by a jury, but by ecclesiastical judges.   Let their passports be marked, so that they shall neither be employed nor harboured, and residence in Russia shall become impossible for them.   Let them be held to be legally incapable of renting, purchasing, or holding real property.   Let their children be removed from their control, and educated in the Orthodox faith."

"Article 187 —Offence: Leaving the Church for another religious community.   Punishment Loss of civil and personal rights.   In milder cases eighteen months in a reformatory

"Article 189.—Offence: Preaching or writing religious works to pervert others.   Punishment: First offence, the loss of certain personal rights, and imprisonment from eight to sixteen months; second offence, imprisonment in a fortress from thirty-two to forty-eight months,   third offence, banishment.

"Article 196.—Offence: Spreading the views of heretics or dissenters, or aiding such.   Punishment: Banishment to Siberia, Transcaucasia, or other remote part of the empire."

.   That the resolutions of the Congress and the suggestions of the Procurator were not to be a dead letter, was speedily proved by the violence

of the persecutions which broke out against the
Baptists everywhere.

In 1892, Elias Liavovi, of the province of
Kiev, sent out the following pathetic letter, which
came into the hands of members of the Baptist
Churches in England and America and to those
of the Society of Friends of both countries. As
a human document it hardly has its equal in
the literature of any time.

"I describe to you, my dear brothers, what
happened to us here. The elder of the village,
the village policeman, and other drunkards, torment us most unmercifully They compel us every
day to do forced labour in Babenzy or our own
village. We men are put every night on guard;
and these cruel sots, the village officials, enter our
homes when we are out, frighten our children,
and behave in a disgraceful manner towards our
wives. Late in the night of December 11 they
came to my wife, Chenia, and tormented her as
much as they liked in the same way as is mentioned
of Susanna in the Bible; but they acted worse
still. It is dreadful even to speak of it. They
threw her on the floor and outraged her, first
the drunken companions of the village elder, and
then the latter himself. They then compelled her
to make the sign of the cross, and threatened,
in case she did not do so, to submit her once more
to the same treatment; and all the time the poor
woman was *enceinte*. They twisted her hands

out of joint; and left her half dead. They smashed all the crockery and kitchen utensils, and broke all the windows. Even to the present day our house is without windows. With tears in our eyes we beseech you, brothers, to assist us, and let it be as soon as possible. Do not delay. They torture us so. With our eyes flooded with tears, we entreat you to plead our cause Perhaps our Heavenly Father will grant us grace and protect us."

A Russian political exile, writing his experiences in the *Friends of Russian Freedom*, relates an incident which came under his own observation. "On the way to Kiev, two men in chains, and with shaven heads, were placed in our railway carriage; their wives accompanied them, one with four children, the other with three; the eldest boy was twelve years old. The appearance of these prisoners instantly attracted our attention; both of them had fine faces, and there was a quiet, straightforward look about them which impressed us pleasantly.

"On seeing us, they at once asked us what we were, and why we were being transported, and when we answered, 'Socialists,' their faces brightened, and they held out their hands to us, calling us 'brothers.' They were members of the religious sect of Stundists, and had been tried several years ago in the district of Kirigin, as being among the first promoters of heresy. The

l

sentence passed upon them was, 'Transport to the Caucasus, and forfeiture of all civil rights' When the priest of their parish accused them of heresy, they were dragged, with blows and insults, through their village, and brought before the authorities. In prison they were treated with a barbarity worthy of the Middle Ages: the priest who had denounced them struck them in the face, demanding the names of their co-religionists. Whilst waiting for trial they were deprived of their one consolation, the New Testament, though by law every prisoner may possess it. On arriving at Kiev, we bought a New Testament, and gave it to them with the consent of the officer in charge. Their delight on receiving our present, and the passion with which they at once began their propaganda, was something to remember."

In the province of Kherson stern measures were taken to stamp out the heresy. Men and women were scourged and imprisoned, and three of the leaders were put to death by the "Orthodox" at the instigation of the clergy.

In the depth of winter they were taken to the river, and water was continually poured over them until they were frozen to death. Some of the brutalities exercised against these men and women are too vile to be described even in veiled words.

In September, 1892, the Pennsylvanian Society

of Friends received the following petition from the Baptists in the Province of Kiev:

"We implore you, beloved brothers, with tears in our eyes, take this account of ours and give it to somebody who can speak out loudly, and perhaps people will hear us in our most terrible distress. We are, as it were, stifled, and cannot cry aloud ourselves; awful and unspeakable is our distress."

The appeal is signed by all the members of the local Church, and is supplemented by personal narratives of wrong and iniquity practised against them.

Not content with "legal" persecutions, the clergy, with the connivance of the police, stirred up the brutal mob to wreak vengeance upon the "heretics."

They were flogged over and over again, compelled to cross themselves after the Orthodox fashion, made to kiss the Holy Icon, vodka was forced into their lips, tobacco smoke was blown into their faces, indignities and insults were heaped upon them, if by any means they could be forced to recant.

George Savarieff tells in *Free Russia* the story of Elias Sukhach, whom he knew intimately whilst they were both in exile in Eastern Siberia, and whose story he learnt during the long winter nights in that frozen land.

Elias was a devout "Orthodox" until he

L

became a Baptist, and was closely attached to
the Church and her services He was "server"
to the priest, and neglected his own home affairs
to minister to the needs of the "Little Father."
His conversion, through the preaching of Rjabos-
chapka, annoyed the parish priest, and the goodwill of the latter was speedily changed into violent
hatred. The priest spoke against him incessantly,
denounced him as an enemy of God and a traitor
to the Russian nation. He declared that it was
a mortal sin against God to leave a Baptist un-
molested. At the ceremony of the Blessing of the
Waters, which takes place on January 6, O.S.,
when the weather is at its worst in Russia, he so
aroused the animosity of the villagers against
Sukhach and his fellow Church members that they
rushed to the houses of the heretics, demolished
their cottages, broke into pieces their furniture,
smashed the crockery and cooking utensils, and
dragged the offenders to the river-side, where
the priest was awaiting their coming. He exhorted them to abjure their heretical doctrines;
he threatened them with divers pains and
penalties; he upbraided them as bringing calamities
upon the village whilst continuing in such sin.
On their quietly stating their adherence to the
new doctrines, the priest was so enraged that
he ordered a hole to be cut in the ice, and they
were forthwith plunged thrice into the ice-cold
water in mock baptism, each time being called

L

upon to forsake their heresy. Sukhach, with teeth chattering with the cold, on emerging from the water the third time, loudly said, "Forgive them, O Lord, for they know not what they do."

"Be damned, you impenitent heretic, in this world and in the future!" the infuriated priest made reply.

Sukhach was taken to Kiev and tried for criminal blasphemy and sentenced to two years in the "penal battalions," deprivation of all civil rights, and perpetual exile in the most distant part of Siberia. His wife Maria, and his two children, accompanied him into exile.

Eighteen months after his settlement in Siberia Elias received the following letter from his former fellow-villagers:

"Beloved martyr, and our true brother in Christ, Elias! Will you forgive us, the wretched perjurers and persecutors, our many offences against you? Truly you were right when, after we had railed at your sufferings, you, remembering in your misery the words of our Saviour, thrice exclaimed, 'Forgive them, O Lord, for they know not what they do!' And we, unworthy, instead of falling at your feet, committed a villainous outrage upon your house, and have falsely testified against you, throwing you into prison and bringing upon you condemnation and exile to Siberia."

Other letters followed. The heart of the exile

was cheered. His sufferings had not been in vain, for his very persecutors had embraced the new doctrine and had forsaken their old ways of enmity against God's men. Although he was never permitted to return home, and died a lonely exile in the wretched Saghalien district, his faith was firm until the last.

Another form of persecution was adopted in Kapustrizy. The village authorities arrested the brethren in a body, and sent them to forced labour on the public buildings. They were set to repair the fabric, men to do the woodwork, women and children to work the clay and plaster the walls. Some of the women had their babies with them, so that whilst carrying the child on one arm, or slung in a shawl, they had to carry the wood and clay in the other. The little ones could not be left at home, for all the elder children (from ten and twelve years of age) were forced to work with their parents, and oftentimes the work to be performed was four or five miles away from their homes.

In the evening the men were set on night watch for the whole night, and to every two brethren an Orthodox overseer was told off to see that they never sat down to rest, but walked to and fro the whole night through.

In the village of Pavlovka, the estate of Prince Khilkoff before mentioned, the elder, with the Dean and two priests, were reproaching the

L

peasants at the meeting of the *Mir* for their tolerat-
ing Baptists in their midst. "In other places in
Russia they are torn to pieces," said these worthies,
alluding to the province of Kiev. But their hearers
had themselves been newly awakened to faith in
the risen Christ, and were no longer susceptible
to such incitements.

Pamphlets, cartoons, and books were scattered broadcast over Russia, mainly written by
the higher clergy, denouncing the Baptists. Some
of them are too vile in their accusations to be
reprinted; the temper of them may be judged by
the specimen issued by the Archbishop Ambrosius.

Another wrote: "Better had it been for us that
the pestilence of cholera had broken out amongst
us, than this heresy. For the spiritual disease is
far more deadly, and much more to be dreaded
than the physical malady."

In spite of the wholesale persecutions, or
perhaps because of them, the movement spread
with rapidity throughout the whole of Russia
With his usual thoroughness, the Russian, when
in the grip of a new idea, will go to any length
He not only manifests "patience through tribulation," but perseverance in propaganda. Every
convert becomes a missionary, women as well as
men. I was in conversation some years ago with
Sonia Krepankov, of Tiflis, who had been in prison
for six weeks for distributing tracts to people in
the street (a heinous crime). I asked her if she

was going to continue her work, and naïvely she
answered, "I have nearly eighty left at home,
and they must not be wasted." In railway-trains,
on the great steamers of the Volga, in tram-
cars, in railway-stations, everywhere, these men
and women find opportunities to "tell the glad
tidings."

Petrovitch Ilija, of Eupatoria, when asked to
sign a promise not to speak to others of the
"doctrine" on penalty of going to prison, replied,
"The blessed Lord has said, 'Go ye everywhere
and preach the Gospel,' and I cannot disobey Him;
I would rather go to prison"; and to prison he
went.

No mention of the modern Baptist movement
in Russia can be complete without a reference to
W. A. Fetler, of St. Petersburg, who has rapidly
come to the front as a leader. He was originally
the minister of the Lettish Baptist Church in St.
Petersburg, but his energies and boundless enthusiasm led him to preach to the Russians, and
the response to his Gospel-call has been stupendous.
In less than five years he has become the head
of a great religious and social movement, the head-
quarters of which are to be found in the "Dom
Evangelia" (the House of the Gospel) in Vasilli
Ostrow.

I had the privilege of laying the foundation-
stone of the building in 1910, when representatives
of Baptist Churches from All Russia, including

Siberia and the Caucasus, were present   Hundreds have been converted under his ministry, and his enthusiasm and energy have inspired many to carry on the work in places hitherto considered impregnable to the Evangelical appeal

Although the severe and monstrous persecutions of the "nineties" have passed away, and are not likely to be resorted to again, and the Tsar's Manifesto of October 30, 1905, granted a measure of liberty and toleration, yet the spirit behind the persecutions has not been abolished, and Baptist leaders are still being arrested upon trivial pretexts and imprisoned for "blasphemy" and acting "contrary to the Imperial will."

The Metropolitan Antonius of St. Petersburg, one of the most powerful of the Russian Ecclesiastical hierarchy, issued a proclamation in 1908 in the following terms:

"The Orthodox Church is a Divine Institution. We teach that salvation can only be obtained while remaining in fellowship with the Orthodox Church.   By fellowship we understand general prayer, Church charity, the sacraments, all one's activity sanctioned by the Church, good works done in the name of Christ and the Church, and not in one's own.   We agree that it is possible, though abiding outwardly in the Church, to be a weak member of the Orthodox Church, but it is perfectly certain that a man who separates himself from the Church breaks his fellowship with

24

L

her, ceases to be one with her in spirit.   Separating himself from the Church, a man separates himself from Christ.

"Thus teacheth the Orthodox faith.   Except of the Church, the Grace of Christ does not exist.

"Therefore, when the Orthodox Church speaks of enemies of the Church, her meaning is plain. Enemies of the Orthodox Church are all those who profess any other religion, who deny that the Orthodox Church is the only true source of the Grace of Christ.   Enemies of the Orthodox Church are all those belonging to any other denomination, Raskolniks, Sectarians, Masons, the Godless, and so on.

"To leave the Orthodox Church and be in enmity with her is the greatest sin, for which there is no justification.   No sin or failure of the clergy can serve as an excuse for apostasy. These must be warned and fought against while still remaining in the Church.   But if any, in fighting against the evils existing in the Church, reaches so far as to fall away from the Church himself, he only proves by this that he is far worse than those whom he has been trying to convict of sin" (see *Under Three Tsars*).

Reliable statistics are exceedingly difficult to obtain, largely owing to looseness of organisation and the immensity of the country, but in the Russian Baptist Union there are more than 1,000 Churches, with about 97,000 members.

THE JEWS

BIBLIOGRAPHY.

PRELOOKER   *Russian Flashlights.*

                Experiences of a Russian Reformer.

JOUBERT   . *Russia as it really is.*

L

ι

THE JEWS

ALTHOUGH there are less than four and a half millions of Jews out of a population in European Russia of one hundred and forty millions, this book would not be at all complete without some reference to the "Ancient People." Not that they have had any influence upon the development of doctrine in either the Holy Orthodox or Sectarian Churches, but they have certainly a place in the development of the Russian nation, socially, politically, and religiously.

Three factors have militated against their wielding a greater influence upon the religious life of the people:

First: Until the reign of Paul I (1754-1801) the Jews had equality before the law, and they were allowed to settle freely in Russia, but comparatively few of them moved from their homes in Poland, Livonia, and Lithuania, mainly by reason of their language, religion, and customs being vastly different from those of the Russian people. Under the Tsar Paul I. the first law was passed prohibiting the Jews to leave the regions in which

L

they were settled. In 1804, Alexander I. held an inquiry into the cause of the famine in the province of Minsk, and the report presented to him declared that the economic pressure of the Jews was the primary cause of the distress, and Jew-baiting became the order of the day.

Nicholas I. tried to absorb them into the Russian peasantry, and the policy was continued under Alexander II. (1856).

Zones were fixed within which Jews could live, including fifteen provinces in Poland, Lithuania, and Bessarabia, outside of which it was not legal for a Jew to live or carry on trade, or hold real estate, save under certain well-defined exceptions.

In 1865 Jewish artisans were given the right to settle in Russia proper, with a view to developing the infant Russian industries, and in 1872, Jewish chemists and merchants received the like permission.

In 1874, Jews were admitted into the Tsar's army, and could even obtain officers' commissions. Schools were opened for their children, and the policy of assimilation went forward, but with little success.

The wave of Nihilistic propaganda of 1874 and the complicity of Jews in the "days of terror" brought about severe restrictions and savage reprisals. A complete change came over the policy of the Government towards its Jewish subjects.

Within a month of Alexander III. ascending the throne (1881) the first popular manifestations against the Jews began to take place.

On May the third of the same year, a *provisional* law was passed "in order to allay popular excitement against the Jews," that in future no Jew would be allowed to go into the country, nor in future could Jews purchase property in the country or hold a mortgage on property in the country. Under this law, Jews were not only confined to the pale, but members of the race were driven from towns where previously they had been allowed to settle, and were compelled to live in the ghettos.

In 1886 the number of Jewish children allowed to use a Government school was restricted to five per cent. of the scholars admitted, and later, the same restrictions were imposed upon them in reference to the universities

In 1892 they were deprived of the franchise for the municipal elections. These successive restrictive measures, coming in rapid sequence, fanned the flame of hatred against the Jew in the hearts of the Orthodox, especially those who unthinkingly believed the gross stories told by the priests as to Jewish religious customs. This policy has led the Jew to cling tenaciously to his own people and race. Until 1901 the anti-Jewish demonstrations had been mostly confined to the destruction of property, but in the following year the Kischineff "pogrom" took place, and since then there have been frequent outbursts against the Jews, sometimes instigated by the police, at other times by the priests, each of them using the "Black Hundreds" (The Union of the Russian People) as their willing tools.

Secondly: From time immemorial the Jew has been persistent in clinging to the ancient religion and ritual. The Russian Jew of the present day is a survival of the long ago days of the Sanhedrin. Their religion, laws, customs are the same as when the Romans destroyed the Temple at Jerusalem and destroyed the national character of the people. The Talmudic Law is still observed wherever Jews are to be found in Holy Russia. No Orthodox Jew will live in any town in Russia unless he is within easy reach of a Rabbi. I have seen in a railway-station, lamps burning before the Holy Icon, a priest conducting a service in the waiting-room, but in the corner, a Jew, with praying shawl over his shoulders, face to the wall, *wailing* his prayers, apparently unconscious of the wonder gaze of the "uncircumcised." The great gulf fixed between the two religions, the superstitious fanaticism of the ordinary moujik, the persecuting policy of the clergy and the police, all have had their effect in keeping the two races estranged.

Thirdly: Whilst the economic factor must inevitably have its place in estimating the aloofness of

the Jew, the persecutions and repressions on
account of his religion loom very largely. The
belief that the blood of a Christian child is secured by the Jews on Passover day, and that
this human sacrifice is an indispensable adjunct
to the Jewish ceremonies of that day, is shared
alike by many well educated people and the most
ignorant peasants. The trial this year of Beiliss at
Kiev (after two years in prison) on this charge
shows that the monstrous falsehood has not yet
been killed. We have it on the authority of
Count Tolstoi, Minister of Education, that in the
High School for young ladies, St. Petersburg the
students were taught that it was a vital part of
Jewish ritual, and it was only upon his stringent
orders that teaching of that kind ceased.

As a general rule, Jew and Christian live in
amity and peace all over Russia, and little kind-
nesses are shown to one another all day long But
when the order goes forth, and the peasant, well
primed with vodka, is led by a gang of the Black
Hundreds, then, for the Jew, "Hell is let loose"

I shall never forget the day when the rebel
battleship, *Kniaz Potemkin*, sailed into the harbour
at Theodosia, July 1905. Rumours of massacres
of Jews at Kischineff and Kieff had reached the
town, and many remembered the scenes of carnage
in Theodosia on June 2, 1881, when a "pogrom"
of Jews took place. Within an hour every available vehicle was purchased at a greatly enhanced

L

price, and the Jews were fleeing into the country for their lives Nor can one easily forget the burnt and blackened homes of the Jews in Odessa, Kischineff, and Kiev during that dread year.

A peculiar sect of the Jews is to be found in the Crimea—the Karaites. They adhere to the strict letter of Scripture, and reject oral tradition and depreciate the Talmud. They have existed since the middle of the eighth century, and found their home on the shores of the Black Sea, after the time of the Crusades, when they were driven from Jerusalem by the invading Christians.

In the early eighties, Jacob Prelooker, a Jew of Odessa, had been reading the New Testament, and discovered that the essence of Christ's teaching was love, forgiveness, and the brotherhood of man. He continued to study the Gospels in all earnestness, and the general history of Christianity.

Gradually, though only a young man of twenty years of age, he began to teach the necessity of a reconciliation between Jew and Christian. By some he was repulsed with hatred and contempt, whilst a few listened to him, and subsequently there was formed the " New Israel Brotherhood."

The founder calmly put on one side the authority of the Talmud, declared that circumcision should be of the spirit only, that the Jew might partake of food clean enough for the Christian, that a Christian Church was as holy as a

Jewish synagogue, and (most daring of all) that Jews and Christians might intermarry.

The new movement was, for the time being, wrecked by the fanaticism of the Orthodox Jews and Prelooker suffered bitterly at their hands. He was excommunicated from the Synagogue, but despite the "Sanhedrin," he retained for a while his position as a master in the Jewish School. For eight years he carried on his propaganda and received recruits to the new idea, but at last he decided to leave Russia and breathe the freer air of England

For a full account of this turning-point in Russian Jewry, those interested should read his fascinating book, *The Experiences of a Russian Reformer*.

TOLSTOI

BIBLIOGRAPHY.

TOLSTOI . *My Confession.*
My Religion.
Thoughts on God.
The Kingdom of God is Within You.
The Christian Teaching.
That Whereby Men Live.
Where Love is, there is God also.
The Two Old Men.
The Three Old Men.
The Penitent Sinner.
God Sees the Right, Though He be Slow
to Declare it.
Labour, Death, and Disease.
The Godson.

SAROLEA . *Life of Tolstoi*

MAUDE . *A Peculiar People.*
Tolstoi and His Problems.

STEINER. . *Tolstoi, the Man and His Message.*

RAPAPERT . *Tolstoi, His Life, Works, and Doctrine.*

KENWORTHY *Tolstoi, His Life and Works.*

L

For me the doctrine of Jesus is simply one of those beautiful doctrines which we have received from Egyptian, Jewish, Hindoo, Chinese, and Greek antiquity. The two great principles of Jesus ; Love of God, (in a word, absolute perfection), and Love of one's neighbour (that is to say, Love of all men without distinction), have been preached by all the sages of the world, Krishna, Buddha, Laotze, Confucius, Socrates, Plato, Epictetus, Marcus Aurelius, and among the moderns, Rousseau, Pascal, Kant, Emerson, Channing, and many others. Religion and moral truth is everywhere and always the same. I have no predilection whatever for Christianity. If I have been particularly interested in the doctrine of Jesus, it is ; Firstly, because I was born in that religion, and have lived among Christians, secondly, because I have found a great spiritual joy in freeing the doctrine in its purity from the astounding falsifications wrought by the Churches

TOLSTOI, 1909.
(*Sarolea—Life of Tolstoi.*)

TOLSTOI

IN estimating the influence of Tolstoi upon the development of the "Soul of Russia," we need to take into account two main factors, firstly, his life and teaching are of too recent a date for any full and just appreciation of the extent of his influence to be made; and second, so far as the overwhelming majority of the ordinary Orthodox peasants are concerned, the fact of his excommunication from the Holy Orthodox Church would tell against his teaching, even where it would be possible to obtain his works and to read them.

As far as one can judge from personal observation in Russia, more especially away from the large centres of population, Tolstoi's influence upon the social and political evolution of the Russian Empire will be more far-reaching and permanent than upon its religious life. In many of his later works, i.e., those written since his "conversion," there is a deep, true, and even passionate spiritual note, and from them emerge his three articles of belief, his creed, if you will:

1. The easing of the heavy burden of labour on the masses of mankind. "Even now only a few have really begun to divine that work ought not

L

to be a byword or a slavery, but should be a thing common to all, and so ordered as to bring all happily together in peace and unity."

2. The right to and the human need of happiness. Tolstoi's scheme for happiness in life is laid down in his book, *What I Believe*, and may be summarised, as much as a philosophy of life can be, into the following cardinal principles: Life in the open air; sufficient manual labour for each day; a full share of the pleasures of family life; to be on good terms with one's neighbours and to invite and enjoy their fellowship; to have a sound mind in a sound body; always to be in good physical health.

3. To seek by faith in God for a solution of the mysteries of life, and for courage to meet death calmly and with a good heart. In the parable, *Master and Man*, Tolstoi describes the "Master" Vassili Andreitch, caught in a blinding snowstorm, slowly sinking into a long sleep, the sleep of death, and vividly portrays the thoughts passing through the mind of the dying man. " Then he began to think about his money, his store, his house, his sales and his purchases, and Mirinoff's millions. He could not understand how that man whom men called Vassili Brekhunoff could bear to interest himself in such things as he did. ' That man can never have known what is the greatest thing of all,' he thought of this Vassili Brekhunoff. 'He can never have known what I

know. Yes, I know it for certain now. At last —I KNOW.' Once again he heard the MAN calling him who had called to him before, and his whole being seemed to respond in joy and loving-kindness as he replied: 'I am coming, I am coming' For he felt that he was free at last, and that nothing could hold him further. And indeed, nothing further than that did Vassili Andreitch see or hear or feel in this world."

Tolstoi taught that underneath all social and economic problems, whether in the individual or the community, there is a tremendous factor, the condition (good or ill) of the soul.

Aylmer Maude writes: "When the clamour of partisans and of detractors has died down— when Tolstoi's errors and exaggerations have all been frankly admitted—it will be only the more distinctly realised how immense is the debt humanity owes to this man, whose intellectual force, love of the people, courage and out spokenness, have given to his words a power of arousing men's consciences, unapproached by any of his compatriots and unequalled by any of his contemporaries."

Until early manhood, Tolstoi was a typical product of the aristocratic society of St. Petersburg. His rank and his fame as a writer opened all doors to him, and to a man of his temperament the life was alluring. The Crimean war, and later, his marriage, led him to a crisis. He was no longer

25

ι

content with what birth or opportunity had given to him, he was not satisfied with his selfish philosophy of life. He started out on the great quest for Truth. His *Confessions*, written some years later, dealing with the spiritual crisis in his life, will rank as one of the world's great masterpieces of devotional literature. In them he does not spare himself; he lays bare his inmost thoughts and feelings; one can clearly trace his severe spiritual struggles; the inner strivings as flesh contended with spirit for the mastery of his life; and gradually the emergence into light and the deeper culture of his own soul.

When turned fifty years of age he passed through a severe spiritual crisis, and of the emotions of that time he writes: " Five years ago something very strange began to happen to me. I experienced moments of perplexity and arrest of life, as though I did not know how to live or what to do."

He made vain attempts to put his perplexities on one side. He plunged resolutely and with absolute conscience into his work as a great landowner, as a working farmer, as a practical agriculturist. His days were filled with hard and arduous toil in the fields, but the solution of his problems was not to be found in manual toil. Again and again the thought of suicide came to him. To end his life would be to end his perplexities. He plays with the idea, and seems at times to become fascinated with it. But to him suicide was not the way out. The meaning of life was an enigma. The burden of life seemed to be too heavy for him. The sorrows of life were too poignant for tears.

Then the thought came to him, "You cannot understand the meaning of life, so do not think about it, but just live, live for the day." "Two drops of honey diverted my eyes from the cruel truth longer than the rest—my love of family, and of writing.

"Family—said I, but my family are also human.

"Writing—I soon saw that that too was a fraud.

"The question came again and again: 'What will come of what I am doing to-day, or shall do to-morrow? What will come of my whole life?' Then I began to consider the lives of the men of my own kind, and found that they met the problem in one or other of four ways. The first way was that of ignorance. Some people, mostly women, or very young or very dull people, have not understood the question of life; but I, having understood it, could not again shut my eyes.

"The second way was that of the Epicureans, expressed by Solomon when he said: 'Then I commended mirth, because a man hath no better thing under the sun than to eat, and to drink, and to be merry.' . .

ι

"The third way of escape is that of strength and energy. It consists in understanding that life is an evil and an absurdity, and in destroying it. It is a way adopted by a few exceptionally strong and consistent people. I saw that it was the worthiest way of escape, and I wished to adopt it.

"The fourth escape is that of weakness. It consists in seeing the truth of the situation, and yet clinging to life as though one still hoped something from it, and I found myself in that category. . . .

"On examining the matter I saw that the billions of mankind always have had, and still have, a knowledge of the meaning of life, but that knowledge is their faith, which I could not but reject. 'It is God, one and three, the creation in six days, the devil and angels, and all the rest that I cannot accept as long as I retain my reason,' said I to myself.

"My position was terrible. I knew I could find nothing along the path of reasonable knowledge, except a denial of life; and in faith I could find nothing but a denial of reason, still more impossible to me than a denial of life.

"What am I? A part of the Infinite. In those few words lies the whole problem. . . .

"I was now ready to accept any faith, if only it did not demand from me a direct denial of reason—which would be a falsehood. I studied Buddhism and Mohammedanism from books, and most of all I studied Christianity, both from books and from living people."

Tolstoi began to question people in his own circle of society, then theologians, monks, sectarians, Evangelicals, but he could find no satisfaction. He then turned to pilgrims, travelling monks, peasants, poor, unlettered, simple folk, but again he was baffled. For two years he had a time of introspection, and again and again the thought came to him, Why not end it all? a noose or a bullet would soon solve the problem.

"All that time . . . my heart was oppressed with a painful feeling which I can only describe as a search for God.

". . . I turned my gaze upon myself, on what went on within me, and I remembered that I only lived at those times when I believed in God. As it was before, so it was now; I need only be aware of God to live; I need only forget Him, or disbelieve in Him, and I die . . . 'What more do you seek?' exclaimed a voice within me. 'This is He. He is that without which one cannot live. To know God and to live is one and the same thing. God is life. Live seeking God, and then you will not live without God. . . .'

"And I was saved from suicide. . . ."

For a time Tolstoi found a measure of relief from his doubts in the dogma of the Infallibility of the Church.

l

"I told myself that Divine truth cannot be accessible to a separate individual; it is only revealed to the whole assembly of people united by love."

He commenced to attend the services of the Orthodox Church, to fulfil her rites; he humbled his reason, submitted to tradition. Of this period in his experience he writes:

"When rising before dawn for the early Church services, I knew that I was doing well, if only because I was sacrificing my bodily ease to humble my mental pride, and for the sake of finding the meaning of life. . . . I fasted, prepared for communion, observed the fixed hours of prayer at home and in Church. During Church service I attended to every word, and gave it a meaning whenever I could." This phase lasted but a short while. Doubts and perplexities crowded upon him. They were brought to a head when he was about to partake of the communion service.

"Never shall I forget the painful feeling I experienced the day I received the Eucharist for the first time after many years. The service, confession, and prayers were quite intelligible, and produced in me a glad consciousness that the meaning of life was being revealed to me. The communion itself I explained as an act performed in remembrance of Christ, and indicating a purification from sin and the full acceptance of Christ's teaching. If that explanation was artificial I did

not notice its artificiality, so happy was I at
humbling myself before the priest   . . But when
I approached the altar gates, and the priest made
me say that what I was about to swallow was
truly flesh and blood, I felt a pain in my heart:
it was not merely a false note, it was a cruel
demand made by some one or other who evidently
had never known what faith is. . . ." Three years
were spent after this in struggles to find a living
faith acceptable to him, but at last he came to
the conclusion that he could no longer remain
in the fellowship of the Orthodox Church He had
been probing to the very roots of religion as
manifested in the Orthodox Church. He could
not reconcile the attitude of the Church to other
Churches—to Catholics, Old Believers, Sectarians,
and the relation of the Church to war and capital
punishment. He set himself to study and investigate the writings and traditions of the Church,
to a close examination of theology.

"I must find what is true and what is false,
and must disentangle the one from the other   I
am setting to work upon this task."

Dr. Sarolea says: "He set himself to establish
the Christian religion, but purged of dogmas and
mysticism, a practical religion, not promising
future bliss, but giving bliss on earth."

Most of his parables and short stories were
the direct fruitage of this period of soul unrest
and quest for Truth. The reader is referred to

l

them for a fuller idea of the attitude of Tolstoi to essential Christian teaching. It is by his parables, published singly and in cheap form, and scattered broadcast in Russia, that he will ultimately affect the development of a purer form of Christianity in that land. In them he deliberately turns from the husks of religion, ritual and ceremony; to the kernel, "by their fruits ye shall know them."

In Tolstoi's creed, religion must inspire all individual and social morality, but religion, to Tolstoi, is based on a simple conception of brotherly love, the desire to do to others as we would have others do unto us.

He defines religion as an attempt to establish the relation of man to the world and its central principle. God is the principle of the world, but the will of God is to bring about the welfare of man: the end of religion is social service The end of society, on the other hand, is God. "For man, through man, to God," is Tolstoi's latest formulation of his social creed. God's will is the spiritual welfare of mankind.

Whilst Tolstoi is influencing his thousands, the simple Evangelical preachers are winning their tens of thousands, and their influence upon the "Soul of Russia" is immeasurably greater and more far-reaching.

ι

INDEX

L

L

l

The Kingsgate Press, London and Bedford.

L

X-81455

ι

Lightning Source UK Ltd.
Milton Keynes UK
UKHW021943100921
390383UK00002B/236